## ALSO BY JUNE SPRIGG

*By Shaker Hands*

*Domestick Beings*

*Inner Light: The Shaker Legacy*
(with Linda Butler)

*Shaker Design*

*Shaker: Life, Work, and Art*
(with David Larkin and Michael Freeman)

*Shaker Woodenware*
(with Jim Johnson and Paul Rocheleau)

*Shaker Built*
(with Paul Rocheleau and David Larkin)

# SIMPLE GIFTS

# SIMPLE GIFTS

## A Memoir of a Shaker Village

*by* JUNE SPRIGG

*with illustrations by the author*

*Alfred A. Knopf* · *New York* · *1998*

THIS IS A BORZOI BOOK
PUBLISHED BY ALFRED A. KNOPF, INC.

www.randomhouse.com

Library of Congress Cataloging-in-Publication Data

Sprigg, June.
Simple gifts : a memoir of a Shaker village / June Sprigg ; with illustrations by the
author. — 1st American ed.
p.    cm.
Includes bibliographical references.
ISBN 0-679-45504-3 (hc)
1. Shakers—New Hampshire—Canterbury. 2. Sprigg, June—Childhood
and youth. 3. Canterbury (N.H.)—Biography. I. Title.
BX9768.C3S67    1998
289'.8'0974272—dc21            97-49157
                                                        CIP

Manufactured in the United States of America

First Edition

*In loving memory of*

Sister Alice Howland
Sister Ethel Hudson
Eldress Bertha Lindsay
Sister Lillian Phelps
Eldress Gertrude Soule
Sister Miriam Wall
Mildred Wells

Eric Ashworth
Sister Mildred Barker
Harold and Mary Brinig
Marjorie Emery
Albert and Mary Karabinus
Bert and Mary Karcher
Margaret Nielsen
Sister Ethel Peacock
Gus Schwerdtfeger
Mildred Shuttleworth
Jennie Starkweather

# CONTENTS

# ILLUSTRATIONS

# ACKNOWLEDGMENTS

With special thanks to: Dorothy Sprigg; Ann Sprigg Morris; Dan, Sean, and Erin Morris; Alice Schwerdtfeger; all the Macombers—Viola, Bruce, Karen, Bruce Jr., Deana, and John; all the Karchers, especially Bruce and Doreen; Bud and Nancy Thompson; Darryl and Dayne Thompson; David and Steven Lamb; all the Wymans—David, Midge, Teresa, and Jimmy; all the Maynards—Jan, Clancy, Tom, and Cathy; Barry and Claire Roche; Tom Davenport; and all the Otts—John, Lili, Jennie, and Mike.

I am grateful to those who read the manuscript before publication. As this is the story of my experience with the Shakers, the opinions expressed herein are mine and are not necessarily shared by the people I wish to thank, who include: Priscilla Brewer; Sister Frances Carr and Brother Arnold Hadd of the United Society of Shakers, Sabbathday Lake, Maine; Jerry Grant; Alice Schwerdtfeger and her daughter Viola Macomber and family; Dr. Scott Swank; Darryl Thompson; Bud and Nancy Thompson; and Teresa Wyman.

Darryl Thompson deserves special thanks. His unfailing friendship, generosity with his time and knowledge, and above all, his insights—which combine heart and intellect in equal and great measure—have played an important role in this book. I am also grateful to my editors, Jane Garrett and Sarah McGrath, whose ability and wisdom encouraged me and helped shape the book.

Thanks and appreciation to: Canterbury Shaker Village, Inc., Canterbury, New Hampshire; The Shaker Museum and Library, Old Chatham, New York; Nancy Symmes and the staff of Barnes and Noble, Pittsfield, Massachusetts; Faith Vosburgh, Jim and Karen Border, and Peggy Levesque, Berkshire Community College, Pittsfield, Massachusetts; Gus Nelson, Kathy Moriarty, and the 1997 Berkshire Shaker Seminar; my friends at Hancock Shaker Village, Pittsfield, Massachusetts; Pastor John Beattie and the United Methodist Church of Lenox, Massachusetts; Bill Wilson, Dr. Bob Smith, and friends; Neil Olson; Eve Bowen; Susan Carroll; Kate Scott; Karen Deaver; Virginia Tan; Webb Younce; Bobbie Bristol; Angus Cameron; Alice Quinn; Betty Anderson; and Peter Parnall.

Love and thanks to all the Tooleys—
Ruth, Jeff, Phil, and Jill,
and most of all

TO JIM

# SIMPLE GIFTS

# "I Was a Teenage Shaker"

Well, no, not really. It's not as if I wanted to join the Shakers, or that they would have accepted me, even if I could have joined. By the summer of 1972, the Shakers at Canterbury, New Hampshire, had long since closed their doors to converts, figuring that it wouldn't do for a young hopeful to enter a celibate, religious community that now consisted of a half dozen old ladies on the decline—"members of an endangered species," Eldress Gertrude would say with a grin.

No, it's not that I actually lived as a Shaker. But I did live with them for three sweet summers half my lifetime ago. What might have seemed like the unlikeliest of friendships—me at nineteen, a miniskirted college sophomore, and six Shaker sisters in their seventies, eighties, and nineties, soft and wrinkled as old plums—made sense, perhaps to our mutual surprise. The contours of our lives fit comfortably. We were snug. The fit we formed in that first summer led to a friendship that lasted through the next twenty years, as long as they lived, and laid the foundation for my life as a grown woman.

Of course, nothing about this story is important because it happened to me—except to me. What is important is that it happened at all, what it reveals about the Shaker spirit. Never mind that the United Society of Believers was dwindling in numbers. The power to ignite was still there, the light still bright enough to kindle another small flame. My three summers with the Shakers changed me, inwardly and outwardly. They gave me a path to follow and work to do. Most of all, they taught me the wisdom of faith—the last thing I expected and the gift of a lifetime.

This is a simple story that means the world to me.

But first things first. The Shakers were the remnants of America's longest-lived and best-known communal utopian society. There had been Shakers in America since 1774, when Mother Ann Lee left England for the New World with a handful of followers in search of religious freedom. Their official name, the United Society of Believers in Christ's Second Appearing, presented the heart of their belief in a nutshell. Ann and her followers, dissenters who thought that the Church of England had more to do with royal politics than genuine Christianity, were millennialists who believed that the spirit of Christ had come again and had appeared to and through Ann in visions.

If you believed her and embraced the example of the earliest Christians, the spirit of Christ would live in you, too. It was simple (although not easy): all you had to do was turn away from the rotten values of "the World," hand over your property, and love everybody. Ah, yes, and renounce sex. The Shakers called themselves Believers, but it wasn't too long before they themselves adopted the nickname a mocking world had given them: at times the powerful presence of the Christ spirit caused some Believers to tremble and shake.

When I had been studying the Shakers for many years, I thought it was interesting that Ann was a contemporary of Abigail Adams, the wife of President John Adams, and another woman who spoke her mind. In letters to her husband and friends, Abigail offered vigorous opinions on topics, including politics and sex, that were not considered to be the proper province of ladies. Still, Abigail kept her comments within the family circle. As a dutiful wife and mother, she remained a lady in the eyes of the public. Ann, on the other hand, was no "lady" by the standards of the eighteenth century. Oh, she was a model of chaste living, all right—a vision had revealed to her that sex was at the heart of human troubles, so she was an adamant advocate of abstinence (to the dismay of her husband). No, the trouble was that she spoke out in public, sometimes barging in on church services in England to set the Anglican congregations straight. In America, congregationalists were no more able to appreciate Ann and her followers. Ann was beaten and jailed from time to time on both sides of the Atlantic. The vision of original sin came to her, in fact, during one period of incarceration.

In spite of these controversies, the Shakers took root in their new American home and flourished as never before. By 1800, several thousand converts lived and worked in a dozen villages in New England and New York. By 1825, a half dozen more communities were thriving in the west, which at the time meant Kentucky, Ohio, and Indiana. Shakers were famous in America for their unusual communal, celibate lifestyle, for the dance worship that simultaneously entertained and scandalized observers from the World, for the prosperity of their extensive farms and enterprises, and for the excellence of their products, which included vegetable seeds, brooms and brushes, botanic medicines, chairs, bonnets, buckets, and oval wooden boxes. Over time, their steadfast commitment to peacefulness, charity, and honesty won them grudging admiration. Like islands in the tumultuous sea of American growth in the nineteenth century, Shaker villages weathered the storms of national expansion, panics, booms, the Gold Rush, industrialism, and the Civil War.

For the United Society's survival, that was probably the

problem. As the world changed enormously around them, the Shakers clung steadfastly to their foundation principles. By 1850, it was clear that conversion was slowing down. For the celibate Shakers, who depended entirely on converts for life and growth, the situation was serious. With each new decade there were other opportunities for people, especially men, in search of their own particular notion of the Grail, whatever it might be. Doors were opening more slowly for women, so Shaker Sisters began to out-number Shaker Brothers by something like two to one. By 1900, three out of four Believers were women.

The particular attraction that Shaker life held for women in nineteenth-century America was easy to understand. In "the World," the Shaker's term for non-Shakers, an unmarried woman had little opportunity for anything like financial independence or personal autonomy. At best, a single woman of ordinary means might hope to find a place in the home of relatives. Married women and mothers made single by the death, desertion, or incapacity of their husbands also faced extraordinary challenges, especially if they had children. For women like these, Shaker life could look very good indeed. The Society offered emotional and financial security, the companionship of a loving Sisterhood, and—ironi-cally, given the strictures of Shaker life—a degree of independence unknown in society at large. Shaker women were in charge of their own lives. Collectively, they earned their own income from trades and industries and managed their own internal concerns, just as the Brothers did.

At all levels, Shaker leadership was divided equally between women and men, a remarkable practice in light of the gender inequities sanctioned by American custom and law. Throughout Shaker history, two of the four members of the Central Ministry, based in New Lebanon, New York, were women. The Central Ministry was to the Shakers what the Pope is to Catholics. As the ratio of Shaker women to men grew in the latter half of the nineteenth century, these Sisters bore ever more of the responsibility of maintaining the United Society. In the twentieth century, when the Believers ran low on men, the Central Ministry was entirely female. On the whole they did just fine. Declining population or not, the Shakers continued their forward spiritual march.

In time, the United Society of Believers' focus turned from growth and expansion to simple maintenance, and finally to sheer survival. The United Society's membership turned downward from the 1840s on. One by one, the communal family groups that made up Shaker villages closed owing to shrinking numbers. In 1875, for the first time an entire long-lived community went belly-up. From that point, it was all downhill, in terms of numbers, anyhow. By 1972, the six Shaker Sisters at Canterbury represented about 35 percent of the world population of Shakers—all fourteen of them. Eldress Gertrude was right; they were an endangered species.

The other surviving community, in Sabbathday Lake, Maine, had been founded in 1782 and organized in 1794, a couple of years after the founding of Canterbury Shaker Village. The imminent demise of the United Society had been steadily forecast for about two hundred years. Throughout the nineteenth century, outsiders continually predicted the Shakers' inevitable end. The tone of these prognostications depended on the observer. Most opinions from the first three quarters of the century were not sympathetic. Nathaniel Hawthorne, who survived his own youthful skirmish with an experiment in communal living, was not kind when he expressed his sentiments about the Shakers' coming end: the sooner, the better. Well, in 1972 he was long gone, but they were still here. They were few but tough, these valiant last Believers. Their numbers were down, but not their spirits. Although their long-heralded demise seemed truly inevitable at last, the Shakers looked forward, not backward, with optimism and hope. Maybe the United Society would continue in the flesh and maybe not, but the *spirit* of the Shaker way would go on nevertheless.

From this remove, it is easy to see that the Shakers and I became friends because we needed each other. My summer job as a tour guide through the museum part of the village was what had brought me there, but it proved to be the least important aspect of my service. I was a girl, and these celibate Sisters had spent their young and middle lives caring for girls like me. Brought to communal Shaker villages themselves as young girls when their own families had fallen asunder, the Shakers I knew had chosen to spend their lives in the faith when they grew up in spite of the cost—no marriage, no sexual expression, no children of their own. As they grew to womanhood, their motherly hearts found reward in the care of girls.

By the early to mid-twentieth century, of course, the girls in their care were not making the same commitment to stay with the United Society, which was dwindling in numbers and ever less attractive to the young. One by one, the Shakers' girls left, drawn to the promise of the world outside. So when I came and showed enthusiasm for Shaker history and affection for the Sisters, I entered a place in the heart already prepared but long vacant, although I didn't realize it at the time. I was just glad that they liked me. To the Shakers, it must have felt as if a door long closed were opened and the room made up fresh once again.

I needed them, too. I felt it at the time as a kind of unthinking yearning, like a newborn pup who blindly seeks the teat, but now I understand more clearly. If they were glad for one last girl to care for and teach, then I was equally grateful for all the additional grandmothers I could find. I was blessed with three of my own, including my father's stepmother and my namesake, each very different, each a teacher to her granddaughters in her own way. But even three weren't enough.

In the Shakers I found a half dozen more grandmothers. I could not have explained why at that time, but I knew without question that I hungered for teachers and that they had to be women and old. Why women? Well, how else could I learn to become a woman myself? Who else could teach me? And why old? Well, weren't the oldest those with the greatest wisdom and perspective? The longer they lived, the more they had learned. Life's currents had tumbled them longer, smoothed them more. If they couldn't teach me, who on earth could? Ironically, I became aware that the closer I grew to womanhood and the more I needed them, the fewer female elders I encountered among my teachers. They were all around us in grade school, and we adored most of them. There were fewer of them in high school, and we were much less kind. There were hardly any at all in college.

At nineteen, like most young people, I felt bewildered by my passage from childhood to adulthood. Overnight, I was an adult, more or less. I could drive, vote, and do all the things that adults did, for better or for worse. But I didn't know who or what to trust. My peers said, "Don't trust anyone over thirty," and I could understand that. The rules handed to me were from

*Shaker Sister Miriam Wall and the author*

another era. They may have worked for Mom in the 1940s or Grandma in the 1920s, but they didn't fit my world. On the other hand some of my generation were going off the deep end with sex, drugs, and rock and roll. I wasn't sure they were so trustworthy, either.

Where else might I turn? Mom took us to church when we were growing up, which I appreciated, but it was a dry affair that seemed to consist of boring sermons, lousy singing, and too many "Thou shalt nots." So religion was suspect, too. I was lucky to have a loving family, but we were not a smooth fit. I wanted to go on peace marches. Mom, who'd served in the Navy (so had Dad) said no, the "peaceniks" were a bunch of Communists. It was so confusing. I needed a book of instructions to life, or a map that matched the terrain of my life, but it seemed I was going to be on my own.

I was lost and confused. By 1972, two years of college had taught me everything from books, but little about life. At nineteen I was half in and half out of the egg, older than my years in some ways, younger in others. I had learned how to work hard and how to play hard, how to swear, and how to drink. But I was more baffled than ever about the single thing that mattered most: how to become an adult, to live at peace with myself and with others, and to live decently and remain undiscouraged in a dirty old world.

I had a long way to go.

That summer with the Shakers gave me something to trust. It's not why I went, and it was the last thing I expected. Who would have thought that a handful of little old ladies who belonged to an offbeat religious sect could make sense to a teenager like me? Not only that, their faith was built on the strictest principles of discipline—celibacy, temperance, selflessness. Yet the attraction I felt had nothing to do with dogma or harsh and rigid rules, to which I have always been allergic. No, it was the spirit of their faith, not the letter of their law, that grabbed my attention and then my trust. They expected the best of themselves and others, every day and in every way. In fact, Shaker society was famous for its commitment to perfectionism. Well, in that they weren't necessarily so different from other people I knew. The difference came in the consequences of their own and others' inevitable *failure* to achieve perfection, which is after all part of being human. Amazingly, they accepted shortfalls with patience and grace. In their actions and words, the Shakers lived the Golden Rule. It was as simple as that.

They were human beings, not impossibly perfect saints, and that made all the difference. Doing unto others as I would have them do unto me didn't mean that I had to be perfect, or a Goody Two-shoes, or a Holy Roller, thank God. I could be my own real self. In fact, God wanted me to be my own real self. All I needed was to keep in mind that kindness is never a mistake, that we all make mistakes, and that forgiveness is the key. The heart of the Shaker way was so powerful that I knew I was onto something big within my first week at Canterbury. I could sense a door opening to hope. Maybe I *could* find a wise and safe way to maturity. By the end of the first summer, it was clear what I'd found: a North Star at last. If I didn't always know exactly where I was going, or got lost and wandered off the path, at least I'd know which way I wanted to turn.

I hadn't gone looking for that. It was a gift.

# CHAPTER 1

# Gus and Alice

I arrived at Canterbury Shaker Village, about twelve miles north of Concord, New Hampshire, in late afternoon at the end of May 1972, with Mom and Grandma in the old blue Chevy station wagon. It had been a long drive from Martin's Creek, Pennsylvania, but my course had been steered in this direction years earlier, through a series of life's coincidences. When I was very young, our family had vacationed every summer in Maine, where we stayed at the lakeside cottage of Uncle Bert, across the water from the village of the Sabbathday Lake Shakers, Maine's only surviving Shaker community. In the late 1950s, there were only two other Shaker villages left in America: one in Hancock, Massachusetts (which became a museum in 1960), and the other in Canterbury, a couple of hours' drive away.

The lake was lovely, especially for us kids. The bottom sand was silky smooth between our toes, but you had to watch out for sharp mussel shells. We rowed the old boat up and down the inlet for hours.

It was hard to pry us from the water. But on rainy days we'd go poke around some antique shops or take a trip over to the Shakers. My sister Ann and I must have been slightly odd little kids, because we went willingly and behaved ourselves, even in the small museum there. There was an old woman with a long dress who showed people the furniture, clothes, baskets, and so on in the plain white Meetinghouse, which we learned was the Shakers' church. The old wavy window panes did funny things to the apple orchard on the hill above. Across the road was the village's biggest building, more than three stories tall, made of brick, with lots of windows. We were told that it was the Dwelling, where most of the remaining Shakers lived. Some of them lived in the Office and in the Girls' Shop. The village, which consisted of about a dozen buildings along Maine's Route 26, was quiet and mostly white clapboard, like any other small New England town. There were big old trees along the road and around the lawns, which sloped down and down to fields, then to woods, and finally, way down, to the shore of the lake.

The Gift Shop made the biggest impression on us kids. It was in the Office and Store, a white building a short distance from the Dwelling. The Shop was a big, pleasant room with large windows facing the road. We put our noses against glass cases filled with Shaker handiwork for sale: knitted baby bonnets and booties, cardboard and cloth needlebooks, pincushions, beautiful oval wooden boxes with lids. There were racks of old-fashioned black-and-white photo postcards. We always got maple-sugar candy. One year we each got a small china-headed doll. Ann's was blonde and mine was dark and wore a pale blue thin cotton dress, tied at the waist and neck with pink satin ribbon. On another visit Grandpa bought me a dollhouse Shaker stove, made of real cast iron. We went back to Sabbathday Lake Shaker Village year after year. Nothing seemed to change, which was nice. It seemed to be something you could count on.

The years went by, until one summer I was fifteen; Ann was a year older. Tadpoles and rowboats didn't have quite the thrill that they had had a few years before. Our new hobby was boys, and there weren't any up at the lake, at least in our inlet. Is it possible that we were bored? Is it possible that we mentioned that we were bored, repeatedly? At any rate, that was the year my involvement with the Shakers grew, thanks to the suggestion that we go visit the Shakers' neighbors, just down the hill, a retired couple who made high-quality miniatures. In fact, the dollhouse stove Grandpa got for me in the Shaker store years earlier was one of theirs. We piled into the car and drove around the lake to a small white house with a wooden sign in the yard: "Gus and Alice Schwerdtfeger—Miniature Shaker Furniture." The lady who answered the backdoor smiled and invited us in. There was coffee heating on the stove, so we must have arrived at around three, which was when Gus and Alice took their afternoon break. I was to learn that you could set your watch by it.

The kitchen led into the dining room, which was clearly used for dining no more. Every tabletop and surface was covered with miniatures, mostly their own work. On a table next to the wall was a small shadowbox Shaker room, filled with wonderfully authentic furnishings, one inch to the foot. There were chairs and candle stands, washstands, and wood boxes, each of which could rest comfortably in your palm. I didn't know a whole lot about Shaker furniture, but from our yearly visits to the museum, we could tell that these small-scale replicas were very well done indeed.

Gus used maple and pine, just like the antique originals. The furniture that was painted was all the right colors: barn red for the cupboard and washstand, dark green for the bed. The attention to detail was amazing. The bed was strung with twine "rope" and there were tiny wheels on the feet that really rolled (the Shakers put their beds on wheels to make them easier to move for thorough housecleaning). He made tiny brass hogscraper candlesticks out of cup hooks and the tubes of ballpoint pens. One ladder-back chair had perfect little "tilting feet" on its back legs. Just as in the full-size originals, Gus hollowed out the bottom of the back legs and threaded a half-round tilter into place. The device, used by the Shakers since the 1820s, was designed to keep the chair's feet flat on the floor when the sitter leaned back, to keep the floorboards like new, free from little dents.

The dustpan and brush hanging from the peg on the wood box were hardly bigger than a postage stamp. Alice smiled proudly when she told us that Gus stuck precisely twenty bristles from his old shaving brush into each tiny hole in the brush handle. In workmanship, Alice was Gus's equal. She wove the checker-board cloth seats of the chairs with colored tapes barely an eighth-inch wide. The carpets she braided of embroidery floss in subdued colors were just the right scale. The little shadowbox room was presided over by a dollhouse lady with white hair in a bun, outfitted by Alice in a perfect little Shaker dress, complete with long pleated skirt and cape, or "bertha," over the shoulders.

When we had admired everything in the dining room, Alice led us down the hall to Gus's workroom, a cubbyhole about the size of a pantry. Gus sat at a huge rolltop desk that practically filled the room. Every pigeonhole held little wooden parts or some kind of tool. Everything in the room, including Gus, was slightly blurry with sawdust. It smelled wonderful. In one enormous hand, knobby and callused from years as a master welder in the shipyards in nearby Bath, Gus held a one-eighth-inch dowel. In the other, a penknife deftly moved: one stroke, two, three. In the time it takes to describe, the end of the dowel was a perfect little drawer knob that would have been dwarfed by an aspirin tablet.

*Gus: hands to work*

By now, it was time for coffee. We sat around the kitchen table and listened to the story of how they came to be making Shaker miniatures. They took turns talking, companionably. Gus was tall and bony in khaki work shirt and pants, with big hands and a long, good-humored face. His voice was pleasantly rough from the endless stream of short, stubby Camels he smoked. Alice, small and quick with big dark eyes, was his match in the smoking department, too. Gus had moved to Maine in his youth to work as a welder in the shipyards. He was New York City born and bred, but you'd never know it. His boyhood accent was long gone, replaced with the broadest of Down East. The shipyards were in Bath—"Baahth," when he said it. Alice Mallett was working as a waitress when she and Gus met. Mama Mallett was not happy. Gus was considerably older than Alice, and he was divorced, besides. When they married, in 1936, Mama gave the marriage a year at best.

We all laughed. It was now 1968 and they were still going strong, many years later. In time, Gus and Alice had had a little girl and had settled into a big connected Maine farmhouse and barn, which happened to make them the Sabbathday Lake Shakers' nearest neighbors to the south. More than a half mile of field stretched between the two places, so they weren't exactly placed to develop a gab-over-the-back-fence kind of friendship. But everything changed one bitter winter night in the forties, when the house caught on fire. They all got out safely, but the house and barn were destroyed. The Shakers up the road didn't waste a minute inviting the family to stay with them in the community until they got back on their feet. The Shaker Family was shrinking, and there was plenty of spare room in the Office. Gus and Alice grinned when they recalled Eldress Prudence Stickney's generous offer. Coming from this tiny autocrat, it sounded like an order.

They obeyed, and moved into their own quarters while Gus went about moving and altering a one-room schoolhouse into a new home. Alice got to know the Sisters as she helped them with chores, and little Viola went to the Shaker school with other neighborhood kids as well as children cared for by the community. Gus made friends with Elder Delmer Wilson, at that time the last Shaker Brother at Sabbathday Lake (and one of a tiny handful anywhere else). In time, Gus and Alice moved back down the hill, but the bonds of friendship remained and grew.

Gus assisted Delmer from time to time with repairs and odd jobs around the village. Gus and Alice both recalled the Shaker man with respect and affection. Late in life he had been made Elder, but he was a simple man who preferred his old title of Brother. Delmer, born in 1873, was placed with the Shakers in Sabbathday Lake when he was eight. His mother, widowed when Delmer was three, sent his brother, too. At fourteen, Delmer had charge of the community's herd of cattle. As he grew, he became the self-taught master of a number of trades. At eighteen he built and steam-fitted a large greenhouse. When he was thirty-six, he bought a book called *The Steel Square and Its Use* so he could build a garage for the Family's new automobile, purchased in 1909. The beekeeping came after he read *The ABC's of Bees*. It was a good thing that he was clever that way, because there were fewer and fewer older Brothers to instruct him. Among them, his fine teachers included Elder William Dumont, Brother Washington Jones, and Brother Eben Coolbroth.

Delmer was a good old-fashioned Shaker, adept at any number of things. One of his loves was the orchard that spread over the hill behind the Meetinghouse. Alice told how he used to bring them bushels of apples and potatoes for a Christmas gift. He became dear to them, a sort of kindly godfather who hovered nearby and shared in their family's growth in his Shaker Brother's way. He thought and spoke like a man of the earth. When he saw their first newborn grandchild, Alice recalled, he said in awe and wonder that the baby was the "greenest thing" he'd ever seen—new and tiny and tender, like a freshly sprouted seedling. I wondered if he had ever seen a newborn baby so close in person before, and thought, probably not. He was also an accomplished carpenter, furniture maker, photographer, and artist. It was Delmer who had taken the crisp, nicely balanced black-and-white pictures that the community still sold as postcards. It was Delmer, too, who had kept alive the tradition of making fine oval wooden carriers, long after other Shaker communities had stopped making them. A carrier was an open oval box with a fixed or swinging bail handle that served like a basket in function.

The oval carriers we had seen over the years in the Shaker Store were not Delmer's, however. When Delmer felt that it was time for him to retire from the craft, after making thousands of carriers in his lifetime, he and the Sisters thought that Gus might take over the business. He knew Gus was a good craftsman and he also knew that the carriers sold well for the Shakers in their Store. When Gus agreed to give it a try, Delmer dropped off some parts and tools, but no instructions. Gus said that he figured Delmer had faith that he could work out the process himself. Gus said that it took a week before he had made a box that he felt was up to Delmer's high standards. When Gus handed it to Delmer for inspection, the Elder gave it a good thorough once-over in silence—then smiled his approval and told Gus that he had himself a job.

It meant a great deal to Gus that Delmer held him and his way of working in such high regard. The Shakers' motto, "Hands to work, hearts to God," was a quote of Mother Ann. As far as hands and heart went, Gus would have made a fine Shaker, and in fact Sister Lillian at Canterbury joked with him and Alice about this. The Camels and nightly thimble of medicinal whiskey would have had to go, of course, as well as a few of Gus's pithier expressions and the ancient pin-up girl on the calendar in his big workshop out back, which survived the fire. Gus pointed out that the pin-up came with the shop when they bought the place, but I noticed that in several decades he had never felt moved to take her down. She made a striking appearance, naked as she was alongside a magnificent black stallion. The first time their dear friend Sister Mildred paid a call to the shop, Gus recalled, she glanced at the calendar, was quiet a moment, and then said, "My, what a beautiful horse."

Yes, all this would have had to go, as well as Alice, so Gus's conversion was hardly likely. But his manner of working shed light on a way of Shaker life that had passed. "Do all your work as though you had a thousand years to live, and as if you would die tomorrow," Mother Ann also said. As a boy and young man, Delmer had witnessed the great Shaker workshops and mills in action. Now they were silent, some in ruins, and Delmer, too, was gone, but not before handing Gus something that meant a lot to them both.

When Gus retired from the shipyards, he began fooling around with miniatures in addition to making boxes. Alice began to add her ideas and handwork, and before long, they had a nice little home business going, with sales to the Shakers' Store as well as to individuals who either saw the sign or heard about them and stopped at the backdoor, like us. By the time we met them, they had a permanent waiting list of appreciative and devoted collectors. I had no money to speak of at fifteen, but I knew if I ever got some, I'd like to join the list.

We thanked Alice and Gus for the coffee and a lovely time and piled back into the car and drove back around the lake. That was the end of our first visit, but just the beginning of my long and wonderful friendship with them. It was partly that I liked miniatures and truly admired Gus and Alice's fine workmanship, but even more that I was crazy about Gus. My father had died before I was two and Mom had never remarried. Grandpa was a good man, but stern and hard to get to know.

When we went home to Pennsylvania, I wrote to Gus and Alice. Alice wrote right back, a friendly letter that encouraged a reply. Before long I got the idea of drawing miniature versions of Shaker "gift" or spirit drawings like *The Tree of Life* by Sister Hannah Cohoon, and sent off a few samples. Gus and Alice liked them and offered to take orders from their customers. It was a deal! We stayed in touch for the next three years, while lots of things changed. Ann and I graduated from high school. When the package postmarked "Maine" came in the mail, I couldn't believe my fortune. Gus and Alice had sent me a little open display case complete with furnishings, including a rocker, a table, and one of Alice's beautiful braided carpets, in gray, maroon, and green. The walls were painted white, like Shaker walls, and there was a perfect section of peg rail on the wall. Each peg, carved by hand, was only a quarter-inch long. This was no toy for some kid. It was the beginning of a real collection, exquisite and valuable, the kind of thing that adults had, and it was my proudest possession.

There was sad news, too. Grandpa died that summer, leaving a big hole in our little family of five. The visits to Maine ended. Ann and I both went to work that summer and then to college in the fall. When summer rolled around, I wasn't really a kid anymore, but I wasn't all grown up, either, so Alice's letter was perfectly timed. Why didn't I plan to visit her and Gus for a week at the end of the summer she asked. I could stay on the fold-out sofa bed in the living room. This was not the same old family trip. It was the first solo invitation of my young adult life. At eighteen, I could not have been more pleased.

It was nice but also strange to be there for real. We had written for three years now, but I had never spent more than an hour or two with them in person, and never without my family. Over coffee at the familiar kitchen table, the strangeness quickly wore off, and I felt at home. To Gus's surprise, I couldn't be pried from his elbow at the big rolltop desk in the workroom. When he offered to show me how to do what he did, I was in heaven. We sat there for hours that week. He showed me how to carve a tiny peg and a tiny pull from maple dowels. Then I was promoted to carving something bigger: a smooth pine oval the size of a large nutmeg, which he finished into a miniature standing bonnet mold. I was entranced—it came out well. The next job was even tougher: the shaped pine seat for a low-back Windsor-style Shaker dining chair, the kind they had made at Canterbury.

It was a pleasure to watch Gus work, especially when he was figuring out something new. He was a natural-born mechanic in the old sense of the word: an artisan, someone gifted by God in the art and mystery of making things. His economy of motion fascinated me. He'd ponder a bit, then pick up whatever tool or make whatever jig was needed for the next step. He didn't make a false move. It was a kind of grace I'd never seen, and I realized later that we don't get to see much of it now that the Industrial Revolution has changed how things are made.

I, on the other hand, had a knack for going at things "bass-ackwards," as Gus put it. I didn't mind his kidding, but I took to watching him like a hawk to catch him in a mistake. Maybe I did, once. In spite of my awkwardness, the things I tried came out well. I don't know who was more surprised and pleased—Gus, at my dedication, or me, at my success. I had never carved anything more ambitious than a bird out of Ivory soap at day camp. Since he stamped his work with a small *S*, we agreed that my work should be marked *JS*. During that week, I made about a half dozen pieces, with Gus's help.

More than anything else, I came to love our evenings around the kitchen table. Its enameled metal top was pleasantly cool to the touch. While Gus and Alice talked and smoked, I traced the brown and red enamel patterns with my finger. The only light in the house was the lamp on the wall that washed us in its warm yellow glow.

They told me more about their friendship with the Shakers. Over the years, Gus and Alice had also become friends with the Shakers from New Hampshire. In time-honored Shaker tradition, the Canterbury Shakers had made regular visits to their sister community at Sabbathday Lake, and vice versa. In the old days, by horse and wagon, the trip took much longer. Early in the twentieth century, the Shakers in both communities had acquired automobiles. This was not a break with tradition, since the Shakers, unlike the Amish, embraced modern technology. For two hundred years, Shakers had seen no conflict between the spiritual life and technological progress. This made sense, when you considered that the Shakers got their start in Manchester, England, a major early factory town, during the birth of the Industrial Revolution.

Anyway, the visits back and forth had introduced Gus and Alice to the Canterbury Shakers and they, too, became friends. Gus and Alice shared so many fond recollections of their New Hampshire Shaker friends that I began to feel that I knew them myself. Sister Lillian Phelps, in her nineties, was the spiritual center of the community. She was a fine musician who loved to play the piano and organ. Gus really liked her sense of humor, and the way she kidded him right back. Lillian thought so highly of Alice that she gave her friend one of the few treasures she'd kept from her life before Canterbury Shaker Village—her tiny china doll, bought with the weekly nickels that Lillian earned by shining her father's shoes.

Bertha Lindsay, in her seventies, was the brand-new Eldress, appointed to that office following the death of Eldress Marguerite Frost earlier that year. Gus and Alice both adored Bertha, who was like a daughter to Lillian. They had respect for Bertha, too, because it wasn't easy running a Shaker community, tending to Lillian's health, and also being in charge of the communal kitchen. Bertha fed eight or ten people every day in the summer, and she was an excellent cook.

By the summer of 1971, going to Canterbury from Sabbathday Lake was no big deal, just a couple of hours' drive across the New Hampshire border. You could make it a comfortable day trip if you didn't stay too long or leave too late. So when Gus and Alice had a delivery of miniatures to make to the shop at Canterbury, I went along.

The sun was shining in a New England sky the color of the cornflowers that grew along the road. We made our way along Route 202, through one small Maine town after another, over shallow, rocky rivers and past old mills, Grange halls, and tall white churches.

En route, Gus and Alice talked about Bud Thompson, who had helped found the museum at Canterbury, and who gave tours. They liked Bud a lot. He had visited the Canterbury Shakers years ago as a young folksinger, wanting to learn more about Shaker music, like the sacred song "Simple Gifts." Intrigued with everything he found, he had hung around and become close friends of Lillian and Bertha. In time, he married and had two boys, who were as dear as grandsons to the elderly Shaker Sisters. When he saw that the community's heritage was in danger of disappearing, he worked with Lillian and Bertha to open a museum. The Shakers had made visitors welcome since 1792, so offering guided tours was nothing new. Bud fixed up a fine exhibit of Shaker workmanship in the Meetinghouse. Gus said that if we were lucky, Bud would be on duty when we got there. Bud's tours were famous. He was knowledgeable and funny.

Shaker Road, not far from Concord, was definitely a country road. It was paved—"hard-topped," the natives said—but narrow and full of potholes as it climbed steadily through scrubby woods.

As we rounded the final bend, Gus slowed the car so we could appreciate the approach. Before us, Canterbury Shaker Village floated at the top of a long, green rise, a rare stretch of open field in a state long since abandoned by farmers. At the crest, a magnificent row of sugar maples rose slightly from the road on the left to the neat white gambrel-roofed Meetinghouse, a twin to the one in Sabbathday Lake. Behind the Meetinghouse was the taller roof-line of an enormous Dwellinghouse, also shining white clapboard, with a domed cupola crowning all. The maples shielded the rest of the buildings from sight. To the right, at the far end of the wide field, an apple orchard curved down the hill. Beyond the orchard was forest.

Gus drove slowly up the last hill. A stately double row of maples arched their branches overhead. Just beyond were the Shakers' stone walls, or more accurately, fences. Even in a first glimpse from a moving car, you could tell the workmanship was remarkable. These walls were not just heaps of piled cobbles, but consisted of huge, angular chunks of granite, fitted so neatly that the surfaces were nearly as flat as pavement. Some of the rocks were a yard across. The walls reminded me vaguely of pictures I had seen of the ancient Incan stonework at Machu Picchu. This wall was not so big and grand, but it was impressive just the same. As Gus drove slowly forward, we could see the field basking in the sunlight to the right; to the left, thin woods crowded up to the wall.

And then we were at the top of the hill. From here, on the right, the Meetinghouse lay at the far end of a broad green lawn flanked by maples even older and craggier than those along Shaker Road. It looked so cool and refreshing. The Meetinghouse itself faced the road, and even at this distance, we could see the twin doors on the front, just as at Sabbathday Lake—one for men, one for women. A fence separated the Meetinghouse and its lawn from the rest of the village buildings, which sloped up a rise along a straight granite walk, one after another, gleaming white in the early-afternoon sun. Perched at the far end of this yard was a small house that faced the road. That was the Girls' House, where Bertha had lived as a child. Now that Bud and his sons lived there, Gus and Alice joked, it would need a new name.

We could see more buildings behind this first row, but they would have to wait for the tour. In the meantime, Gus pulled over to the only principal building on this side of the road. It was a large, handsome brick house with two small Victorian porches, really more like covered doorways. To the right was a small open addition, a kind of porch roof on columns over a driveway. I knew it was a porte cochere, a covered place to park a buggy or automobile and go inside without getting wet in bad weather. The Trustees' Office was where visitors stopped, Gus and Alice said, and also where Lillian and Bertha lived. The big, heavy door was open to the hallway, and in we went.

You'd think that the details of my first meeting with Bertha and Lillian would be clear in my memory, but they're not. There was so much to take in that the rest of the afternoon remains a pleasant blur. I know that we went on tour with Bud, and it was every bit as lively as promised. His warm good humor shone over what he showed and told to bring Shaker history to life. I know that we sat and visited with Lillian and Bertha, although I can't recall whether it was in the bright bubble-gum pink sitting room (*that* was a surprise) or out on the other little porch, which was screened. Their rooms were comfortably furnished with ordinary chairs and sofas, not classic Shaker chairs. It was a home, not a museum. There was a cheerful clutter of knickknacks in the sitting room, an upright piano, and a TV. Everything was spotlessly clean. The Sisters wore long dresses in vivid colors (another surprise) and white net caps, the sign of their commitment to the

Shaker faith. I know that we must have been offered refreshments, because hospitality in a Shaker village was as inevitable and natural as breathing.

The details don't matter, anyway. What I do remember is how much I liked being there, and how much I enjoyed the easy laughter of these good old friends. Lillian was lovely, and she was also older than anyone I knew except maybe Auntie Rader back home. Her spirit was bright with the light of intelligent goodness, and I could tell it was only her physical self that was falling to age. Everything about Lillian seemed soothingly low and slow. She had droopy hound-dog jowls and she spoke deliberately in a voice that was clear and low. Her deep, gentle chuckle would have melted the heart of Scrooge. Everything about Bertha was higher and lighter—her voice, her laugh, the relative quickness of her hands and legs. They were devoted to each other, that was for sure.

We didn't stay long. Gus and Alice knew that Bertha had plenty to do, and besides, we wanted to get home well before dark. We turned in early that evening, worn out. But that night, sitting up in the sofa bed for a few last moments of wakefulness, I turned the day over in my mind, and felt the echoes of warmth and light.

My week with Gus and Alice ended all too soon and then it was back home to college and classes. When spring rolled around, I gave thought to a summer job in a museum in New England. I was turning nineteen and getting ready to fly. Off went a dozen letters of application, including one to the Canterbury Shakers. I hoped for one offer from the lot. One came from the Canterbury Shakers, who were hiring summer tour guides, and I'm sure that my association with Gus and Alice put me in a favorable light. Because I was from out of town, they would give me room and board so I could afford to go. The only other offer, coincidentally, was from another Shaker museum in Massachusetts, Hancock Shaker Village, where there were handsome buildings and a fine collection, but no living Shakers anymore. They needed a clerk in the gift shop, and I'd have to find a place to stay.

In hindsight, the choice seems obvious. I'd like to say that there was no contest at the time, but that's not true. I had my eye on a young man, and the plain truth is that I chose Canterbury because it was slightly closer to where he lived. Never mind that it was a one-way crush. Gus and Alice, who knew of my initial indecision, told me later that they'd held their breaths, knowing how special an opportunity it would be to live and work with the Shakers, and hoping I'd choose well.

God works in mysterious ways, and I did make the right choice.

# CHAPTER 2

# Memorial Day

Afternoon, Saturday, May 27, 1972. For the second time in my life, I was standing at the big door to the Trustees' Office in Canterbury Shaker Village. Mom, Grandma, and I were tired after the long drive on a warm day. The aging Chevy had old-style air conditioning—you cranked down the window for cool, and

28

cranked it back up for warm. Now, as the sun faded, so did we. It was good to be here at last.

This time, we made our approach to the Shaker village the other way, through Canterbury Center from the interstate. The "downtown" was even smaller than Martin's Creek. There was a store, a church, a cemetery, a little town hall, a tiny public library, and a few houses. The town green was hardly bigger than Grandma's lawn. It didn't have any traffic lights. Even my hometown had them (well, one). Everything seemed to be painted white. It was dinky, all right, but it was also pretty. We passed through town in less time than it has taken to write this paragraph and continued on Baptist Road, narrow, winding, and pocked with potholes.

Bertha met us at the door, gracious and kind. We gathered in the sitting room and all the ladies hit it off. Grandma presented a tin of her delicious sugar cookies, her standard gift to friends old or new. Bertha made us welcome to supper, but Mom declined

*Canterbury Shaker Village*

Bertha's invitation to eat and stay overnight. It was a Shaker tradition to extend lodging to friends and visitors from the World, and the old Trustees' Office had tucked in thousands of weary visitors during its hundred and forty–something years. But to Mom, the village seemed like the end of the earth, dark and desolate at night. She politely but firmly declined, insisting that she didn't want to put Bertha to extra work and that she and Grandma would stay in a motel in Concord. Bertha was gently amused. Her peaceful Shaker village seemed a much safer place than any city.

That first day was a blur. There was so much to take in and I was all eyes and ears. As it happened, my arrival coincided with a day that was twice blessed. It was the day of Bud's wedding to Nancy, whom the Shakers liked very much, and it was Bertha's "Shaker birthday," sixty-seven years ago to the day that she had been brought to the Shakers when she was seven years old in 1905. How many changes had come to pass in that lifetime, I thought with wonder, in the World, in the United Society, and in her own individual life. Sixty-seven years . . . more than twenty-four thousand mornings of awakening, twenty-four thousand afternoons of work, and twenty-four thousand nights of rest in this place. I had yet to live through one such day.

For Bertha on this day, the first order of business was to settle me into my new quarters. I would share the old Infirmary with Jennie Starkweather, Bertha's helper in the kitchen. Like me, Jennie had room and board as part of her pay. Unlike me, Jennie had a home nearby, where she went every weekend. Jennie was there now, at her brother's in Wilmot Flat, so I wouldn't meet her until Monday. Jennie lived downstairs, and a room upstairs would be mine for the summer. The white clapboard building was built in 1811 and served as the village's Infirmary, but it hadn't been used to house the sick and infirm for many years. With the passage of time and the decline of membership, the Shakers had let go of their reliance on their own medical practitioners and turned

to worldly doctors, instead. Now, the Infirmary was really just a
house for Jennie, with the upstairs rooms vacant. Until her death
the year before, Eldress Marguerite Frost had lived here downstairs
with Jennie.

The Infirmary was the first house in the row across the
road from the Office. It was two stories with an ell out the back. It
didn't look that big until I realized that I was comparing it to the
Trustees' Office, which had maybe twenty rooms on five levels,
and the really big Dwellinghouse, with more than fifty rooms. The
Infirmary was much larger than any of my friends' houses, and it
was certainly bigger than ours. Bertha walked me over, through
the old gate and up the few steps of the narrow stone walk, and we
went inside. Whew! Bertha had mentioned that Jennie had cats,
but my nose would have told me that. We were in a narrow hallway. Jennie's rooms were on the left, facing the road. She had a
sitting room, a bedroom, and a kitchen at the far end of the hall.

There were two rooms on the right, the old "Medicine
Room" in the back, where Shakers had worked with herbal reme-
dies and other nostrums, and a front room, now the village's
library, which consisted of a glass-fronted case of books about
the Shakers, to help the tour guides learn more. The Medicine
Room was now Jennie's laundry, outfitted with a modest washing
machine. A small bathroom, no doubt installed sometime early in
the twentieth century in what had been a closet, separated Jennie's
sitting room and bedroom. It had an old-fashioned claw-foot tub.
Bertha said that I would share the bath with Jennie. That was okay
with me. I wasn't expecting a modern shower. Besides, we had a
tub like that at home.

About the only other thing in the hall besides a nice old
grandfather clock was an enclosed staircase. Bertha lifted the latch
and pulled herself up the narrow stairs, with me and my bags in
tow. Her knees were not in the best of shape, and I knew from an
occasional "oof" that the climb was painful, but she didn't make a

big deal about it. A few steps took us to my room in the front, over Jennie's sitting room.

Many years later, when I had the opportunity to show my old room to a colleague, she took one look and said, "How depressing." Her reaction astonished me. I guess I could see the room through her eyes that day, and okay, maybe the plaster was a little dingy with age and the white paint on the woodwork needed a good scrubbing, but all I could really see was the sunlit, airy room of my first Shaker summer. Heaven! I had shared a room with my sister Ann my whole life. We got along all right but I craved privacy. Now I was in college, sharing a room yet again. My roommate and I were the best of friends, but boy, it was grand to have a room of my own for the first time in my life.

Bertha gave me a brief tour of the amenities: an adjacent toilet in a tiny closet, an old-fashioned sink with two taps (*H* on the right and *C* on the left, backward, in the old-fashioned way), a white-painted iron bedstead (single, of course), a nightstand, three Shaker rockers, a chest of drawers, and a TV—all this, just for me. The only decorations were a couple of doilies on the chest of drawers and an old framed print of a tiny plane coursing through a sky of improbably billowing clouds, entitled *The Spirit of St. Louis*. The TV, which I spent very little time watching, was not a surprise because I knew the Shakers were at ease with technology. I learned that they had been given their first television set as a gift the year I was born, 1953, long before my family ever thought of owning one. There certainly seemed to be a lot of TVs in the village. I think my count that summer was seven or eight.

The original Shaker fixtures were the best thing about the room. I liked the built-in drawers and pegs; maybe they could keep me more tidy. There was a small, built-in wood box, over by the closet, and a built-in set of drawers and cupboard. The walls were fitted above our heads with a peg rail, like all classic Shaker interiors, only in this room the original turned wooden pegs had

been replaced with cast-iron hooks. The hooks were just one indi-
cator that this room had been modernized, probably around the
time that Grandma was a teenager. The woodwork, originally finished with a warm ocher stain in classic Shaker style, had been
repainted white, and the original wooden floor had been covered
with linoleum, a subdued pattern in shades of brown. The indoor
plumbing was an update, as was the electricity. The newest thing
in the room, beside the TV, was a relatively modern gas heater, a
replacement for the original Shaker wood-burning stove. Well,
that was good; I didn't know how to build a fire, anyway, and the
last thing I wanted to do was burn down an irreplaceable historic
structure.

I was glad for all the windows, too. There were four of them,
two on the south wall and two on the west, facing the road, so my
room was flooded with light. Sheer dotted-Swiss curtains hung
over old-fashioned dark green window shades. Each window had
a set of sliding, interior shutters, which were the neatest thing
of all. All you had to do was pull on the wooden knob, and the
paneled shutter slid smoothly into place over the panes. Bertha
called them "Indian shutters," adding that it was merely a figure of
speech because the Shakers and the local natives had gotten along
just fine.

Bertha smiled and told me to make myself at home. As she
"oofed" off down the stairs, I unpacked my bags. I hadn't brought
much, just some clothes and books, plus the old Pink Lady bike
that my sister had cast off. It had fat tires and no gears, but it
was my only source of transportation and I was happy to have
it. The bright flower-garden quilt that Grandma had made went
on the bed, along with my battered old teddy. My prize possession, the miniature room from Gus and Alice, went on the nightstand. There . . . now I was home. *The* most essential items, my
oversize rollers and hair dryer, the kind with the bonnet and the
hose, went into the top drawer of the chest. It was 1972. Frizzy

hair was for hippies, and I didn't qualify. It took time, skill, and the right equipment to tame my hair daily into submission, especially in humid summer. It was a losing battle, but I stubbornly fought the good fight.

I peered into the mirror on the small medicine cabinet over the sink. Here I was, way off my turf. Was I any different? Who was I, anyway? The same old questions rolled around in my head. The same old face peered back at me, with the same old automatic assessment: face too long, nose too big, chin too pointy. "Spare Parts"—that's what one friend's older brother called me.

I had a pretty good sense of humor, so I didn't especially mind the teasing, but I wished someone could tell me how to make the most of what I did have. The wire-rim glasses were in style but they didn't seem right on me, somehow. I often pulled my hair back into a bun, which looked pretty on other girls, but I suspected that it looked goofy on me. Olive Oyl . . . Stan Laurel . . . these were not the faces that smiled fetchingly from the glossy pages of *Seventeen* and *Glamour*, but they were the faces that looked back at me.

Nope, I wasn't any different, not yet, anyway.


I stuck my head into the rooms across the hall, just to see what they were like—full of old stuff in piles, evidently—but I didn't take time to explore the rest of the Infirmary yet. That could wait. All of a sudden I felt chicken about heading over to the Office. Sure, the Shakers were wonderfully friendly. Yes, I knew that everything was going to work out fine this summer. And yet . . . and yet . . . three months suddenly seemed like an awfully long time. What if I didn't like it here after all? What if they didn't like me? I had been away from home a couple of years earlier, but not for that long, and with people my age.

I was on new ground. The youngest Shaker here was more

than fifty years my senior. The thought of giving up and going home never entered my head as a possibility. In our family, once you made a decision, you were supposed to stick with it. "You made your bed, now lie in it"—I'd heard that about a million times. My experience that other time had been unhappy, in spite of (or maybe because of) being entirely with people my own age. Those weeks had convinced me that I was hopelessly inept socially, and it had taken guts to make this trip. The sun was still bright outside, but I felt a little shiver. Well, nothing to do but go on over. I couldn't hide in my room for the summer.

It was nearly time for dinner, only they called it "supper" here. (Lunch, or the noon meal, was "dinner.") The group at the table tonight was going to be small: just Lillian, Bertha, Eldress Gertrude, and I. Lillian and Bertha, of course, were familiar to me from Gus and Alice's stories and from our brief meeting the summer before. Eldress Gertrude was new, not just to me, but to Canterbury. Oh, she'd been a Shaker for years, all right, but not here at Canterbury. Eldress Gertrude was from Sabbathday Lake. Bertha explained merely that Eldress Gertrude was "visiting," and no more was said to me that day about it.

For my part, I was charmed. The Eldress from Maine was small and straight as a poker in her handsome wine-colored dress. A net cap covered her white hair. She looked just like the other Sisters, except for her feet. Lillian and Bertha wore sensible shoes— what my sister and I called "old-lady shoes." Eldress Gertrude's tiny feet sported a chic pair of navy blue espadrilles. Her language was slightly different, too. Instead of "yes" and "no," she used the traditional Shaker "yea" and "nay." Behind a pair of rimless spectacles, her blue eyes snapped over a jack-o'-lantern grin that split her face. I could tell she was going to be fun.

Bertha was down in the Office Kitchen, on her own today because it was Jennie's day off. The housekeeper, Margaret, was off for the weekend, too. Bud and Nancy were away on their honeymoon. With her two boys to be added to his two, the village would soon be a livelier place. The other Shakers did not eat with us in the Office, I learned. Up in the Dwellinghouse, Alice and Ethel got their own meals. Miriam fixed hers, too, in the Enfield House, the building next to the Infirmary. Bertha gave the tour guides noon dinner during the season, but the rest of them weren't here yet because there was a day or two to go.

Precisely at six, a little bell chimed, the signal for us to go down to eat. The Sisters told me that they customarily ate breakfast and sometimes light suppers in a sort of kitchenette on the first floor, in the back of the building. Dinners and most suppers were served in the Dining Room downstairs, off the Office Kitchen. You could tell at a glance that this was not the big communal dining room for the Shaker Family, which in this part of the village had once numbered perhaps a hundred—there wasn't nearly enough room. That large dining room was up in the Dwelling-house. This dining room was where the Shakers had served (in fact, still served) visitors from the World who came to the Office on business or a pleasure call. It was also where the hired help had been fed. Were still being fed, I realized. Jennie, Margaret, and the guides who ate here, including me, were part of that tradition, too.

When Bertha was my age, the workers had been mostly hired men. In their heyday, of course, the Shakers had relied on their own membership for all the farmwork. But as the nineteenth century passed into the twentieth, the number of Brothers dwindled severely. By 1900, Shaker women vastly outnumbered Shaker men. The last Canterbury Brother, Irving Greenwood, had died in 1939, and the Sisters had run the village since then. The problem was universal throughout the United Society in America from the later 1800s. Faced with the choice of selling off farmland or using hired help, the Shakers in most communities reluctantly employed hired men. They got the work done, but they weren't always the best influence on the young people, especially the girls. Like the

Brethren, the hired men were now long gone, too. The Shakers had sold much of their acreage and now leased the remaining fields to local farmers.

Although the Office dining room was small by Shaker standards, it was still a good-sized room. The dining room and adjacent kitchen were not gloomy underground rooms, even though they were on the basement level, because the land sloped down from the road on this side. The kitchen, in the front of the building nearer the road, was lit by two big windows on the south. The dining room was flooded with light from windows to the south and west. This room had been modernized around the turn of the century with showy pressed-tin panels over the original plaster ceiling and walls. The tin was painted in two shades of green. The room was like a box gift-wrapped on the inside. The good company china was stored in a built-in cupboard with glass doors, over drawers for the silverware. Over by the sideboard was a small opening in the wall. Bertha said it allowed the Kitchen Sisters to pass food to the hired men. I understood that it was also meant to limit contact between the young Sisters and the hired men—to avoid illicit romances.

We took our places at the dining table, which comfortably seated eight. It was apparent that Bertha was sold on plastic, because our place settings were neatly arranged on plastic place mats over a plasticized tablecloth. In the old days, the Shakers ate from the plainest of dishes on bare tables, honoring Mother Ann's counsel of simplicity. Purists might have shuddered, but the plastic made sense to me. It was easy to wipe and it protected the table. Cleanliness, efficiency, care for communal possessions—what wasn't Shaker about that?

Our meal began with grace. Like the Quakers, the Shakers preferred silent prayer. I thought that was fine; spoken prayers usually embarrassed me. We all joined hands and bowed our heads. After a few moments, Eldress Gertrude murmured "Amen" and we knew it was time to dig in. I can't remember exactly what Bertha served at my first Shaker meal, but it was abundant, varied, and delicious. She had been cooking professionally since she was thirteen. Feeding a communal Family of more than a hundred on a daily basis was like running a restaurant.

Bertha seemed incapable of presenting a meal that included fewer than a half dozen offerings. There was a main dish, of course, and a nice variety of sides, served family style: two different kinds of vegetables, a salad or two, a big bowl of mashed potatoes, little pressed glass dishes of pickles and other "sauces." What a quandary. I loved to eat, but I was also diet-conscious. I paled at the momentary vision of myself waddling back to school in September. As it turned out, I needn't have worried. Bertha was trying to mind her waistline, too, and Margaret needed low-fat meals because of heart problems.

I learned to fill my plate with a spoonful of this and a taste of that. I found as the summer passed that I actually ate less when there was so much variety, so I could always have a serving of dessert, which was blancmange that evening. I had heard of this old-fashioned dish but I'd never had it. It was a delicate, pearly pudding, thickened with Irish moss, a kind of seaweed. I wasn't too sure about the seaweed, but I tried it and it was delicious. The others told me about Bertha's pies: apple, delicately flavored with rosewater, or Maine blueberry, with juicy fresh blueberries in a sauce, or sweet-sour lemon meringue.

I wasn't the only one whose mouth was watering. Someone else, someone with furry ears and big brown eyes, lurked under the table and drooled, too. During dinner, I noticed that Eldress Gertrude kept sneaking tidbits to Bertha's dog, Honey. When she caught my eye, she put her finger to her lips and grinned in conspiracy. This was forbidden fruit, not just for Eldress Gertrude, but for the dog as well. Bertha's dog had to watch her waistline, too, with all her friends wanting to treat her, so Bertha had laid down the law. Bertha was nearly blind, so Eldress Gertrude seemed to figure that she could get away with just shoving a bit of food under the table by her knee.

Bertha was nobody's fool, however, and she always cottoned on to what was up. It amused the rest of us to watch the guilty parties get caught red-handed, as Bertha would lightly say, "I think my Honey is getting something she shouldn't." Eldress Gertrude would laugh and Honey would snuffle for more. In this and other little ways Eldress Gertrude seemed to receive special dispensation, which I was to understand better as the summer passed. The rest of us obeyed Bertha's wishes, so Honey didn't seem in grave danger of getting too fat.

When it was time to clear the table, Bertha politely tried to shoo me upstairs because I was "company." I said that no, I wasn't, I was here for the summer, so she laughed and let me help. There was a routine in the cleanup. Bertha tended to the leftovers, which she called "little foxes," although she couldn't say why, it was just what she'd always heard. Meanwhile, Eldress Gertrude whipped the dishes into the double sink. She was quick, like a bird. *Plop* went each dish into the soapsuds on the right, then *plip*, into the scalding, clear water on the left.

Lillian's job was to dry. She fished the dishes and utensils out of the rinse water, then wiped them dry and stacked them on the counter. She insisted on doing her part and the others expressed their pleasure in and respect for her help. This attitude was a time-honored part of Shaker life. The most aged members were encouraged to keep busy at simple chores for as long as they could, and were praised for their contributions.

It was decided that my job could be to put things away, since I had the youngest, spryest legs of the bunch. As I went, Bertha told me where to put everything. "A place for everything, and everything in its place," the Shakers said. The kitchen was so well organized that it didn't take long to remember what went where.

Order, a Shaker tradition that Bertha especially honored, served her special needs well. In spite of her failing eyesight, she could put her hands on anything she wanted, as long as the rest of us put things away where they belonged. Memory was never Bertha's problem, just occasional confusion originating down in the ranks with me and other well-meaning but occasionally inept assistants. I wondered if Bertha would let me help out in the kitchen when she was making dinner, as Grandma did.

When everything was tidied, we made our way upstairs in a slow and stately procession. I had admired the smooth, simple beauty of the banisters on the way down the stairs, but now I could appreciate their utility. The handrail was just the right size and shape for a good grip to hoist a tired old body up. Quick-stepping Eldress Gertrude went first. Next came Lillian, who made her gentle joke: "With my cane, I am able." Bertha said I should go ahead of her, because I was faster, but I made some excuse and went behind. If she took a wrong step and toppled backward, at least she'd land on a padded cushion—me. It was only my first day, but already my protective instincts were aroused. If there was something I could do to help preserve these lovely old ladies, then, by God, I would.

The rest of the evening passed quickly because I was tired from the trip and the newness of everything. We gathered in the sitting room and watched TV—Lawrence Welk and then *All in the Family*. Later, when I became Bertha's "eyes" and read aloud to her, someone gave her an autobiography of Lawrence Welk. She asked me to read it to her, so I did, which was truly a labor of love. I got a kick out of the fact that Eldress Gertrude got a big kick out of Archie Bunker.

At nine we retired to the back kitchen and had a cup of something warm—tea for Bertha and Postum for Eldress Gertrude. I thought I'd give the Postum a try—hmmmm, like molasses dripped on shredded wheat. It was time for Honey's biscuit and

rest stop out back. Here was something else I could do to help—
the last thing Bertha needed was one more trip up and down those
stairs. I made up my mind that this would be my nightly chore.
Bertha always protested, but in time her protests grew mild and
weak, and I could tell that she was glad.

Morning dawned early and I was awake with the first light.
Breakfast was promptly at eight in the back kitchen on the first
floor, I'd been told, so I had some time to write in my diary and
think.

The second day went fast. Since the museum was not yet
open, Bertha said, the Sisters were still free to take it easy after
breakfast, perhaps spend some quiet time in the sitting room. After
dinner, she would take me and another new guide through the
tour so we could learn the spiel. When Bud came back, he would
tell us some more. Visitors and their guide began at the Trustees'
Office, built in 1831 of Shaker-made bricks, and stopped first in
the Summer Kitchen, a cozy ell tacked to the Office Kitchen. The
Office was built on land that sloped sharply down from the road,
so even though it was a story below the first floor, the Summer
Kitchen was at ground level, like the basement kitchen. In the late
1800s the Shakers had built it for the convenience of the Office
Kitchen Sisters as a cooler place to work during hot weather. Now
it was an exhibit room, and was the first stop on the tour.

It was a pleasant room, well lit by large windows. On the wall
were old framed portraits of some of Canterbury's distinguished
Shaker leaders. One nice-looking Sister was Mary Whitcher, a
granddaughter of Benjamin Whitcher, a farmer and early convert
on whose property the Canterbury community first gathered to
worship in the 1780s after a Shaker missionary from Mother Ann
came through town. As they felt the "gift," the Believers made an
oral covenant to consecrate themselves and their property to the

Church, or Church Family. In 1792 the Canterbury Shaker Society was formally sanctioned by the Central Ministry in New Lebanon, New York, or "gathered into order." Sister Mary's face beamed gently from its frame. Her face was haloed by a more solid version of Bertha's cap and she had a kerchief crossed neatly over her bosom.

Mary had died before Bertha's time—in fact, just before Lillian came to the village—but Bertha said that she felt especially kindly toward Mary because she was so well loved and had earned the respect and affection of the outside world for her business acumen. She was also a good cook. In 1882 the United Society published a cookbook, the Shakers' first, *Mary Whitcher's Shaker Housekeeper,* a pamphlet that featured daily menus and recipes for goodies like "Very Nice Cookies" and "Poor Man's Cake" among advertisements and testimonies for Corbett's Shakers' Sarsaparilla, "The Great Purifier of the Blood and other Fluids of the Body." Bertha confided that she wanted to write a cookbook, too, and hoped that she would live to see her goal accomplished.

There were a handful of artifacts in the Summer Kitchen, but the most interesting things were built in. Under a trapdoor in the floor, there was a drain, beautifully carved out of granite. Bertha recalled that it was a great help for the Kitchen Sisters when they were canning or doing other such work in the summer. And there was a neatly made cat door cut into the big door that opened into the Office Kitchen. In the old days, the Shakers had not allowed pets because they were too worldly. Cats were for catching mice and dogs were for guarding livestock. Animals were for work, not mere pleasure. But as time went by, some of the old strict rules were relaxed. Bertha sighed when she patted her dog. She was glad for the company, she said, but really wished that she still had some little girls to love.

We continued up the wide green Lane to the Meetinghouse, which was the main part of the museum. As we walked, Bertha recounted early Shaker history, telling how Mother Ann brought seven followers to America in 1774, and about a vision of angels that miraculously saved the good ship *Mariah* from sinking in a storm. Mother Ann didn't live to see any communities formed, but in time there were nineteen principal villages with a total population that Bertha said was about six thousand around 1860. As she talked, I scribbled madly in my diary. There was so much to remember!

I followed her into the Meetinghouse. For more than ten years now, Bud and other guides had shown visitors the assortment of Shaker objects that he had installed in the first floor. There were all sorts of wonderful curiosities, some of which I remembered from my brief visit the year before: a china doll dressed in a small and perfect Shaker bonnet and cloak (much older and more detailed than the simple dolls that my sister and I had gotten in Maine), a clever wooden mold for making strawberry baskets, a Shaker dentist's chair, sleek and simple and far less forbidding than the clutches of the cold white-and-chrome contraptions of my experience.

There were textiles—linens and woolens from this village, silk from the Kentucky Shakers, wrinkle-resistant cloth from Sabbathday Lake—and baskets, ironware, tinware, brooms and brushes, old photos of the Sisters making maple-sugar candy, chairs, tools, oval boxes, and a print of the famous industrial-scale washing machine that won a gold medal for the Canterbury Shakers at the 1876 Philadelphia Centennial Exposition.

The crowning glory was a very large map of Canterbury Shaker Village, as big as the top of a dining table, drawn and colored in 1848 by Brother Henry Blinn when he was a young man, just five years older than I was that summer. It showed the main part of the village at its peak: three communal Families on four thousand acres of woodland and farmland, with seven connected man-made ponds and their mills out back to the east. Most of the

SIMPLE GIFTS · 44

buildings were long gone. Bertha explained how the Shakers had systematically razed structures that had fallen into disuse, not only to avoid unsightly disorder, but to save on taxes. Although the Shakers were a religious society, they were not tax-exempt. When the United Society first settled in Canterbury, there was already enough suspicion, or at least dismay, about the unconventional sect, so the early Shaker leaders deemed it prudent to pay taxes like all other good citizens. Besides, they felt a responsibility to support the government that guaranteed their freedom, and taxes were an acceptable alternative to military service, which as pacifists they could not in good conscience provide. But what did survive was just as young Henry drew it. There was the Office; there was the Infirmary; there was this very Meetinghouse in which we were standing, built in 1792. That made it fifty-six years old when Henry sketched it. Now it was 180 years old. I couldn't wait to spend more time poring over the map's details.

Near it there was a large black-and-white portrait photo-graph of an older Henry, now Elder, in a gilded frame. He wore a plain Shaker Brother's suit and his silver hair was shaped in the regulation Shaker haircut: straight short bangs in front, shoulder-length in back. I wasn't supposed to think this way, I guessed, but, my, he was handsome. What a nice face. From the frame he gazed out over the room, a quiet, peaceable perusal that seemed to rest content in what he saw. The more I heard about him, the more I liked him.

We had things in common, I learned. Like me, Henry had been drawn to this village young, even younger than I. He came of his own volition at age fourteen, attracted from his home in Providence, Rhode Island, by the promise of a large and whole family of Believers, as well as an education. Like me, Henry had lost his father early in life. The bones of sea Captain Blinn lay dreaming in the rich, moist soil of Jamaica, far from New England's frosty ground. Navy Lieutenant Sprigg was swallowed by the greedy, gray Atlantic in 1954, down, down, down into the black water at the bottom of the sea. Henry and I were even the same age when our mothers became widows, not yet two years old when we learned the heart of loss before we knew any language but crying.

Bertha limped on through the village, talking all the while. We didn't go into most of the buildings that we passed—they weren't restored yet, Bertha said, but she and Bud had a plan to open one more every season if they could. We went by the Ministry Shop, finished in 1849 behind the Meetinghouse; the enormous Dwellinghouse, started in 1793, with its fifty-six rooms; the Sisters' Shop; the Laundry; the North Shop; and one of the community's "newest" buildings, the Creamery, built in 1905, the year Bertha was brought to the Shakers.

Then on past the incredible drive-through Cow Barn, two hundred and fifty feet long, including a ramp at each end. The prize herd of thoroughbred Guernseys was long gone, but Bertha remembered them well. Lily Bell of Canterbury was the queen of the herd. Bertha smiled and added that cows were fine but she preferred the horses kept by the community when she was young. We continued on past other "new" buildings—the Garage, built in 1908, and the generating station from 1910. The next-to-last stop was the two-story Schoolhouse. It had started life as a one-room schoolhouse in 1823, but some years later, the Shakers enlarged it by raising it twelve feet and adding a second story underneath.

The schoolroom, well equipped and cheerful, was fitted with old-fashioned desks and chalkboards that were made of frosted glass painted black. Bertha talked about the progressive leaders before the turn of the century who made Shaker life more appealing to young people, in the hopes of keeping more of them as converts. Eldress Dorothy Durgin and Elder Henry Blinn had both served as teachers here, but not at the same time, of course—boys went to school in winter, girls in summer. Here was the little parlor organ brought into the community in the 1870s, one of the first musical instruments allowed under the new, relaxed interpretation of the rules—rules that prohibited the use of instruments other than the human voice. Music was a big part of Shaker education.

The last stop was the Carriage House, and then we wandered back out onto the road and back to the Office. Bertha said that it was always nice to invite company back to use the rest room or to visit the Gift Shop. She meant it, too. In her eyes, visitors were not tourists, they were guests. Hospitality and courtesy were the rule.

I had enjoyed my first two days with the Shakers, but I was beginning to feel strange and out of place. I didn't realize how stressful it was to fit into a new household and a new routine, even though I was willing and they made me feel welcome. I definitely needed some quiet time to myself. Was it all right if I explored around the village on my own? Bertha said sure. Now I was free . . . still glad to be here, but maybe more glad for a time to be alone with my thoughts.

It made sense to retrace the path of the tour, and I already knew that the Meetinghouse was a peaceful place. The walk up the Lane was a pleasant stroll. It was so quiet here. To the right, as far as the eye could see, an unbroken sea of trees rolled away to the horizon. There was no hint of the houses and trailers, garages and gas stations that busied themselves along Route 106. At the top of the Lane, a white picket fence enclosed the Meetinghouse in its own small yard. I remembered what Bertha had said about the fence. The wooden pickets were held above the ground on granite posts. The fence builders had gone to this trouble to preserve the wood from rot and spare themselves the work of replacement, and the original pickets were still in good shape after about 125 years. They were beautiful, too. The top of each was shaped like a candle flame, or a signpost to guide weary saints home.

Two gates in the fence opened to two short stone walks that

led to two sets of stone steps to the two front doors of the Meetinghouse, so even if you didn't know that the Shakers were a celibate, egalitarian society, you could see at a glance that something was up. The twin doors and stairs seemed a fitting icon for the way that the Shakers regarded men and women—forever different (and in the Shakers' world, separate), always equal, in balance, neither one before the other, but comfortably marching to salvation side by side. It seemed so simple. I didn't see why it was so hard for the World outside to grasp.

The Meetinghouse was a pleasing equation: wooden-shingled gambrel-roof angles plus white clapboard, divided by narrow windows, whose panes appeared black in the daytime. Back home, I had always sought the hilltops on my daily after-school walks, but I had seldom sensed such serenity as here. It surprised me, because until now I'd experienced peacefulness only in the natural world, far from anything man-made. In 1792 the Canterbury Shakers had pooled their resources and labor to build this house of worship first; the Dwellinghouse, where they ate and slept, waited until the next year. In this Meetinghouse, the Canterbury Shakers had danced and sung for the love of God.

I love old trees, and I sat and looked at the double row of maples. Bertha had talked about them as if they were friends, and I could see why. Elder Henry had set them out in 1859 and 1860, or rather had supervised their planting by the community's children. Each child took care of a tree. They'd done a good job. The crowns were healthy and green in spite of their great age. The maples nearest the Meetinghouse were the oldest I'd ever seen, bigger even than the others in the row. Gray-green lichens patched the fissures in their deeply scarred trunks.

The delicate breeze that always seemed to stir in the Lane, like a breath of some long-ago hymn, wandered rustling in the leaves. It was easy to sense that the trees were alive; I wished I could know all that they had seen. At the foot of the maple on the right, a pair of granite gateposts to a fence long gone opened to the field, like a doorway to another time. The rest of the village faded away. The field and wooded hills seemed to go on forever. From this rise, the world below looked like Eden, untouched. A scent of apple blossoms drifted from the orchard, now ragged with age, at the edge of the wide green field.

I sat for a while on the granite steps, feeling my spinning new world come back to its center, until a swarm of blackflies broke the spell and drove me to my feet. There was more to explore. I headed off through the yard to the left of the Meeting-house. Mmm, lilacs . . . I buried my nose in a light purple bunch and thought of the bush in Grandma's backyard. Here was the Dwellinghouse, looming to my left, but in a friendly way. It was a long, tall building of white clapboard with lots of windows. The Dwelling was at right angles to the Meetinghouse. This whole end of the village sloped down to the road, so the first floor of the Dwelling was at ground level on the east but above ground on the west. Steep steps rose to meet the front door under a white Victorian porch. A row of dormers poked through the roof, and up on top, a simple but handsome cupola held the community's big bell.

Sprouting from the roof next to the cupola was—what else?—a TV antenna. The Dwellinghouse was not on the public tour, partly because it needed restoration, but mostly because of Sister Alice Howland and Sister Ethel Hudson. In all those fifty-six rooms these two made their home. Gus and Alice knew of them, of course, but they had never met. Ethel was a bit of a recluse, I understood, perfectly happy to have company, but reluctant her-self to venture beyond the door. It made me smile to think of two old Shaker ladies rattling around in all those rooms. Talk about a room of your own! They could use a different room every day for a month, if they wanted.

This practice of Shakers living in separate buildings was

something new in the later twentieth century. I knew that in old times, virtually all of the Shakers in this part of the village lived together in the Dwelling. Four or five Sisters shared each bedroom, dormitory style. The Brothers did the same, under the same roof, a cheerful, cheek-by-jowl, celibate life that worked fine for the Shakers, while frequently baffling observers from the World who wondered how on earth such an arrangement could succeed. One Elder simply explained, "We're like monks and nuns, without the bolts and bars." With fewer members, however, it had eventually made sense to the Shakers to split up. It was better for the buildings to be inhabited, and the Sisters also enjoyed some privacy, after a lifetime of mandatory sharing. Living in community was never easy. Sometimes a little elbow room was a blessing.

In the United Society's heyday, there had been nearly a hundred Shaker dwellings, one for each communal Family in the network of nineteen principal settlements, plus a number of smaller or more temporary gatherings. They were more or less built to a formula, whether large or small, brick, stone, or wood, or designed for a family of a few dozen or of more than a hundred. There were typically two floors ("lofts," the Shakers called them) with bedrooms or "retiring rooms." Brothers' and Sisters' quarters were on the same floors, but on opposite sides of the building. Above were one or maybe two floors of attic storage, used mostly for off-season clothing. The first floor usually included a communal dining room and a big meeting room, where the Shakers who lived here met for Family business, discussions, worship, and celebrations. The kitchens and food-storage rooms were normally on the ground floor, or in the basement.

I was eager to explore the Dwellinghouse, but that would have to wait until I was introduced to Alice and Ethel. In the meantime, I glanced around the yard at the Ministry Shop, a trim, white clapboard house behind the Meetinghouse where the members of the Ministry lived and worked. I knew from the tour and from my reading that this had been home to the two Elders and two Eldresses who served as the primary authority for every Shaker in the state of New Hampshire. In the old days, the New Hampshire Ministry divided its time between Canterbury and Enfield, about forty miles to the northwest, not far from Dartmouth College.

Bud always spoke with admiration of Elder Henry Blinn of the Ministry as the last of the great old-time Shaker leaders in New Hampshire. As a young woman, Lillian had really loved the old Elder, who, in typical Shaker fashion, was gifted in about a dozen useful trades, including cabinetmaking, printing, beekeeping, record keeping, stonecutting, and more. But the young people at the turn of the century loved him for his kindness and good humor. From what I'd heard, I knew that Elder Henry was a primary reason why Canterbury was still in existence: he was one of the enlightened, progressive members who genuinely enjoyed the spirit of change for the sake of the young. He wanted them to like Shaker life enough to stay.

Between the Dwellinghouse and the Infirmary was the Enfield House, so called because the last few Shakers from the Enfield community had come to roost here around World War I, when their property was sold. The Canterbury Shakers gave them a home of their own. They moved this building, originally the 1826 Trustees' Office of the North Family up the road, onto this site for the Enfield Shakers' use. It was a smaller version of the Dwelling, with two front doors and twin stepped porches.

Sister Miriam Wall and Mildred Wells lived here. Gus and Alice were fond of cheerful Miriam, an avid Red Sox fan. Mildred was something else. She was not a Shaker in the same sense as the other Sisters, but rather a longtime resident who had never signed the Covenant, a legal document that stated the duties and responsibilities of the signer. From early in Shaker history in America, people who wanted to consecrate their lives and their earthly goods to the faith signed the Covenant when they were deemed ready, although the practice was not enforced consistently throughout Shaker history. For members who had grown up in the village from childhood, that step usually took place when they came of age. Bertha and the others had signed when they turned twenty-one. I understood that Mildred had signed some articles of agreement, so she was technically the last novitiate at Canterbury.

I had glimpsed Mildred briefly the year before. She was strange, grim and forbidding, with a dark, powerful German Shepherd almost always at her side. Bertha had already warned me about the dog, who would chase and bite if she broke free. But Gus and Alice had mentioned some good things, too. Mildred was a wonderful gardener. She took Bertha's dog for long walks, a real kindness to both Honey and Bertha. Honey adored her. As Alice said, no one who was that good with flowers and dogs could be all bad. Besides, Gus said that Mildred always saved up a big bag of wood scraps to give him when he and Alice came. She never called him anything but "the man." They were useless for his purposes, but he appreciated the thought, and he always thanked her just the same.

Up at the top, facing the road like the Meetinghouse, was Bud's little house. Soon I'd have more people to meet. By this time I didn't know whether I was more glad or anxious about that, although there wasn't much I could do about it either way. I wandered around the rest of the buildings, but my heart wasn't in it anymore.

Supper was a simpler version of dinner, and afterward I felt tired and shy. When cleanup was finished, I excused myself and retreated to the Infirmary. There was so much to absorb, and I was feeling more and more peculiar. It wasn't that anyone was unkind, or that anything unpleasant had happened. It was just that everything was so *new* . . . or rather, everything was so *old* . . . Well, I knew what I meant. I felt like Gulliver, a stranger in a strange land,

and I was very, very tired. Damn—the mosquitoes flocked through the old window screens in my room. The evening hours stretched ahead, long and wretched. TV held no thrills. I thought about studying my Greek text—I'd actually dragged it along—but the boring conjugations just made me feel worse. Now what?

I wrote a postcard to practically everybody I knew from college, and hoped that somebody from the outside world would remember I was alive. When I tried to sleep, the whine of mosquitoes on reconnaissance for my blood drove me nuts. I thought of books I'd read about the Middle Ages, with pictures of poor souls tormented by nasty, grinning, winged demons. Frustrated to tears, I sprayed the whole room with Extra Strength Yard-Gard. It was like using a hydrogen bomb to kill a mouse, but that night I didn't care.

The streetlight outside lit up my room enough to see shapes, but without my glasses, they were more threatening than comforting. I had never stayed alone in a house all by myself. I realized that the Infirmary was kind of creepy at night. People had died here, in this very room, maybe even in this very bed. Elder Henry himself had gone to glory in this room. I knew he was a loving and kindly soul, but whenever I awoke, I peered anxiously into the gloom, praying that no spirit of Elder Henry would want to visit poor scared me.

The next day was worse. In spite of the Shakers' kindness, I was sinking into more and more of a slough. The weather turned lousy, overcast and sticky. Mosquitoes flourished in the humidity, joining the blackflies, making it impossible to explore outdoors. Everyone had a routine but me. Since the museum was not yet open, I didn't know where I fit in or what to do. My hair frizzed like a used Brillo in the damp heat. I got crabbier and more miserable as the day went on. I fretted that I would feel this bad and worse the whole summer long.

Then a really terrible thing happened. When I crossed the

road, I found Honey in a bloody heap, the victim of a hit-and-run driver. Worst of all, she was still alive, and suffering. Her big brown eyes opened in pain and shock. I felt awful. I couldn't help her because I didn't know how, and she was beyond help, anyhow. I had to tell Bertha that her dear little dog was dying in the road, and I hated to bring her distress. Her voice high with anguish, Bertha rang up Mildred to please come down. The last I saw of Honey, she was being lifted in Mildred's powerful arms into a cardboard carton.

That did it. I got away as fast as I could and burst into tears as I climbed onto the old Pink Lady bike. I pedaled madly up the road, desperately wishing that I had somewhere else to go. But of course that was silly. I didn't know another soul in the state of New Hampshire. Anyway, if I had, the rickety bike would never have made it. So I just pounded along, crying, until I ran out of steam. There was nothing to do but turn the bike around and head back. There was nowhere to run.

It got better, I'm glad to say. I've never been exactly sure what happened, but by the end of the first week, I was in love with my new life. Who knows why? Maybe my moods just needed time to switch gears, maybe a spell of clear weather tamed my run-away hair, or maybe the planets turned a corner in their dance. But I think that my heart began to hear the whispers that linger in a holy and happy place. In the next few days, I met the rest of the village's non-Shaker residents, and it was all good. The tours started and I enjoyed giving them, once I got over the shock of realizing that my job involved public speaking. Somehow I had managed to overlook that fact in the excitement of a first summer job away from home (and the possibility of seeing Mr. Right one more time). I began to settle in, to feel my place.

All I know is that I had a change of heart. By the end of the seventh day, I knew that this summer was going to change my life. No fireworks accompanied this realization, no brass bands, no cannons; the knowledge came with a quiet sigh, like the breeze in the maples at dusk. I have the evidence in front of me now, a postcard that I wrote that week but forgot to mail. I found it in a pile of papers years later. "I love it here," I wrote. "Have a feeling that this summer is going to change my life."

When I look in my memory, the summer of 1972 seems made of moments—dozens and dozens of fragments of time that remain vivid and clear. But their sequence and order have become vague. It reminds me of the road between Sabbathday Lake and Canterbury, which in years to come became more than familiar to me as I visited back and forth. I can still conjure up individual vignettes of the journey: here, the twin farmhouses, linked by one barn, everything big, white, and beautiful, like a wedding cake. In my imagination, a rich farmer had built the place for his two beloved sons, so that they might reside in splendor, side by side, the proud talk of the town.

And here: an old iron bridge over a rocky, shallow river, its banks flanked with stone and brick mills, serene in retirement, once as noisy and demanding as children. Here was the town with the house with the grapevine painted on the porch; here was the hollow where a great patch of orange day lilies blasted summer back at the sun; and here, the stretch of road that raced past a tumble-down farm, set far back from the road, that looked like some dead or dying beast: all shaggy, gray shingles and dead black windows, the yard overgrown, the ancient pickup rusted into place, with never a sign of life. (But once I saw sheets flapping on the line.)

For all the times I traveled that road, however, I could never for the life of me remember which of these scenes was in which town, or in what order they came. I would always recognize them as I passed them yet again, but try as I might, I could not seem to fix them in my mind in one straight line. When I think of the events of my first Shaker summer, time seems like that road. I remember certain moments as if I were there now, hearing those voices, feeling that moment of warmth or coolness, each welcome in turn, breathing the air that my Shaker friends and I drew in and sighed out together.

If I want to know how those moments ordered themselves, I consult the diary I wrote that summer. In its pages, my scribbled notes record the sequence of things, like bird tracks in river mud. Now one bit of information astonishes me. Let me explain.

Whenever I have thought of my time with the Shakers, one image has always come to mind first and strongest, a single moment that seemed to epitomize the whole of that summer. That image is with me still. In my mind's eye on this dismal, gray Massachusetts day, I am again nineteen, rocking and gently perspiring on a summertime porch in southern New Hampshire half my life ago. I can see us and hear us as if the scene were preserved in the smooth glow of amber.

The screened porch—"piazza," the Shakers call it—is small and friendly, bounded outside with bushy, old-fashioned hydrangeas. The other porch on the Office, not far away, is open to the front hall, where tours begin and end. The murmur of a few departing voices blends with the ceaseless rustling of the leaves on the sugar maples across the road. All these sounds fade into a light, cheerful hum.

We are four: Sister Lillian Phelps, ninety-six, Eldress Bertha Lindsay, seventy-four, Eldress Gertrude Soule, seventy-seven, and I, comfortably tipping to and fro in our chairs, every forward surge sending a delicate breeze to foreheads and cheeks. It is the end of a summer afternoon and we are all taking a breather before Bertha goes downstairs to start supper. The ladies are talking quietly of this and that. The words aren't clear in my memory, but that doesn't matter so much. What persists is the tone: gentle, serene, at ease. The sound of their voices is like music. Lillian's low chuckles are the bass notes to Bertha's fluty laugh, which sometimes ends in a sigh. Now Eldress Gertrude introduces the fugue in her reedy contralto.

Thirty knotted fingers rest for a while on summery, flowered laps. Ten young fingers fiddle with a loop of frizzy hair. If the sheer goodness in which I feel bathed assumed substance, it would have the honeyed light of a mature afternoon and the faint scent of roses from Bertha's soap. *This* was Canterbury Shaker Village in 1972. In my memory, this moment lasts all summer long.

So it astounds me to learn that this afternoon must have taken place in the very first days of my arrival, because after June 7, we four never sat together on the piazza again, and the rhythm of life in the village was never the same afterward. By the cold, square reckoning of the calendar, I had twelve days to know Lillian as her own, whole self in her home before everything changed. Yet the impact she made on me, as on many others, was so powerful that her presence persists at the center of the moment I remember best. Lillian was the true spiritual axis of the community, even as time and age pecked at her frail old shell. That summer was a gift to me, a last chance indeed, although not the one I'd come hoping to find.

Never mind the young man near Boston. I caught the tail end of Lillian's life and times, and that's what changed my life.

CHAPTER 3

# Lillian, Bertha, and
# Eldress Gertrude

I got to know Lillian, Bertha, and Eldress Gertrude best
because they lived in the Trustees' Office, the hub of everyday life
and affairs at Canterbury at this time. The Trustees' Office had
always been a center of activity in the village, but in the old days,
there were others, too: the great communal kitchen up in the
Dwelling, the Schoolhouse, the Ministry Shop for the leaders and
their visitors, the mills and barns for the Brothers, the Laundry,
gardens, and workshops for the Sisters.

Now, with the Canterbury Society dwindled from almost
three hundred souls to six, pretty much everything that happened
took place in the Office by the side of the road, where the World
still came to call. With the other three Sisters and Mildred rattling
around in all those rooms farther up the granite walk, plus all the
unoccupied buildings, the Trustees' Office fairly hummed with
life, by comparison.

"The World" was what the Shakers in their early history
called outsiders, something like the way the Amish call everybody
else "the English." In the old days, only the community's spiritual
and business leaders enjoyed the privilege (or suffered the nui-
sance) of dealing with the World. Ordinary Brothers and Sisters
were to stay home and mind their own chores and prayers. By the

late twentieth century, however, the Shakers had long since made peace with the World, or perhaps it was the other way around. The front door of the Office was unlocked and usually open all day long. At night, of course, the Sisters bolted the door, but even on Sundays and Mondays, when the museum tours were closed, a steady stream of callers rang the bell or yoo-hooed and came on in. Some of the Shakers' personal friends were familiar faces. So was the brown-suited delivery man from United Parcel Service. Bertha called him the "ups" man and liked him because he was fond of dogs and had been kind to her Honey.

I spent most of my waking hours in the Office. Tuesday through Saturday, we tour guides waited our turns for the next hourly excursion in the sitting room just off the hall, keeping company with Lillian, who sat in the big dark rocker by the window. In the very early morning, before anybody from the World came near, Mildred would carry a great armful of fresh flowers from her garden into the hall and arrange them in a vase on a small, doily-topped stand by the entrance. Gladioli brandished spiky crowns over all, tall and glaring, like biblical swords of flame. Somehow they reminded me of Mildred.

When the Sisters were younger, years before the establishment of the museum here in 1960, it had been their job to take interested parties from the World or other Shaker communities around to look at the buildings and operations, a tradition combining hospitality and quiet pride that went far back into the nineteenth century. Now, although they hired outsiders like me to do the actual job of touring, they continued to spend time with visitors. When the tours began at nine, Eldress Gertrude took her place in the hall, just outside the sitting room and just inside the front door, to greet the day's company. The Shakers didn't think of the people who came as tourists, or of the village as a tourist attraction. It was their home, and they felt that it was only right to make their guests welcome personally. Bertha and Eldress Gertrude took turns during the day to make each arrival welcome. It was fun to watch newcomers step into the hall and meet a real live Shaker. Not knowing quite what to expect from what they supposed to be a fading society of religious, celibate eccentrics, most visitors were timid and respectful. Some were completely at ease. A few were downright rude. Bertha always laughed when Bud recalled the man who stomped in demanding to know if these were "those Shaker babes" he'd always heard about.

Bertha took her turn as greeter in the afternoon, when she was done with the morning work of preparing the noon dinner. She sat smiling gently in her favorite pink dress, making visitors welcome. Her eyesight wasn't yet completely gone, but she couldn't clearly distinguish faces, especially with the bright light from the door at the visitors' backs. Sometimes Bertha would welcome people who were returning from their tour to visit the Gift Shop or use the bathroom, and ask them politely if they would like to take a tour. She'd just laugh her light laugh when they set her straight. If she felt embarrassed, she didn't show it.

She always asked people to sign the guest register, an old, oversized, leather-bound ledger on a lectern in the hall. If they were shy, she encouraged them, saying that the Shakers liked to know where in the World—literally—their company was from. It was a daily ritual for the Sisters to pore through the register after the last afternoon tour and tally up a list of states and countries for the season. For the first few weeks, I was amazed at how far visitors had traveled to see this little country museum; they came from hometowns in France, Oregon, England, California, Australia. Then I found out that many of them were in New Hampshire for an ongoing series of scientific conferences not too far away. Well, that still counted . . . After all, they didn't *have* to choose Canterbury as a destination in their free time.

Because of Lillian's age she had retired from direct contact with visitors to the museum, but she steadily knit simple items for the Gift Shop while she sat nearby in the sitting room. Lillian occupied a special place in this community of a half dozen Shakers. Bertha and Bud liked to share the circumstances of their beloved Lillian's life with friends old and new. I heard the stories often, and was never bored.

Several factors distinguished her experience. For one, she was the last of the old-time Shakers who chose the Shaker life as an adult convert. Of course, the other Shakers now at Canterbury had made a choice, too, when they grew into young womanhood and decided to go or stay. But they had been placed with the Shakers as young children in need. All but Lillian had come from families broken by death or illness or poor luck. Bertha's parents had died within a short time of each other, leaving her older brothers and sisters to choose a new home for her. Eldress Gertrude and her sister Cora had been left with the Sabbathday Lake Shakers when their father remarried. Cora grew up there but left when she came of age. Miriam's story was much the same, and Ethel's, and Alice's, and I assumed that Mildred's was not so different.

But Lillian had left a happier home near Boston, where she was an indulged and much loved daughter, a gifted young musician with a fine conservatory education in her future. She left something especially comfortable and inviting behind. What happened was that Lillian's health declined and her family sent her to Canterbury Shaker Village for the summer to rest and recover her strength—she was "put out to pasture," she joked. Her mother and father knew the Shakers and felt safe leaving their daughter in their good, country care. A summer at Canterbury Shaker Village restored Lillian to health. She liked to add that the Shakers' famous herbal medicines had something to do with it, too—one bottle of Dr. Corbett's Shaker Syrup of Sarsaparilla, and she got well and was good for another seventy or eighty years.

To everyone's surprise, including her own, something more than physical healing came to Lillian that summer, long ago. She felt a calling to join the group of Sisters and Brothers whose life and work she had come to know in one short summer. Lillian was sixteen years old—young, yes, but an adult, nevertheless, acting on her volition, not a child at the mercy of other adults. Her face lit up when she talked about her decision and the "heavenly power" she believed had led her there. This summer, Lillian and the community would celebrate her eightieth "Shaker birthday." Eighty years a Shaker. The sun had risen in almost thirty thousand dawns of her waking here, being useful, and growing closer to God, the life work that the "old Shakers" simply called "laboring in the vineyard." I could not begin to comprehend that number of days or years.

It seemed fitting that Lillian's first Shaker summer took place in 1892, the Canterbury society's centennial year. What better way to celebrate one hundred years of a commendable past than to welcome a bright young soul who would, God willing, carry the flame into the next century? The Elders and Eldresses (including Elder Henry Blinn) must have rejoiced at Lillian's decision, and I bet they were surprised, too. By the end of the nineteenth century, converts like Lillian—intelligent, virtuous, competent, sincere— were not exactly beating down the doors for admission. The people who came were more likely to be in need, to have more of the nature of takers than givers.

So, Lillian was a rare gift, the kind of Believer who typified the very best of the first generation or two of converts, drawn by conviction, not convenience. Given Lillian's lifelong belief in reincarnation, which she and Bud sometimes described as the "evolution of souls," and Elder Henry's mysticism, I came to wonder if Lillian or Henry or both ever glimpsed the possibility of the great unseen wheels of life in motion. Maybe she, or she-who-was-now-Lillian, simply came home again.

Lillian's personal belief in reincarnation may not have been part of conventional Christianity or orthodox Shaker belief, but it was (to my surprise) part of a time-honored tradition of spiritual open-mindedness among the more progressive Shaker leaders in several communities around the turn of the twentieth century, particularly New Lebanon, New York, and Canterbury. Being unconventional was hardly likely to bother the Shakers, who after all had no problem believing that the Christ spirit could return to earth in a woman and that God was both Father and Mother—the sanest, most reasonable notion I'd ever heard, but an outlook not readily palatable to conventional Christians then or now. A few of the most enlightened Shaker leaders (or most deluded, if you happened to disagree) went so far as to consider their entire United Society a reawakening to the divinity of humankind's most ancient deity, the Great Mother.

My own spiritual sense was just forming, so I thought that was pretty wild. At nineteen I had trouble enough trying to comprehend the idea of God. I had no ordinary experience of a father, and if God was stern and distant like Grandpa, I was in trouble. Being adolescent and female, I naturally had zero interest in buying the concept of God as a mother. In fact the whole notion of God as a parental authority of any kind didn't sit well with my teenage soul. But the seeds of my mature conviction were sown. If we were made in God's image, and God was the pattern for men like Gus and women like Lillian, then I could believe we all were in good, good hands.

I came to understand quickly that, in this time and place, Lillian held the key to understanding Shaker life. She had been witness to—not merely witness to, but a living part of—the great United Society of Believers in its prime. Yes, it's true that she became part of it in 1892, on the downhill side of the curve, but Lillian at sixteen got to know much older Shakers, many of whom were loved and respected relics of the Shakers' real heyday. Besides, I felt sure that Lillian at sixteen had powers of perception beyond those of an ordinary teenage girl. Just as I listened to and learned from Lillian, whose memories kept alive a world the better part of a century older than I, so had she paid heed in her youth to others who offered her a similar glimpse. Lillian was like a stereoscope—a wondrous lens that transformed flat sepia photographs into three-dimensional life. Time was telescoped through Lillian, whose long life and sure memory formed the bridge across all of Shaker history, between the twentieth and the eighteenth centuries.

I knew that Lillian had particularly loved Dorothea Cochran, her best friend and mentor. In Lillian's first Shaker summer, Dorothea, born in Scotland in 1844, was fifty-one, with some thirty-five years' worth of Shaker life experience. Bertha also knew and loved Dorothea, who had been made Eldress by the time Bertha arrived. Dorothea called Bertha her "golden child." I guessed that it had nothing to do with her hair or physical coloring, since Bertha had dark hair and dark eyes, but with something that Dorothea saw inside her.

Then there was Eldress Dorothy Durgin, the prominent progressive leader on the "female side." When Lillian was sixteen, Eldress Dorothy was sixty-seven, with personal memories of Canterbury Shaker life that dated from 1834, when she was brought to the Shakers as a child of nine or ten. In turn, Eldress Dorothy had had a long association with kindly Mary Whitcher, whose portrait hung in the Summer Kitchen. Mary's firsthand memories of Canterbury Shaker life went back to 1826, when she too came to the village as a child of about ten. Mary herself died two years before Lillian's arrival, but her spirit lived on, strong and real, in the collective memory of the communal Family.

I could understand how that worked because I felt an odd but pleasant kinship with Elder Henry, although by the calendar we had missed each other by a mile. He had in fact died in 1905, just weeks before Bertha's arrival. She always wished that she could have crossed paths with him in person even for a short while. But she knew Lillian, and I was getting to know Lillian, and Lillian had known and loved the fatherly Elder Henry, so the connection was there, vital and genuine. Lillian was our unique link to the past. It wasn't only her personal experience that she passed on, it was what she had learned from her elders, those traveling the same spiritual path, who had passed this way just like us, only a little earlier on.

Elder Henry, in turn, had stories of his own. It was clear from his voluminous writings and historical interest that young Henry liked to hang with the old folks to learn what he could. Later, he wrote with affection of Brother Peter Ayers, an old-timer when Henry was a young convert. Peter was something of a legend at Canterbury, a lusty, vigorous fighting man whose boxer's arms weren't all that well concealed under his Believer's sleeves. When he became a Shaker, he became a spiritual warrior instead. Converted, Peter threw his energy into Shaker life and especially into the worship dance. But I bet that what impressed young Henry the most was hearing about Peter's own youthful face-to-face meeting with Mother Ann years earlier, the reason for his conversion. The experience of the earliest American Shakers like Peter, whom the old Shakers reverently called "Mother's First Born," was treasured by Believers, much as the early Christians valued the testimony of those who had actually known Jesus.

The spiritual lineage that I glimpsed through Lillian smote me. That's an old-fashioned and curious word, I know, but such was the impact. I knew and loved Lillian, held her arm when she climbed the stairs, felt her hand in mine. She had known and loved Henry, who had known and loved Peter. And Peter was a Shaker because he had met and trusted Mother Ann. It was that simple to believe in the goodness of Ann and the early Believers.


As the days passed, the strange and pleasant feeling grew that I might be part of Lillian's work, one more young soul willing to learn. Bud knew that she was failing in body, although not spirit. and said it was too bad I hadn't known Lillian in her prime (oh, say, in her seventies). But I was glad just for the overlap we did have. I wanted to be like her when I was ninety, of that I was sure.

So did Bertha, who in this goal had hands down the advantage over the likes of me. For starters, Bertha and Lillian had been best friends through good times and bad, in sickness and in health, for going on seventy years. Let's see. I'd known Lillian for going on seventy *hours*. Bertha also had sixty-seven years of practice in acquiring all the qualities that I admired in her and wanted for myself—serenity, optimism, kindness, clarity. I was just getting started, and none too soon, at nineteen. It was clear that I had better look to Bertha, too, if I had any hope of staying on the path that Lillian trod.

If Lillian was the spiritual axis of the Canterbury community, the apparent stillness at the center, then Bertha served as spokes and rim, the parts that are seen to be carrying out the hub's heart of momentum. At seventy-four, Bertha was more active than many people I knew who were years younger. She may have been plagued with the physical infirmities of advancing age—bad knees, slight deafness, and severely failing eyesight—and Lord knows she had wrinkles, but she seemed young nevertheless, I think because she felt young, for better and also for worse. I heard her say any number of times that she felt seventeen, which completely baffled me. How on earth could she feel that young, younger even than I? I understand it now, but at nineteen it made no sense that I could see. Bertha laughed gently at my youth sometimes. One afternoon when I remarked that I never felt like taking naps, she just smiled and said, "Wait until you're seventy-four." I haven't had to wait nearly that long.

I could understand, however, that she had reason to feel young, because she was actually the youngest of the surviving members of the communal family and of course had been the youngest of that particular lot for almost seventy years (if you didn't count Mildred, who was six years her junior.) Young as I was, I could already comprehend that special arithmetic. One of the nicest and most considerate things about my sister Ann is that she was, is, and will be, as long as we both shall live, one year older than I. When she is 101, I'll be merely 100, which will allow me to preserve a sense of myself as young in comparison.

Besides, Bertha used Shaker standards for judging old age, and they were definitely skewed, according to the World's guidelines. Retire at sixty-five? The Shakers thought not. "Golden-ager" or "senior citizen" at fifty-five? No way. Historically, the United Society had earned a reputation for the robust longevity of its members. That was certainly true at Canterbury. All you had to do was consult the cemetery chart or the vital records to see how long many Believers lived. A lifetime of good nutrition, moderate exercise, sensible hours, peace of mind, and abstinence from smoking and drinking no doubt had something to do with it,

*Lillian, Bertha, and Honey*

although one Shaker Brother in the late nineteenth century printed a pamphlet that gave the credit to celibacy. The promise of long life seemed like a reasonable marketing ploy to win much needed recruits, although in hindsight it obviously didn't have the selling power the author intended.

At any rate, seventy-something was kid stuff for Shakers. Eldress Gertrude, who was a few years older than Bertha, concurred wholeheartedly. She would say with a perfectly straight face when tour buses of retirees pulled up that she loved to see the "old people" come. She was literally of an age in some cases to have been their mother, but she did not see what made us giggle.

The occasion of Bertha's sixty-seventh Shaker birthday was an opportunity for her and the others to tell her story again, although it was brand-new to me. Bertha, christened Goldie Ina Ruby Lindsay, was born in July 1897 to the Lindsays in Braintree, Massachusetts. She said that her parents had given one of her brothers the right to name her. She shook her head and laughed as she spelled out the initials he chose: G.I.R.L. Before the year was out, the family moved back to Laconia, New Hampshire, not far north of Canterbury. She said that her parents were Baptists who were friendly with the Shakers and sometimes attended their worship services.

When she was about four, her mother and father died within a month of each other, leaving little Goldie in the care of a much older sister. When her sister decided to marry and move west, she brought Goldie to the Canterbury Shakers. In some ways, the United Society was to nineteenth- and early twentieth-century Americans what welfare, The Department of Social Services, and foster homes are now: a way to provide physical and emotional care for children who have fallen through the cracks of the nuclear family.

Goldie, seven going on eight, did not like this plan at all and threw herself down sobbing in the middle of Shaker Road when her sister drove away. While this was by no means approved behavior for Shaker children, the Sisters in whose care she was left showed compassion and tenderness. Bertha recalled how Sister Helena Sarle gently told her not to cry, that now they would be sisters, and how Helena held good to her word for the rest of her life. In traditional Shaker fashion, Goldie went to live in the Girls' Order, located at this time in the little house at the top of the yard. Here, a pair of Sisters served as Caretakers for the girls in their care. These women were true adoptive mothers. They made sure the girls were clothed and fed, educated in school and in the useful arts of housekeeping, and, most important of all, loved.

This system of child care had served the United Society since the beginning. Although the celibate Shakers did not have babies of their own, there were always children in the villages. Sometimes, especially in the early days, whole families would join, and the children would finish their growing up in their new Shaker homes. That required parents and children to separate and break their earthly ties. It was a sacrifice, but the Shakers believed wholeheartedly that the best and perhaps only way to recognize the larger brotherhood and sisterhood of all humankind was to dissolve the self-centered focus of the biological family. They pointed to the teaching of Christ, who urged followers to give up their mothers, fathers, sons, and daughters to enter the new creation.

Because of this practice, outsiders might have judged that the Shaker life was bent on eradicating love, but they were wrong. It was all about love. The Shaker focus was simply broader, on what they called universal love, rather than on private, selfish love. That made sense to me as a fatherless child. What if Gus and Alice, who had their own loved daughters and grandchildren, had told me, you're not ours and who needs an extra kid around, anyway? I was very glad that some people had spare room in their hearts.

While some Shaker children had their own biological family

members, including parents, scattered throughout the community, it was much more typical for Shaker children to be there without mother or father or both. The United Society was a haven for the survivors of broken families, for widows and widowers and orphans. As an orphan, little Goldie didn't have to deal with the emotional trial of glimpsing her mother or father from a distance. Nor did she have brothers or sisters who were placed with the Shakers, too. Was that sad? Yes and no. Few would choose complete separation from their family of origin, but Goldie had no choice in this, and in one sense, it was a blessing because it gave her complete freedom to accept the Shakers as her new family.

There were six other little girls in the Girls' Order, so Goldie soon realized she'd have playmates and "sisters" her own age, too. It was luck or providence that Goldie's first Sunday with her new communal family happened to be Blossom Sunday, which the family celebrated annually in the apple orchard up by the Meetinghouse. Under the blue sky, surrounded by birds and sweet white clouds of petals, the last bulwark in young Goldie's heart melted. She knew that she was home.

More apple blossoms came and went as Goldie the girl grew into Bertha the young woman in the years on the eve of World War I. She went to Shaker school and learned how to cook and sew. When she was ten, the Kitchen Sisters taught her to cook potatoes in a variety of ways, an easy introduction to the kitchen and cooking. By the age of thirteen, she had graduated to making pies for the entire family. At eighteen, she was head bread baker, which she enjoyed.

When she was nineteen—my age—Bertha was appointed as head cook in the Office Kitchen, which was akin to being the chef in a large, fine restaurant. The community operated two principal kitchens. The Dwelling Kitchen was for the Church Family. The

Trustees' Office Kitchen was for company, hired men, and the business-minded Believers placed in positions of financial trust who worked in the Office. Meals in the Office Kitchen tended to be slightly nicer than those made for the Family. That first summer, Bertha cooked for twenty-five men, an unusually large crew, hired to do painting.

The Shakers rotated jobs, so between four-week stints in the Kitchen Bertha also worked in the Sisters' poplar-ware industry. The Brothers cut and shaved poplar boards into thin strips, which the Sisters wove into a kind of stiff cloth glued to cardboard boxes. Lined with satin and fitted with sewing notions, the poplar ware and other fancy-work articles sold well enough to keep the United Society afloat during lean times in the twentieth century.

As she grew, Bertha learned more than lessons in the classrooms of the Schoolhouse and the Kitchen, more than skills in housekeeping, needlework, music, astronomy, and geography. Her principal education was in life itself. She learned lessons of the heart from that very first day, when Sister Helena reached out to her in comfort and love. Through her adolescent years, Bertha grew stronger in the bonds of motherly and sisterly love and affection that I could see were the glue of Shaker life and the secret key to the surprising longevity of this entirely celibate society. Because Shaker life was communal, and the focus was consistently on the collective, not the individual, it was easy to overlook the fact that conversion took place one heart, one soul, one life at a time.

As Bertha neared the age of twenty-one, she naturally gave thought to her future. The Shakers had already provided her with a range of useful skills to get her started in the World, from reading and writing to cooking, housekeeping, sewing, and child care. Most of her age mates were choosing to leave. If, however, she chose to stay, she could expect to live with Lillian and the other Sisters she had come to love as her own true family, and to grow old in service to God and her companions, fellow travelers on the path.

At twenty-one, she signed the Covenant. Now she was officially Bertha, having chosen her adult name in honor of Lillian, whose full name was Bertha Lillian Phelps. Was becoming a Shaker an easy choice? Yes and no, she said. When she was around my age, she thought long and hard about leaving for a married life and home of her own. In the end, she chose to stay. It was a decision she said she never regretted, and I believed her. Bertha was smart, talented, and nice. She could have made her way in the World, of that I was certain, and I bet that she knew that, too. That mattered, because the same couldn't be said of all Believers. It seemed fitting to me that Lillian's protégée should in her own way have also made a genuine choice.

Although I scarcely realized it at the time, Bertha's life had begun to turn upside down when we first met in 1971 and 1972. Why? Because the United Society was turning inside out, carrying the handful of surviving members into rapids in which they were soon to find themselves out of their depth. In brief, the United Society's two surviving communities, Canterbury and Sabbathday Lake, were splitting over issues of membership and property. It was like a divorce, or squabbling over a will. And into this sorrowful mess walked Bertha, newly appointed in 1971 to the position of Church Family Eldress and also Central Ministry Eldress in her seventy-fourth year. It took her breath away, and not because she was filled with pride and ambition.

Now she felt very young, indeed, and unsure of her ability to meet the challenges of leadership. All her life, Bertha had been a "simple Kitchen Sister," in her own words, laboring away over rows of cabbages and carrots in the great vegetable garden and over the sink and stove. In her Shaker eyes, the Eldresses, Elders, and Central Ministry were awe-inspiring beings on a higher spiritual plane, burdened like parents (albeit spiritual rather than biological) with the responsibilities of caring for their "children," the ordinary Brothers and Sisters. In fact, the most respected early leaders were addressed as Mother and Father.

Throughout their history, Believers recognized a hierarchy of spiritual development that brought order to their egalitarian world. That chain of command had begun with Mother Ann Lee herself. When she died in 1784, she was succeeded by Father James Whittaker, her protégé from England, and when he died three years later, his successor was the American-born Father Joseph Meacham.

Father Joseph immediately instituted a brilliantly successful form of government that served the Shakers for the next two hundred years. Under his guidance, the orders of leadership were established. In every communal Family, an Elder Brother and Elder Sister, each with a junior associate, had spiritual charge of the Brothers and Sisters, respectively. (The titles were changed to Elder and Eldress in 1862.) Deacons and Deaconesses managed internal practical concerns and Trustees handled temporal affairs with the World. It was harder to maintain pure equality of the sexes in the business world, so the female partners in the Trustees' Office leadership were first known as Office Sisters rather than Trustees, but even that changed over time. In any one village, the Elder and Eldress of the Church Family, or Senior Order, were the most important spiritual leaders.

For each bishopric, typically two or three Shaker villages in one state or region, there was a Ministry: an Elder and Eldress, again each with a junior associate, who were, as Eldress Marguerite Frost aptly put it, "the Elders of the Elders." Just as ordinary Shakers confessed the private matters of their hearts to their Family Elder of the same sex, so in turn did the Family Elders and Eldresses

make confession and turn for guidance and instruction to the Ministry of their bishopric.

At the top of the pyramid was the Central Ministry in New
Lebanon, New York (usually called Mount Lebanon after 1862).
Knowing how much Mother Ann valued a convert named Lucy
Wright, Father Joseph asked her to be his partner in the New
Lebanon Ministry as the female lead. The two men and two
women in the Central Ministry served as the group "Pope" of the
Shaker world. Since Father Joseph died in 1796 and Mother Lucy
continued to guide Shaker life during its critical formative period
for the next quarter century until her death in 1821, it has always
seemed to me that credit for the success of the Shaker system of
government can be fairly shared between them.

Beginning with Mother Ann, the Elders and Eldresses of each
Family and Ministry hand-picked their successors and groomed
them for service as the junior associates. The system allowed for
flexibility. Sometimes the seconds were good companions, but not
good leaders, so they were skipped over. Appointments had to be
ratified by the approbation of the community, so the Brothers and
Sisters had a say of sorts. The leaders consulted with the Family
to help the candidate they approved. These individuals typically
served for decades, providing stability. Often the men and women
who became Elders and Eldresses were first chosen to serve as
schoolteachers, which was wise, since they were able to form
bonds of loyalty, affection, and trust with the rising generation of
potential converts. Obedience to one's lead was part of Shaker
order at every level. What your lead said, you did, and that was
that. The members of the Central Ministry at New Lebanon, having no earthly superiors, were understood to be so highly spiritually advanced that they received guidance directly from God
through prayer and meditation. If your leaders were wise and kind,
you probably had a happy and peaceful communal family. If they
fell short, the communal family had problems, too. Naturally, this

happened. But on the whole, the system worked remarkably well, even when dwindling membership and closing communities began to unravel the traditional structure of Shaker life.

That unraveling accelerated in the twentieth century. In 1947, the New Lebanon community closed its doors finally and forever, so that for the first time since the days of Father Joseph and Mother Lucy in the 1790s the Central Ministry was seated somewhere else. From 1947 through 1957, the Central Ministry was based at Hancock, Massachusetts, only five miles from New Lebanon. There was another unprecedented change: for the first time since the days of Mother Ann, the supreme authority in the Shaker world was in female hands only. With the death of Elder Irving Greenwood in 1939, who was the last in the succession of the male leaders that began with Father Joseph Meacham, the Central Ministry consisted entirely of Shaker women. While there were still a few Shaker men in existence, the Central Ministry did not select any of them to fill a vacancy in the male lead.

The seat of the Central Ministry moved one last time, in 1957, with the death of Frances Hall at Hancock and came to roost in Canterbury, home of Eldress Emma B. King, an assertive leader, known privately to some as "Emma Be King." When Emma died in 1966, Marguerite Frost of Canterbury replaced her as the Canterbury representative in the Central Ministry. Marguerite died in early 1971, and Bertha was appointed her successor as both Family Eldress and member of the Central Ministry.

By 1972, Bertha was among the pair of Central Ministry members left holding the bag, which was beginning to seem like a sackful of skunks. In this she found herself shoulder to shoulder with Eldress Gertrude of Sabbathday Lake, Maine, a member of the Central Ministry since 1957 and now the senior Central Ministry member.

The differences of opinion within the United Society about the best course for the future had widened into a painful schism, making 1972 a particularly difficult time for the Shakers. Yield with grace to what seemed like the end? That was Bertha's way, and it had been the decision of her predecessors in the United Society's leadership, who had formally closed membership in 1965, she said. "New bees don't return to an old hive," she added, and accepted what she perceived as the handwriting on the wall. It made Bertha sad to think of Canterbury without Shakers, and sadder still to imagine America and the world without Shakers. There was nothing she would have liked more than to welcome new generations of Sisters and Brothers to carry on the work. But she didn't see it happening in villages like Canterbury or Sabbathday Lake. Converts were the lifeblood of the Shakers—they had to be, because the whole United Society was celibate. The World was growing more and more interested in Shaker life and design—that was true, judging from the increase in visitors and a spate of new books—but hardly anybody expressed interest in joining. Like it or not, Bertha had made peace with the inevitable passing of her beloved old Shaker community and the historical United Society. She had taken steps to ensure that the buildings and grounds at Canterbury would be preserved as a museum, and that the spiritual message would continue to be taught, when she and the others there were gone.

Bertha was open, however, to the possibility of new life for the Shaker spirit, perhaps even felt a conviction that the Shaker life would continue in another guise. As she saw it, the new incarnation would have to be legally and financially separate from the established, historical United Society, so that its members might be free from any but spiritual motives. She turned to the parable of the wineskins to explain what she meant. Just as new wine would burst old wineskins, so would an influx of young people disrupt the lives of the aged Shakers. More important, any new flowering of Shaker life would have to suit the economic life and times of the twenty-first-century industrial world. The old farming villages of traditional Shaker life were simply outmoded for now. You had to hand it to Bertha; she had vision. She was able to imagine a way of life so different from that of the "old Shakers" that she couldn't even properly forecast it. It might be urban, for example, and it might not be communal. Whatever it was, it would have to suit young people during these times, just as the Shakerism of the founders (Mother Ann, Father Joseph, and Mother Lucy) fit its time and place.

Other Canterbury Sisters saw another possibility. Some dreamed instead that seeing what the Shakers had accomplished would simply inspire people to go back into the World refreshed and ready to live more kindly, charitable, loving lives. Either way, the Canterbury Shakers were clear that their museum was central to the continuation of Shaker life as a means of spiritual witness to the principles of the faith. Whether you came and were simply refreshed, or came and were inspired to begin a new movement altogether, the museum operation was at the heart of teaching the Shaker way.

So, watch the flame flicker out in the old villages . . . or try to keep it blazing? The Shakers in Sabbathday Lake saw it another way. They outnumbered the Canterbury Shakers and were on the average somewhat younger. They had been able to take in enough children to maintain the Girls' Shop until 1966, and continued to have children in the community until the late 1960s—for three decades longer than the Canterbury Shakers. When it came to continuing traditional Shaker life in Shaker villages, they were not ready to throw in the towel, and who could fault them?

The difference of opinion would probably not have mattered, except for the good old problems that power and money bring. By 1972, the United Society of Believers had drifted into uncharted territory in terms of the ratio of members and assets. The circumstances that the Society faced in the late twentieth century were unprecedented, so it's no wonder there was confusion. In the very beginning of Shaker history, there had been few members and fewer assets. With time and work, by about 1830, there was lots more of everything, both members and assets. The Society had grown rich, thanks to hard work, simple living, and a refusal to buy on credit. Over the years, many Shakers with sound business sense had invested the communal resources wisely.

When Shaker communities began to close in the mid-to-late nineteenth century, the balance shifted again. Now there were fewer people again, but overall there was more money in the United Society's pot every time another Shaker village closed. Income accrued from the sale of yet another property. But the extent of the United Society's assets was not generally known among the Shakers until the death in 1957 of Frances Hall of the Central Ministry at Hancock.

Eldress Emma King of Canterbury, now senior in the Central Ministry, was stunned to learn that the United Society controlled about a million dollars' worth of holdings. She took steps immediately to organize the assets into the Shaker Central Trust Fund. Within two years, in 1959, she had the requisite signatures on a trust agreement that ensured that the signers would receive support from the interest generated by the monies in the Shaker Central Trust Fund. There was also a provision that anyone who signed the Covenant in the future would also be eligible for support. The proviso was residence in a Shaker community for at least five years before signing. That took care of Mildred Wells, who had spent her life on Shaker ground but had never technically joined the Society.

The Central Trust Fund was a mixed blessing. It was good that it provided income, since it meant that the Shakers had food to eat and money to maintain the buildings, pay the power company, and meet other necessary expenses. I could imagine that the winter heating bills for these enormous buildings were outrageous, and hospital care and nursing homes for aging, infirm Believers didn't come cheap. To be sure, the Sisters kept busy making small items for sale in the Gift Shop, and they got the money from the tours, but none of that would have kept them afloat.

On the other hand, everyone knew that the love of money was the root of all evil—or at least that it would hard-top the road to trouble. The Fund existed for better and for worse. It was inevitable, even understandable, that any potential newcomer might be thought to have an eye on easy living—not necessarily, just maybe. That was no one's fault; it was simply a fact of human nature. The problem was the Trust Fund itself—or maybe it's fairer to say, the troublesome possibilities that inevitably accompany money like fleas on a dog. Without the Fund, there could be no question of a nonspiritual motive for anyone's wishing to join. I could understand these problems because of what was happening in my own family. Granddaddy, my father's father, had amassed enough money so that what happened to it affected his family in ways that hurt more than they helped. It seemed clear to me that having enough was a blessing, but this business of having more than enough often resulted in a big mess if the money came to matter more than other values.

This dilemma was not new to the Shakers, however. By the summer of 1972, they had dealt with the problem for 150 years. Long before the Fund had been formed, the tidy, prosperous Shaker villages of the 1820s, 1830s, and 1840s attracted people who were drawn more by the security of the existence than the opportunity for spiritual growth. They were so common that the Shakers had names for them—"bread and butter Shakers" or "loaf Believers"—but they were made welcome at God's table just the same. "Winter Shakers" were a specialized subset who felt a spiritual call when it was cold and hot meals and a warm bed looked mighty attractive, but lost their zeal come spring, when the hard work of farming came on.

"Some people are more interested in the loaves and the fishes," observed Bertha in her deliberate manner, than in a true commitment to the spiritual rewards and demands of Shaker life. The Shakers had traditionally accepted repeat loafers, as part of their commitment to charity and in the hopes of a genuine spiritual awakening, except when such persons were known to be severe troublemakers. Then, the doors were closed.

In 1972, in addition to the Shaker Central Trust Fund, there was another dilemma in regard to potential new converts. The last Shaker Elder and Brother at Canterbury had died in 1939, and with the passing of Elder Delmer Wilson in 1961 down in Maine, there were no old-time Shaker men to provide instruction to male converts. It was poignant. The Shaker Sisters in both surviving villages seemed to feel the loss of the Brothers as an imbalance in the pattern of life (and they missed them for practical reasons, too, like for fixing the screen doors and doing other chores). So everybody agreed in principle that it would be grand to have Brothers around again.

Once again, however, there was a difference of opinion about how or whether to make this happen. For Bertha and her predecessors in the leadership at Canterbury, it was not possible to imagine a Shaker woman serving as the spiritual leader for a Shaker man or vice versa. Her attitude was based solidly on almost two hundred years of Shaker experience and wisdom, which insisted on the separation of the sexes. Clearly, the system had worked successfully in a celibate society—even if the price of that celibacy was eventually the Shakers' dwindling membership.

But there was another way to look at the situation, which the Shakers in Sabbathday Lake seemed to take. Why *not* have a Shaker Sister instruct a male convert, especially if the age difference and/or other factors made it unlikely that any kind of romance would bloom? Preventing romance was, after all, the underlying reason for the Shakers' separation of the sexes in the first place. Perhaps more progressive spirits could justify the exception in these exceptional times. Besides, hadn't Mother Ann been a woman spiritually advising men? Hadn't Mother Lucy Wright guided the United Society for twenty-five years, and hadn't she successfully counseled many men during that time? What about the Central Ministry, who had been all female since 1939?

None of these concerns would have mattered if they had been merely theoretical, if no one new had wished to join. And I suspect that they wouldn't have mattered either if dozens or hundreds had come knocking at the door seeking membership. As it was, they mattered a great deal because someone did wish to join, and that particular someone was not universally acceptable to the whole Society. The circumstances in which the United Society found itself were indeed unprecedented. As in the United Society's beginning, there were very few members. As in its heyday, there were significant assets. The problem was the combination and how it concerned real people with heartfelt wishes that did not jibe.

It boiled down to this: In the 1960s, a prospective convert named Theodore Johnson sought to join the Shakers, and members of the Sabbathday Lake community made him welcome. In time, however, his presence caused a difference of opinion between Eldress Gertrude and other members of the Sabbathday Lake Family. Some of the members liked him and wanted him to stay; others, including Eldress Gertrude, disagreed. Their personal exchanges grew increasingly tense. The Shakers, like other Christian monastic orders since the time of St. Benedict almost fifteen hundred years earlier, required obedience to one's spiritual superior. To challenge Eldress Gertrude was the Shaker equivalent of open revolt. Eldress Gertrude departed for Canterbury and Theodore Johnson, now Brother Ted, settled in. There were all kinds of questions. Was he really a Shaker? Had he signed the Covenant? Could anyone join the Shakers or sign the Covenant anymore, anyway? In time, even Bertha's status as Eldress (and that of Marguerite Frost before her) would be challenged by those who claimed that the Central Ministry had not filled the vacancy left by the death of Eldress Emma King. There were far more questions than answers, and things were a long way from being resolved. The situation was sad and painful for all concerned.

Bertha and Lillian were circumspect in their discussions of what they rightly considered as family problems, but Eldress Gertrude was more outspoken. When I came, Bertha explained to me that Eldress Gertrude was visiting from Sabbathday Lake, having arrived a few months earlier. It wasn't long before it was clear that the visit was probably going to last for a long, long time. Eldress Gertrude was in fact in exile from her home, an exile that the Sabbathday Lake Shakers said was self-imposed. We were both new here, but my arrival was entirely voluntary and hers perhaps really wasn't. She was so newly uprooted that parts of her were still raw, chafed with pain and anger, only slightly soothed by the relief of being out of the fray. It seemed to be good for her to talk about how she felt: betrayed, sad, upset with her Shaker Family and with herself for failing to work out a more peaceful conclusion to the situation at hand. Sad, most of all.

Yet as the weeks passed, some healing was taking place as Eldress Gertrude took root in her new home. You would not have known that she had a care in the world when she met visitors in the hallway, and it didn't seem to be an act. She was genuinely sociable and warm, the merry little fairy godmother of everyone's childhood. She was also a public relations dream because people took to her instantly. She was the grandma who welcomed you to the old family place in the country. What a gift she had, especially with the children—the "little ones," she called them—upon whom she doted, or "made of," as the Shakers said. The time she spent with people really brightened her up. I thought of the petunias and other flowers that she tended along the front walk. Maybe a transplanting into the sunshine was good for people, too.

In spite of their troubles with age, health, and internal Shaker affairs, life with the Office Sisters was cheerful and often fun. Our days began with breakfast in the back kitchen on the first floor. It was a big, airy, comfortable room with a sink, washing machine, refrigerator, small electric stove, and family-sized toaster. The appliances made for an electrician's nightmare. Like most of the buildings, the Trustee's Office had been wired in the early twentieth century by Brother Irving Greenwood, a gifted mechanic and handyman. The wiring had held up all right, but it wasn't really meant for all these heavy-duty "modern inconveniences," as Gus called them. There were extension cords everywhere plugged into an adapter that looked like a tentacled alien life form. I had a tendency to worry too much sometimes, like Mom, so I crossed my fingers that nothing would go wrong—and that if it did, the Canterbury volunteer fire department could make it up here pronto.

Although Eldress Emma had sold off most of the treasures made by the "old Shakers" to museums and a handful of collectors in the 1940s and 1950s, a core of farsighted Sisters that included Marguerite Frost, Lillian, and Bertha had managed to hang on to a few nice pieces of furniture. A few were still in use in the kitchen. One was an enormous cupboard with glass doors that filled the whole south wall. It was tall and wide, but not very deep, so it didn't look clunky. The shallow shelves made it convenient to use—nothing could get buried in the back.

There was a classic side table by the fridge, painted a deep brick red. It had the slim, graceful legs that characterized the best of Shaker design. Under it had been Honey's feeding station; her empty dish and water bowl looked lonely now on the floor beneath the table.

The prize piece was a beautiful pine counter with drawers, painted a rich, bittersweet red-orange, on the wall opposite the cupboard. It was something of a legend among the collectors who caught a glimpse of it, a most desirable object that was tantalizingly unavailable. The idea now was to get things back for the museum, not sell them. The ironic fact was that the Shakers might not have been able to afford the counter if they didn't already own it. Even in 1972, before Shaker design had attracted much national and international attention, a choice piece fetched a good price on the market. Anyway, the pine counter wasn't for sale. It was beautiful and it was useful, too. The Office Sisters kept dish towels, pot holders, and the like in the drawers and cookie tins on the top, which was protected by a neat rectangle of linoleum.

We gathered promptly at eight every morning around a table under a stained-glass lamp in the center of the room. That was the idea, anyway, but more than a few times, Eldress Gertrude's chair was empty as the clock struck the hour. Bertha was used to punctuality, which the Shakers had always found to be a balm that greased the rough places of close, communal living. Long experience had taught the Shakers that everyone and everything flowed more smoothly when the group agreed on set times for events like meals, and those events happened on time. Living in community was tough enough at times, so courtesies like punctuality were appreciated. As the minutes ticked by, we would sit and pass the time. Eldress Gertrude's absence was hard to overlook because she sat at the head of the table.

By and by someone would say, deadpan, "Gee, I guess Eldress Gertrude stayed up late last night." It was true. Eldress Gertrude, alone of the Office dwellers, was a night owl. The others went to bed at a decent Shaker hour, like nine or nine-thirty, but there was no denying it, Eldress Gertrude was just entering high gear when the rest were fading. Midnight and the hours after that were none too late for her. Who knows, maybe she liked the privacy or the simple act of rebellion. The trouble was, of course, that her late hours made it harder for her to get up on time. Her habit of tardiness tickled me. Bertha would smile ruefully and shake her head. That was one of the things I really liked about both of these Shaker Eldresses: Eldress Gertrude wasn't so completely perfect, and Bertha loved her and let her be who she was.

Just about the time that Bertha would begin gentle fretting, we'd usually hear the tap of dainty espadrilles hurrying across the upstairs hall and down the stairs to the kitchen. Eldress Gertrude would slide into her chair with a guilty grin on her face. "Am I a little late?" she'd ask rhetorically, then briskly bow her head and announce the silent grace. When she murmured "Amen," we were back on track.

Bertha was so unaccustomed to her new position as Eldress, and so modest besides, that she usually called herself Sister rather than Eldress. The community tended to be informal, anyway, and it was common for us non-Shakers to drop the "Sister" and simply address our Shaker friends by their Christian names. The use of first names was not a mark of disrespect in Shaker life but a traditional sign of humility. But Bertha always addressed Gertrude as Eldress Gertrude and so did all the rest of us.

Eldress Gertrude was a dab hand at many things—knitting, gardening, tending the birds, and more—but there were two things she couldn't do. She said that she couldn't sing (we heard her once, and we believed her) and she wasn't much of a cook. She spent as little time as possible in the kitchen, and if Bertha was sorry about that, she never said so. Eldress Gertrude did, however, prepare the Sunday noon dinner every week to give Bertha a welcome day off. What she made was simple and came out fine, although she was nervous as a cat. You had to admit that Bertha would have been a tough act to follow even for an accomplished cook. I was no great shakes myself, but I would usually find my way to the kitchen to lend a hand or plain moral support.

The Office Sisters slept late on Sundays—which means they were up and stirring by, say, eight or eight-thirty, instead of six-thirty or seven. I would usually go on over to the Trustees' Office around nine or so to share in the morning's devotions. I knew enough about the Shakers already to know that I wasn't going to see any sacred dance—that had gone the way of the buggy and the kerosene lamp. The Shakers at Canterbury in 1972 had never even seen or taken part in the dance worship, except for Lillian, who had witnessed the last of the traditional service in her youth. She said that the dancing Believers looked like "angels," and she spoke with respect and awe of the effect of the dance on faithful Believers, who found blessed unity in their efforts to move as one.

By the last quarter of the nineteenth century, progressive leaders like Elder Henry Blinn and others were more comfortable with a less unconventional service of praying, preaching, offering testimony, and singing. The old Meetinghouse had long since been abandoned for worship in the Chapel (or meeting room) in the ell of the Dwelling, where Canterbury Shakers had been gathering for more than a hundred years.

By 1972, however, the Sisters no longer met as a communal family on Sunday mornings. It made sense if you knew them, the village layout, and New Hampshire weather. It would have been very difficult for Bertha to make it up the narrow granite walk, and virtually impossible for Lillian. Eldress Gertrude could have made it easily, but what would have been the point? Sister Alice was frail and from what I could tell, Ethel was not exactly feverish with zeal about things like religious services, although Bud's son Darryl assured me that prayer and meditation were important to her.

Miriam probably snoozed late on Sunday mornings after late nights with the Red Sox, and Mildred . . . well, who knew what Mildred did on Sunday mornings.

Instead of public worship or a full communal gathering, the Sisters held private, individual devotions, or met in small groups to worship. What worked for Bertha, Eldress Gertrude, and Lillian was simple and practical. They gathered in the Office sitting room for prayer and some Scripture reading, then watched fine religious programs on TV every Sunday morning. Dr. Robert Schuller in the Crystal Cathedral brought them hours of peace and pleasure, all the way from sunny California. And they were crazy about Dr. Norman Vincent Peale, whenever his program was aired. They loved his message of positive thinking and the courage that comes from faith, and they enjoyed his humor, too. Sometimes observers faulted the Canterbury Shakers for failing to meet in the traditional public services, but they themselves were at peace with the changes. In their experience, prayer and living a Christlike life had more to do with everyday behavior than once-a-week church.

Eldress Gertrude did well on the weekdays, when visitors distracted her from her sorrows, but sometimes the weekends (Sunday and Monday were our days off) grew long for her. She enjoyed the Canterbury Sisters' friends, but she hadn't lived here long enough to have a circle of her own friends who knew and loved her well. As the new kids on the block, Eldress Gertrude and I spent time together. I truly liked being with her and I felt a little sorry for her, too, when she talked about her home in Maine far away.

She seemed to feel better when she talked about days long ago. She recalled being taken to the Shakers at Sabbathday Lake when she was a girl by her father, because, as she said, her new stepmother didn't want her or her little sister, Cora. I thought to myself that Mr. Soule didn't sound like a prize father if he went along with that, but of course I never said anything. She talked about many of the beautiful old Sisters she'd known and loved, but also about some who weren't so nice. Cora had brought a doll, Eldress Gertrude said, and the Girls' Caretaker, who went by the old, strict rules, which prohibited toys and private playthings for children, took it from her and threw it away. Eldress Gertrude still snapped and crackled when she said what happened next. She marched straight out to the dump and plucked up Cora's doll—no one was going to make her little sister cry. I found myself rooting for young Gertrude—go, Gertie, go! She got in trouble for what she did, but she was never sorry.

Cora eventually left the Shakers, like so many others of her generation of Shaker girls, and subsequently got married and had a son. When I met Cora some years later, I just about choked. She was the spitting image of Eldress Gertrude—if you could imagine the Eldress with stretch pants, bright red fingernail polish, and a perm. Not to mention the cigarette. Wow! I had to shake my head a few times when no one was looking to sort out the images in my mind.

Eldress Gertrude loved to know what was going on in the outside world, so she kept up with the news. She was a big fan of the *National Geographic*. She liked to discuss what she'd read, so I should have been prepared one afternoon when she asked in all seriousness if there was just the one "fink" in Egypt, or were there more? I had to bite my lip to keep from smiling as I gravely assured her that I believed there was just the one. Yup, there was the *Geographic* in her lap, open to a picture of the famous stone head of the sphinx. Eldress Gertrude's malapropisms tickled us endlessly. Once when he drove her over a bridge, Bud said, Eldress Gertrude had marveled at the big "girdles" that held up the span. When she wanted to go faster, she asked Bud to press harder on the "exhilarator."

Shakers were supposed to keep their political views to themselves—in fact, they weren't supposed to have political views at all, for the sake of harmony in the communal family, that precious commodity the old-time Shakers called "union." Long before Eldress Gertrude, Believers had wisely decided to let the World run its affairs, just as they wished the World would let them run theirs. So Shakers didn't vote. No vote, no political parties, no divisive "party spirit." Simple enough. I never heard Lillian or Bertha discuss politics or their private preferences, not even once, but Eldress Gertrude was different. She was a Republican and had no use for "lily-livered" Democrats. She thought Nixon was just dandy. Years later, when Reagan was president, she liked him, too, because he stood up for prayer in schools. Just once, in private, Bertha shook her head and said quietly, "We Shakers were taught not to discuss politics." But Bertha, as always, tended the garden of her own soul, and let Eldress Gertrude be.

Eldress Gertrude had other hobbies besides current events. She loved "all God's creatures," as she said, and took good care of assorted plants and animals. She had a flair for growing things and over time developed a nice little collection of cacti houseplants. Her prize cactus had pride of place on a table in the sitting room. About two feet tall and no bigger around than a carrot, it sprouted from a tiny saucer and sported a gay red bow. Outdoors, she tended the annuals along the Office walk, watering them and "making of" them at the day's open or close.

She loved birds, too, and fed them faithfully from the back porch off the back kitchen where we ate breakfast. Ever the tender-hearted friend of the small and weak, she grumbled at and shooed away the big, greedy starlings so that the chickadees could have a chance. She thought that bats were "cunning little creatures" and admired how their wings folded so neatly, like small, dark umbrellas.

Eldress Gertrude's greatest passion of all was her interest in medicine and maladies. She must have had quite a gift, because she could not only detect but also *diagnose* an ailment at twenty paces. We would never hurt her feelings, but we used to giggle behind her back. Even Lillian smiled once and remarked solemnly that she didn't care much for "organ recitals." You'd come into the kitchen in the morning, feeling fine and dandy, and then Eldress Gertrude would peer at you through those spectacles and frown. Wagging her head in concern, she'd eyeball you up and down. Then came the pronouncement—"You looked a little peaked, dear, your gizzard must be enlarged," or, "Tsk, tsk, tsk, my goodness, dear, your hand's as clammy as a dog's nose. You must feel awful bad." (The precise medical details have become jumbled in my memory, but you get the point.) It wasn't over yet, though. After Eldress Gertrude finished telling you in ghoulish detail what happened to the last person she knew with an enlarged gizzard or clammy hand, by golly, you didn't feel quite so good anymore. She was a terror around a real invalid, although she always meant only the best.

I didn't share Eldress Gertrude's fascination with bodily disorders, but I felt a little rush of warmth for her when the others pointed out that although her own health was precarious indeed, she never seemed to complain. That was true. When once she catalogued the operations she'd had and the parts she'd had removed, I was surprised that she was still up on her hind legs at all. Imagine my greater surprise when I learned that Eldress Gertrude's medical expertise was at the heart of a secret. My jaw dropped when someone mentioned that Eldress Gertrude knew so much about medicine because she had cared for people during her time away from the Shakers.

I was astonished, but, yes, it was true, I was assured, she had left the Shakers as a young woman and spent nearly twenty years in the World before returning to the fold. The specifics were never clear, although it was said that she worked as a nurse or a governess. In time she came back. This was by no means unheard of in

Shaker tradition. As they liked to say, the door swung both ways. None of the Canterbury Shakers ever spoke of it, and neither did she. It was her business and it was long past.

But if it was true, maybe the trouble in the United Society made more sense. Maybe there were Shakers who didn't want a onetime apostate to serve in the position of highest authority. Who knew? Of course I was dying to know the details, but I never considered asking her. In the summer of 1972 I was not a historian, not a reporter, just a very new, very young friend from the outside world. As the years passed and our friendship grew, I found that her privacy mattered more to me than my curiosity. It didn't change my feelings. Go, Gertie, go . . . I imagine it took guts for her to leave for the World and I'll bet it took more guts to come back.

In later years, I developed a greater appreciation for the historical significance of my associations at Canterbury. I realized what a privilege it had been to befriend the last two members of the Shaker Central Ministry, Bertha and Eldress Gertrude, the big brass of the United Society of Shakers.

Yet at the time I wanted more than anything to be like Lillian, who was never elevated above Second Eldress, was never given any official title or office in the Ministry—never won the Academy Award, as it were. Bertha herself felt that Lillian should have been made Eldress, but her age and other factors evidently mitigated against that choice. It didn't matter. Lillian was still the true center of Shaker life at Canterbury, which I guess forever shaped my feelings about authority. Her power came from the inside, from God within her, not from anything bestowed from without. In the Shaker history books to come Lillian would have no official status, but she was the real item, the water of life in a plain tin cup.

Writers would have it that heroes and good characters are less interesting than villains and pests because virtue is boring. I'll agree that that's often true in stories, or if you're Dickens, and it may be that this chapter is doomed to fall short of rousing your passionate interest. But in real life, I have to say, I have found authentic goodness magnificent, muscular, tonic, as rare and grand as Yosemite's El Capitan, a mountain whose magnitude stuns you further when you realize that it is a monolith, one whole, seamless rock. I find absolutely nothing boring about true goodness. If you doubt that, consider the life of Christ, or Saint Francis, or Dietrich Bonhoeffer, or someone you may know. Lillian, and later Bertha, made goodness vastly more interesting to me than the alternative, and that was a lesson worth learning, especially at nineteen. Whatever else I wanted from life, I wanted to be like them.

Why? I didn't really ask that question at the time. It seemed more a matter of instinct than reason. Why did I bury my nose in lilacs or linger to watch the slow incandescence of a mother-of-pearl sky at dusk? Why did I like the touch of a hand on my arm? I only knew that Lillian was at peace, serene, glad to be alive, and not afraid to die. She enjoyed life even in her physical decline. She suffered from digestive disorders, which made her very uncomfortable. While the rest of us ate Bertha's wonderful cooking, poor Lillian was obliged to eat the blandest of baby food because it was all she could digest, but she ate what she could with a thankful heart.

Lillian couldn't work much anymore, either, but she kept busy and seemed grateful for simple chores. She sat in the rocker by the window in the sitting room and knitted patiently—not the intricate sweaters and delightful stuffed toys she had once made, but the simplest of small squares, in thick red yarn. A friend collected the finished squares and made them into covers for balls of twine. With a green felt leaf or two stitched on top, they looked like apples when the round ball of twine was stuffed inside. You

pulled the loose end of string from a small hole in the bottom—
like a long, skinny worm, come to think of it. They were not classic examples of Shaker design and craftsmanship, but they were cute
and sold well in the Shop when people learned that one of the last
of the old-time Shakers made them. But their real value was to
Lillian because they allowed her to keep her hands at work in true
Shaker fashion.

Lillian maintained a comfortable relationship with changing
life and times. She had experienced the introduction of automobiles, airplanes, electricity, telephones, woman suffrage, the atomic
bomb, space travel, and the Pill (not all of them personally, of
course). I was unsure of myself and afraid of change—not a comfortable place for a person of nineteen, perched on the inevitable
precipice of new and different experiences. And here was Lillian—
old, nearly blind, and physically rickety, but change and the buck-
eting World didn't throw her. She stayed alert, interested, amused.
The detective-cum-lawyer drama *Perry Mason* was her favorite
show on TV because she liked to figure out whodunit. Yup, Lillian knew how to roll with the punches. Over the years, I saw
Bertha step gracefully down the same path; she had heeded well
the example of her spiritual sister, mother, friend.

I was leaving the protected inlet of childhood for the deeper,
murky waters of adult life, and I needed to believe in something. I
had spent my life so far as a good girl—an obedient, law-abiding,
polite, presentable A-student—but I couldn't take credit for that
because I didn't really want to be good. I was simply afraid to be
bad—to question authority, break unfair rules, to tell people who
were seriously out of line to knock it off. My sister Ann was more
like that, and I admired and envied her.

Knowing Lillian and Bertha made me feel different about
being good. I saw that goodness could be a brave moral choice,
not a mere refuge for the faint of heart. In her day, Lillian had
stood up to forces that she felt were not right or not in the com-

munity's best interest. Even now, she seemed to show that real goodness required powerful character and the strength to choose. Bertha was rising to meet the demands of her new role as Eldress in a trying time. That summer I saw her make difficult decisions, tough calls, with grace and courage. Their strength of character sounded a lot like what I'd learned of Mother Ann, whose attitude fascinated and confused me. I could see that she, too, had taken major criticism for her convictions.

But then, so did Christ. Could it be that looking good and being good were two different things? When I listened to Lillian and Bertha, a new picture began to emerge, of someone far less wimpy than the familiar nursery poster of Jesus, the calf-eyed man with wavy brown hair who looked like a fellow even Gus with his "bum ticker" could beat up on a bad day.

Instead, Lillian and Bertha talked about Jesus as someone who persisted in choosing the way of goodness and love at a terrible personal price and who stayed the course through to the end. There was a pattern here. Mother Ann and the eighteenth-century Shakers had been beaten and scorned for their religious and social convictions. The nineteenth-century Shakers, too, had suffered persecution and prejudice for their stand on issues including pacifism and slavery. Now Bertha was facing the heat of a controversy that grew ever more distressing and ever more public.

But all of them had hung in there and not quit. That sounded like my brave, no-nonsense sister Ann.

It sounded awfully good.

# CHAPTER 4

# *June*

June was a wonderful, terrible month.

On Memorial Day the museum opened for business and our first visitors made their way up Shaker Road. I survived my inaugural tour, which consisted of a single tourist, a pleasant lady who was interested in everything. Bertha's training stood the test. Margaret, the housekeeper, and Jennie, Bertha's help in the kitchen, came back to the village after the weekend.

Margaret was a down-to-earth woman in her sixties with platinum hair and a big square jaw. She was nice, and was a crackerjack housekeeper, but she didn't have much to say. Her life had been tough. She had retired after years in the shoe factories down in Manchester and was divorced from a first husband she mentioned only once in my presence, when she recalled that when they split up she threw her wedding ring as far as she could into the Merrimack River.

That memory brought a big smile to her face. Maybe Mom was right. She was always warning us, "There are worse things in life than being an old maid." My sister and I heard *that* so often that we threatened to have it engraved on her tombstone. Margaret's second marriage, a happy one to a good man, produced three sons. But now she was a widow. The other thing that brought a smile to Margaret's face was her little granddaughter, whose pictures she always had nearby. When she wasn't mopping the floors or putting laundry in the washer, Margaret tended to stay in her room, the one on the right front upstairs. Margaret was serious on the whole but she got a kick out of Bud, who teased her and called her Cuddles.

Bertha prepared me for meeting Jennie by smiling thoughtfully and saying in her deliberate way that Jennie was her "diamond in the rough." When Jennie and I met, I knew what Bertha meant. Jennie was built like a pumpkin. She wore a faded cotton house dress whose buttons strained at the seams and she pulled her stringy gray hair back into a tight ponytail. Sneakers with white ankle socks added the finishing touch. One dark gray-blue eye pointed way over to starboard, but the good one beamed straight at me in greeting. Jennie grinned broadly and grabbed me for a full-body hug. She was as soft and squishy as a feather bed, and I couldn't help but laugh at the picture we made—me, tall and skinny, wrapped in lots of Jennie, whose head didn't quite reach my chin. That was our formal introduction. It was the beginning of a thoroughly enjoyable friendship.

To my relief, Jennie was thrilled to have an upstairs roommate in the Infirmary and immediately pronounced herself my "grammie." God had given Jennie a mixed bag of blessings. She had a heart of gold and the mind and soul of a child of around seven or eight. Bertha related more of her history. After a childhood in the State School in Laconia, New Hampshire, Jennie had been working as a kitchen helper in the State Hospital in Concord for a long time when she was hired to help the Shakers. The hospital looked grim from the outside, like the workhouses of Scrooge's era—big brick buildings with iron bars over some of the windows. Jennie didn't miss it. She had been taken under the wing of Eldress Marguerite Frost, who gave her the upbringing she had missed as a young girl.

Miraculously, Jennie learned how to read and spell, how to cook more than rudimentary dishes. More than that, Marguerite and Bertha taught her how to take care of herself, how to balance a checkbook and manage money, how to practice good hygiene, how to carry herself with manners and self-respect, how to value herself just as she was. The Shakers looked at Jennie and saw a lady in the making, which others less bright and less kind might not have seen. Under their instruction and with their affection, Jennie became what the Shakers saw.

Besides food, which she relished without guilt or shame, Jennie's passions in life were her two big, smelly kitties, Tiger and Tommy, and her cockatiel, Toto. Toto spent his days in a brass cage in the library room of the Infirmary. He seemed fond enough of Jennie, but others didn't want to get too close. He was a one-woman bird. When he cocked that beady little eye, he might lunge from preening his pale yellow wings to plant his beak in your finger. No, thanks. I was happy to admire him from afar.

Bud came back from the honeymoon before Nancy, who needed time to make the move to the village, and I quickly found a new friend. Bud, really Charles, was well nicknamed. He was a true buddy. Bud was the same age as my mom, but he seemed much more like a big brother than a parent to me. There was something ageless about this big, affable man.

As I got to know him that summer, I came to see why that might be so. On one hand, he was deeply spiritual and unafraid to talk openly about his faith, a quality that was brand-new to me. I had never met anyone who seemed to ponder the great, holy mysteries of life, let alone talk about them. Back home, the people I knew all seemed to have a Sunday-go-to-church kind of religion: do the rituals once a week and then forget about it. Bud was as open about the central role of faith in his life as the Sisters were. That made sense. Bertha and Lillian loved him because they shared a foundation conviction in the goodness of God and the Christ-like life.

On the other hand, Bud was earthy and funny. He always had a new joke. On the whole his jokes were really awful, but he shared them with such gusto that you couldn't help but laugh. Bud's good-hearted irreverence was well known to all who knew him, and was appreciated by most. Once in a while, the Shakers would overhear him, and even they had to laugh. Bertha would hide a smile and chide, "Oh, Buddy," in a weak attempt at re-proach that fooled no one. Eldress Gertrude, being new to Bud that summer, was made of sterner stuff. For a while, at first, she pursed her lips and sniffed at some of Bud's punch lines, but over time she, too, melted in the warmth of his good nature. When Bud got a "passion meter" from Margaret as a wedding gift, a gag item that worked like a thermometer, no one had more fun with it than Eldress Gertrude. Poor old Lillian was lowest on the scale at "groovy." Bertha, one notch up, was "old-fashioned but good." But Eldress Gertrude made it all the way up to "zowie!" and laughed for days in mock concern that she'd raise it one step to "oversexed!"

I adored Bud just as he was, lousy jokes and all (and won-dered how the Shakers knew about the rude bits, anyway). I was an ideal audience because I could never remember jokes. I'd laugh just as hard the second or third time Bud told the same story, but no one laughed harder than Bud himself. His booming laugh was infectious. He loved to tell a classic old Charlie McCarthy joke about the wooden dummy's investigation into his geneaology. "I don't know if I'm a son of a beech or a son of a birch," he'd say and I'd grin, "but I heard that my mom was a swell piece of ash." Ha, ha, ha! Bud had a lot of fun, but he was always a class act. He didn't tell that one around the Sisters.

Until Nancy and her boys moved in, Bud had time on his

hands. His two boys, Dayne and Darryl, lived with their mother in a small town not too far away, but in the meantime, his only company was Tag, his beagle. He could see that I was a bit lonesome, and maybe he was too, so he took me under his wing, with Bertha and Lillian's blessing.

He invited me along on errands, which was a treat. Just riding with Bud was a memorable experience. He always had something interesting to say, and threw himself wholeheartedly into conversations. The more he talked, the more he gesticulated and turned his head to peer into your eyes. The more wound up he got, the slower he drove, which was just as well, considering that he spent maybe half the time paying attention to the road. If you were driving behind him, you'd know he was onto something really intriguing when his big brown boat of a car slowed to maybe twenty or twenty-five.

We went sightseeing around the Concord area, stopping at local attractions like Franklin Pierce's grave and an original Concord coach. We went up to Gilmanton Iron Works, where his kids lived half the time with their mother, and took a side trip up a dirt road to see the grave of Grace Metallious, who scandalized all the locals back when she wrote *Peyton Place*. Wherever we stopped for coffee and doughnuts, everybody had a big "Hi" for Bud.

Within days I was as devoted to Bud as Tag was. He simply radiated enthusiasm and encouragement. Bud was funny and nice and I could see why the Shakers, especially Lillian and Bertha, loved him like a son. Above all, he was the soul of generosity. There was nothing he wouldn't give—time, attention, coffee and a sandwich—if he thought it would help. He was the first true friend of my adulthood, and I couldn't have done better.

Nancy moved into her new home before too long and Bud perked right up. Nancy was Bud's equal in generosity and friendliness, and they invited me into their lives. I became a regular in their home at the top of the yard. Nancy was a slim and attractive strawberry blonde with wide blue eyes. She had a great laugh, a sort of loud guffaw that cracked me up coming from someone who was so ladylike. She taught elementary school. Lillian and Bertha were delighted that Bud had found such a good match. They had met in church, where Bud had first heard Nancy's glorious soprano voice. He said that from the moment he saw her, he wondered what it would be like to be married to her, and winked. Well, now he was going to find out, and everybody celebrated.

Nancy's boys came with her and moved into the little house. David and Stephen were maybe twelve and thirteen, so they were too young for me to pal around with. But I liked them. Looking back, I was so wrapped up in my own newness at the village that I didn't really understand how strange it might have felt to Nancy and the boys. For better or for worse, I was just there for the summer. They were here for good. I didn't spend a lot of time with the boys, but we did have a good time one afternoon soon after they came. In cahoots, we committed a crime—breaking the rules about staying out of the Cow Barn. The outlaws were Nancy's Steven, Bud's Dayne, and I.

Along with the Dwelling and the Meetinghouse, the Cow Barn was one of the architectural showpieces of the village. Built around 1858, it was the longest barn in New Hampshire and quite possibly all of New England, more than two hundred feet from end to end. It stretched across the north end of the village, and its west entrance was set back from the road by a considerable distance. Like the Horse Barn across the road, it was covered with ugly asbestos shingles. Bertha's eyes lit up as she talked about eventually restoring the Cow Barn to its original appearance when she warned me about its condition. As far as she was concerned, I was welcome to go anywhere in the village, with the permission of course of any inhabitants. The empty buildings were mine for the exploring—with the exception of the Cow Barn. The Cow Barn had been unfortunately "improved" some years earlier by a hired man who thought that asphalt paving would protect the wooden floors. It had rotted them, instead, and there were places where holes in the main floor gaped into the manure pits below. Bertha was apologetic but firm—no poking around in the Cow Barn, for my own safety.

I don't know whose idea it was—surely not mine, because I wasn't much of a rule breaker—but it wasn't long after we met outside one afternoon that Dayne, Steven, and I found that an illicit trip into the forbidden Barn was just the ticket for the next hour. I felt bad about disobeying Bertha, but I really wanted to see the barn. I figured that the three of us had enough sense to look around without falling into any holes.

Since the only reason for Bertha's prohibition was a concern for our safety, there really wasn't any reason *not* to go in, as long as we stayed safe—right? The boys probably figured that I was responsible, being old, wise, and nineteen, so we wouldn't get into trouble. I guessed that if we were caught we wouldn't get into too much trouble, given that Bertha was very fond of all Bud's boys. We probably wouldn't get caught, anyway. The Cow Barn was far away from the Trustees' Office and Bertha was probably lying down to rest or else down in the kitchen doing things for supper. The Sisters were all hard of hearing, so it was very unlikely that we'd be heard, even if any of them were out and about at this end of the village, which was even more unlikely.

All this rationalization made more and more sense, so in we crept. I had my box camera with me, as I had been taking pictures when I ran into the boys, so I recorded our escapade for posterity. It wasn't technically breaking and entering, because there was no reason to break anything to get in. We just walked through the door.

I'll never be sorry that we went inside, although I didn't like to disregard Bertha's wishes. The three-story Cow Barn was a vast cavern filled with scraps of old hay and pigeons in the cupola. Bertha was right: the hard-topped main floor was a mess, but it was sturdy enough around the holes, and plenty safe for sensible folk with agile young legs like us. We had entered through the front, where a regular door cut into the big wagon doors made it convenient for a farmer on foot to enter without having to swing the heavy doors open. At the far end was a similar set of doors. An impressive granite-and-earth ramp at each end made it possible for hay wagons to drive into this upper story. If I closed my eyes, I could imagine a line of hay wagons creaking through the length of the barn at harvest time, each pitching its load down into the hay mows on either side of the runway.

The Canterbury Shakers had planned and built a very user-friendly Barn, which was typical of their approach to life and work. The whole system worked with, not against, the force of gravity. The hay dropped down into the mows on the floor below, where farmers forked it over to the dairy herd in its stanchions. Behind the stanchions, we discovered a row of trapdoors that opened into the manure pits below. In principle, it wasn't that different from the famous round stone barn built in 1826 by the Shakers at Hancock, Massachusetts, except that it was made of wood and stretched out straight, not wrapped in a circle, which made construction much less expensive.

We had a ball climbing around and through the Cow Barn. My girlfriends assured me that little brothers were a pain in the neck, but our clandestine adventure was a good beginning of a friendship. Dayne and Steven obliged me by posing with manure trapdoors, next to stanchions, and the like. When we finally clambered out the way we came in, we were on our way to being friends.

·  ·  ·

I never got to know Bud's younger son very well, because Dayne stayed more with his mom and stepdad, but Darryl and I became close friends indeed. Darryl was thirteen going on fourteen that summer, an odd and pleasant mixture of age and youth, somewhat like his dad. In some ways Darryl was astonishingly mature for his age, and in others, remarkably innocent. There was nothing smart-alecky about him, nothing goofy or gross, like many boys his age. Darryl was a big, strapping fellow with an endearing gentleness in one so big. The Shakers thought the world of their "grandson," and he loved them with all his big, young heart. The Shakers were as pleased as Bud at the honors Darryl garnered for his studies. They loved Dayne, too, who was more active and high spirited, a guy's guy, interested in things that involved noise and speed and dirt.

I got to know Darryl better than the other boys because he was one of the summer tour guides, too. Darryl was already a veteran with a season under his belt. Visitors who were initially surprised at the young age of their guide soon fell under the charm of Darryl's tour. Who else could talk from the heart about growing up in a Shaker village with a bunch of Shaker "grandmothers"? Darryl had inherited his father's gift of gab and passion for history, especially Shaker history.

Like Bud, Darryl was a fountain of information about the Shakers and a wellspring of generous assistance to the new guides, Jan and me. Jan Maynard was from Concord, a jolly woman with short dark hair and a ready laugh. Her mother-in-law, Grace, had been good friends with the Shakers for years. Her husband, Clancy, was just as rollicking as Jan. Like me, she was a sponge for knowledge in the early weeks of June. We couldn't learn enough fast enough, and Darryl was our main man. If we had a question, he had an answer. If he didn't, he looked it up or found it out. There was always something more to learn. It would take a long, long time to get bored.

By the end of the second week of June, I had met everybody in the daily circle of summer life at the village. There was "Coup," Armand Coupal, Dayne and Darryl's stepfather, who was in charge of buildings and grounds and maintenance, and who drove Miriam to town once a week for the Shakers' grocery shopping. Marjorie Emery, a longtime friend of the Sisters, was a retired schoolteacher who sold tickets for the tour, assisted Margaret in the Gift Shop, and also took tours. Marjorie had tight blue-gray curls and spoke with the voice of authority on everything. The Sisters were fond of her and appreciated the help she gave them, but I'm afraid that I steered clear of her when I could. I knew she meant well, and it was nothing personal, but she treated me (to be fair she treated everyone) to lectures on how to be and what to do, and frankly, at nineteen, I did not want to hear another word of instruction along that line.

I wanted to learn how to be an adult, that was certain, I wanted that keenly, but I wanted people to show me, not tell me.


During June I learned more about life on Shaker Road as I met some of the Shakers' neighbors. In the Shakers' heyday, the Brothers and Sisters had been cordial but distant neighbors. For religious reasons they preferred to keep themselves to themselves, safe from the wicked World, even if that meant just the not-so-wicked farm families trying to pry a living from the same rocky hills and swamps. In modern times, of course, the Shakers made much better friends with some of their neighbors.

Homes were well spaced along Shaker Road, so the nearest neighbors to the south were Alejandro de la Cruz, a Spanish cabinetmaker, and his wife, Lolita. Their neat white house was a good three quarters of a mile from the Trustees' Office. They were friends of Bud's, who had a piece or two of Alejandro's work. The workmanship was incredible. When you closed your eyes and ran a finger over the dovetails in the side of a drawer, you felt nothing but solid smoothness. Alejandro favored beautiful woods like bird's-eye maple in his reproductions of some Shaker pieces, in the tradition of some Shaker craftsmen. Some of the most conservative old-time Shaker woodworkers adamantly preferred plain wood such as pine or maple, but some felt different. Added, man-made ornament was vain and a waste of time, but God's natural patterns were there to be used and enjoyed.

The nearest neighbors up the road to the north were the Wymans. Bud and the Sisters spoke well of the family and said that I would probably hit it off with Teresa, who was my age. (Privately, I feared that the chances were slim that the only two girls the same age in about five miles of road actually would have anything in common—she was probably one of those poised cheerleader types with naturally straight hair.) I met David and Midge Wyman first. David, tall and lanky, was a professor of history at the University of Massachusetts. He had started his teaching career long ago in the Tilton-Northfield elementary school, so that's why they summered here, in a long, low, dark-brown homemade house with a huge garden in the backyard. Mr. Wyman was hard at work on a book about America's abandonment of Jewish immigrants during the Holocaust, they told me. He was mostly holed up in his study, the little converted chicken house beyond the garden.

Mrs. Wyman, short and pleasant, spent a good deal of her time among the beans and the peas. They were vegetarians, the first I'd ever met, and raised much of their own food. Their son Jimmy worked in an ice cream distribution center that summer. Mrs. Wyman laughed and said that no matter if they only had fresh soybeans for supper, they always had dessert—Jimmy brought home gallons and gallons of the stuff.

The Wymans were Quakers, and they embraced simplicity and pacifism. They didn't go in much for fashion, either in their clothes or their home furnishings. Mr. Wyman had served time in jail. As a pacifist, Mr. Wyman had chosen not to fight in the Korean War. He could have served as a conscientious objector, but he chose imprisonment instead. A deeply religious man himself, he nevertheless objected to conscientious objection, an alternative that unfairly excluded atheists. Here, clearly, was a man of principle. It was ironic: he was one of those "peaceniks" Mom had tried so hard to protect me from, and I could tell that I was probably going to spend lots of time with this family.

Bud was right. I did like Teresa, and she liked me, too. Teresa's tastes ran to contradancing and playing traditional New England dance tunes on her fiddle. Her dark hair was longer than mine, and not quite as frizzy, but she was no blonde cheerleader. She liked hiking in the woods and she loved the Shakers. Her particular friends were Alice and Ethel, up in the Dwelling. For Teresa as for Darryl, the doors of Canterbury Shaker Village had swung open from earliest childhood. She and Darryl had grown up together here on Shaker Road, and he would always be her beloved "little brother."

Getting to know the Wymans was going to help with tours, too, when visitors inevitably asked what the difference was between the Quakers and the Shakers. The two religious groups had many similarities and a few differences. The Quakers, or the Society of Friends, were established in England in the mid-1600s under the leadership of George Fox. They were dissenters who thought that the Church of England was far more about royal politics than faith. The term "Quakers" was originally derisive. The Shakers came into existence as a group of dissenters in England in the mid-1700s under the guidance of James and Jane Wardley, who soon hailed the young Ann Lee as their spiritual Mother.

Like the Quakers and many other groups of dissenters, the Shakers were dissatisfied with the Church of England. Both groups experienced persecution in England and in America. Many Quakers moved to the Quaker leader William Penn's colony in the seventeenth and eighteenth centuries to establish a city of their own: Philadelphia, the City of Brotherly Love. The Shakers came to America later, in 1774, and there was no safe haven for them in New York's or New England's cities and towns, as they soon found. In time, their numbers grew through conversion and they built their own villages, including Canterbury, apart from the wicked "World."

The dress, speech, and manners of these two societies were similar enough in the nineteenth century that outsiders likened them to each other and sometimes confused the two. There were significant differences, however. The Shakers were celibate and the Quakers weren't. The Shakers had a communal economy, something like modern kibbutzim in Israel, and the Quakers didn't.

Although both Quaker and Shaker religious services took place in simple surroundings, their forms of worship were drastically different. Quakers traditionally sat in silence until someone felt moved to speak. The Shakers, in vivid contrast, were famous for their sacred dance and song, which raised eyebrows because no one else got up and danced in church in the civilized Christian world.

It was twilight when my first visit with the Wymans came to an end, so they walked me and the dogs down to the village. Tall, ancient sugar maples lined this stretch of Shaker Road, just like the stretch below the village. The leaves overhead rustled darkly against the soft gray dusk. One or two leaves were falling—no, flying—good Lord, they were bats! Don't worry, the Wymans said, they won't land in your hair and they live on mosquitoes. Put that way, they didn't seem all that bad. Any creature that got rid of mosquitoes felt like a friend.

In a few steps we walked past the Shaker cemetery on the right, which bounded the Wymans' land to the south. It seemed peaceful, not spooky, a spacious lawn enclosed with a simple iron fence. To the west, a tall pine tree stood like a sentinel, black against the violet sky. Here by the road, a pretty, compact hawthorn stood guard, its bright pink petals dimmed by the dusk, its worthy thorns concealed by night. There were hydrangeas that dried in autumn into "ghost flowers," as Teresa called them, for the Shaker ghosts.

There were no headstones. Instead, a single large granite monument in the center bore the simple word: SHAKERS. Sometime in the twentieth century, the community had decided to replace the old, individual stones with one monument. To the leadership at that time, it felt in keeping with the Shakers' focus on the group, not the self. Besides, it also made the upkeep of mowing easier. The Shakers in Maine had the same arrangement.

The Wymans had been close to Eldress Marguerite Frost, the most recent arrival in this quiet field of rest, who had died the year before. A good, old-fashioned Shaker, they said. A truly spiritual woman, a saint. A really intellectual type, a respected authority on Shaker mysticism, a gifted and lovely soul. Teresa recalled one visit that she and Midge paid to Marguerite when Teresa was very young. Marguerite was feeling poorly, so she was propped up in bed. Teresa noticed there was a glow of light at her head. Later, when she talked about the light, her mother looked at her oddly and said, "But there is no lamp there." Teresa, who was as down to earth as a dandelion, was more or less convinced that she had seen a halo, although it wasn't something she talked about much, and she only told me after we'd been friends for many years.

The Wymans went on and on about Marguerite, with respect and affection. Then one of them mentioned Ethel—and they all burst out laughing. I gathered that there were different kinds of Shakers, just as there were differences in us of the World.

Some of us ate meat, some ate soybeans, some served in the Navy, some refused to bear arms, and God seemed to have room for us all. I learned a folksong later that seemed to say it best: "All God's critters have a place in the choir."

We moved on down the road, beneath the arching branches, past the beautiful old stone walls. The dogs—sandy-colored Sandy and elegant, willowy Twig, the greyhound—tugged at their leashes and sniffed the evening news. Past the arboretum planted by Elder Henry for long-ago Shaker children, past the Schoolhouse, on by the Horse Barn and down to the Trustees' Office. The lights glowed warm in the windows of the sitting room on the first floor facing the road. The Wymans said good night until the next time, and wandered back up the road toward home. But I lingered a moment in the quiet outside the door, the scent of Eldress Gertrude's petunias spicy in the air. I glanced in . . . I could hear the faint mutter of the television through the window screens. It was getting on toward

*Eldress Gertrude*

nine o'clock, so any minute now they'd get up and head to the back kitchen for a cup of something warm. There was Lillian in her rocker by the window. Bertha was behind, in her place on the sofa. Eldress Gertrude sat bolt upright in her chair by the wall, her knitting needles flying. She was our night owl; she'd be up till midnight, at least. Margaret was nodding in the chair nearer the piano.

God's in his heaven, all's right with the world. These were my people, somehow. I was nineteen, a college coed in miniskirts, and they were old Shaker ladies, but somehow we fit, and the fit made sense.

What do you know . . . I was home.

When Lillian fell and broke her hip on June 7, it broke my heart; the rhythm and rhyme of life at Canterbury Shaker Village changed forever. For many days afterward, it was touch and go. The doctors in Concord operated on her and that went well, but her age, frailty, and preexisting ailments made her recovery very tenuous indeed. Poor Bertha was a wreck. She and Lillian had been friends for Bertha's whole Shaker life. Lillian was Bertha's sister, mother, friend, and spiritual mentor. Newly in the Eldress's hot seat at a particularly distressing time in Shaker history, Bertha was counting on Lillian's loving presence.

The doctors' reports, and Bertha's hopes, went up and down with each passing day. At one point, at the end of her rope, Bertha just sniffed in disgust, fed up. The well-meaning doctor told her not to get her hopes up. What does he know anyway, she grumbled back home, he's awfully young (he was in his forties). She and Lillian had been friends for sixty-seven years, longer than that doctor had been alive. It was so hard for the rest of us to know how to help. There didn't seem to be much we could do. We were scared to death that Lillian would be ripped from us all. It was bad enough that she was far away in the hospital. What would happen to Bertha if Lillian died?

As if Lillian's troubles weren't enough, Sister Alice from up in the Dwelling had a heart attack the same day, so off she went to the hospital, too. She was going to be all right though, the doctors said, so at least we could breathe more easily about that. But now Ethel was in distress, too, just like Bertha. Without Alice, who had been like a mother to her, Ethel was all on her own up in that enormous Dwelling. Jennie and the rest of us would just have to keep an extra close eye on her.

The rest of June seemed to pass in a weird, dreamlike fashion. Life went on for all of us—there were tours to give, meals to fix and eat, postcards and baby bonnets to sell in the Gift Shop. Gus and Alice sent for me and we spent a happy weekend. We mulled over the big Shaker auction at the Sabbathday Lake community and shook our heads over the crazy prices collectors paid, like maybe $35 for a Shaker pincushion, for heaven's sake, or $25 for an oval box lid, sold as a "dresser tray." Gus got a kick out of the fact that a few bidders wound up with his oval boxes, and paid hefty Shaker prices for them, too. The auction itself was controversial. The Sabbathday Lake Shakers, fearing loss of income from the Central Trust Fund due to the schism, let it be known that they needed to raise money. Privately, Bertha mourned the public attention to Family troubles, as well as the dispersal of artifacts that were dear to her as the work of the "old Shakers."

Back in Canterbury we experienced the annual thrill of the great motorcycle races. Bikers from everywhere camped on the roadside from Loudon to Laconia. I didn't even dare tell my worry-wart mom that about sixty thousand Hell's Angels were coming into town, but I did the worrying for her. What if maniacs covered in black leather came roaring into little Canterbury Shaker Village on a weekend? Could I save the Shakers? Could I save myself? When it was all over, I had to laugh sheepishly at my fears. Yes, it's true that there was always some violence when the bikers congregated, and every year one or two people got knifed to death, or shot, or something, but rival gangs pretty much confined the violence they wrought to each other.

Bud would take us for rides up and down Route 106 so we could gawk at the bikers, who camped along the road with their big, gorgeous machines. Wow! This was something new. There were lots of women in short black skirts and skimpy tops with tattoos you could see right here from the road. We had to roll up the windows when Eldress Gertrude rode along, because her voice really carried. "Well, I never . . . Look at *that* one there . . . Isn't that awful!" She clucked and frowned and carried on.

She had a better time than anybody.

I started making sketches in June, too. The inspiration to try came from something a visitor said. One day, three middle-aged ladies came through, bubbling over with high spirits. They said that they were sisters and that they were in the flea-market line. They were funny and enthusiastic, with accents that were pure New York City. One of them was so excited that she said she'd be making drawings of everything in sight, if she lived there. *Click*, the light bulb went on. Weekends passed slowly, especially now with Lillian in the hospital and Bud and Bertha away on Sunday and Monday because they spent time at her side. I didn't have a decent camera, only the boxy little Instamatic that couldn't take close-ups. Why *not* give drawing a go? Pencils and paper were cheap. What was there to lose?

I began to head straight for the Meetinghouse or the Summer Kitchen every spare moment on weekends and between tours. The Shakers were delighted that someone was taking such an interest in their legacy, the works of the "old Shakers." Bertha could barely see the lines, but she was happy. When I shyly showed Bud my sketches, he raved about them (that was Bud—he would encourage anybody, anytime, out of the goodness of his heart), and his words fell on fertile soil. Why *not* publish a book of drawings of Shaker subjects?

A kind of spiritual awakening continued in me, too, to my wonder. Bud and Nancy talked about their faith and introduced me to a circle of friends who got together regularly to share their experience and hope. They were wonderful, with the same feel as the Shakers, serene and joyous, especially two of them who had worked with Norman Vincent Peale in New York. They made me welcome and didn't mind that I burst into tears when they started to pray.

A door was opening. Never mind that I was nineteen and a rank beginner—at drawing, at faith, at life . . . When Bud got enthused and the Sisters smiled their encouragement and blessing, anything seemed possible.

A highlight of the summer was a visit from Tom Davenport in the first days of June. Tom was a filmmaker at work on a documentary called *The Shakers.* The fact that he and his partner had persuaded the Shakers in both communities to participate testified to their sincerity and the power of their vision. Winning the blessing of the Shakers for their project was no mean feat at that time because publicity was suspect in Shaker eyes.

I could understand the historical and religious reasons for the United Society's modest shrinking from the limelight. For the first half century and more of their existence in America, nearly all of the attention the Shakers received, which at the time meant in print, was not favorable. On hindsight this was hardly surprising. Yes, the new nation was a democracy founded in theory on the ideals of toleration, including religious freedom, but it was obviously going to take some time to get that message into the mainstream, out there in the trenches where real people trudged through everyday life.

To many people who lived in towns where the Shakers began to establish settlements, the United Society seemed peculiar and even threatening. Who were these oddballs, anyway, the thinking of many on the outside seemed to run, and what on earth were they doing shaking and hopping around in church? And what was this nonsense about celibacy and breaking up families? What if your own spouse or child got some fool notion to join up, for heaven's sake? And scariest of all—they were obviously succeeding. Their numbers were growing, their acreage expanded yearly, their plain but costly new buildings sprouted up as fast as toadstools in the damp. They didn't fight, they didn't scramble to get rich, they didn't vote—why, they seemed downright un-American.

Given this general line of thinking, the reaction of the Shakers' neighbors varied from community to community and indeed from individual to individual. At worst, gangs of local rowdies rode through quiet Shaker streets and dooryards, yelling taunts and threats, sometimes armed and dangerous in their violence and ignorance. At best, a few neighbors might be inclined to live and let live. Most left them alone but were critical and suspicious.

This general popular reaction could not help but attract the attention of writers of books and newspapers. From the Shakers' earliest days in America, observers with pen in hand descended upon them like fleas to Jennie's cats. It wasn't hard for them to gain access to Shaker villages because Believers made all travelers welcome. That policy, instituted fairly early in Shaker life, made sense from the standpoint of the United Society.

In Mother Ann's time, it had been necessary for missionaries to venture forth into New England and "open the gospel" to congregations willing and able to hear. Once the communities had been established and organized, however, in the days of Father Joseph Meacham and Mother Lucy Wright, the United Society withdrew its energy from proselytizing and instead focused on meeting the World on Believers' home ground, letting it be known that visitors would be treated courteously and given tours of the grounds and operations. Good meals were available at reasonable prices in the Trustees' Office, which also featured a neat shop where the ladies could purchase mementoes, mostly well made and useful items for the home: baskets, pincushions, poplar ware, oval boxes, and dainty confections like candied walnuts or sugared violets.

By the early 1800s, Shaker villages became tourist attractions of a sort in their regions. In a world that was still agricultural, the operations were something to see: huge, well-tended farms and gardens, large herds of sleek stock, the most modern barns and mills, and big dwellings and workshops. On Sundays, the Shakers held public worship services, the biggest draw of all. Visitors sat along the perimeter of the meetinghouse (gentlemen and ladies separate, please), heard a brief sermon, and then watched the Shakers dance.

It must have been impressive to spectators, at the very least as theater, although the Shakers of course always hoped for a sparking of the conversion flame inside the visitors' breasts. Inside the large white hall with deep blue woodwork, dozens or hundreds of Believers stepped in unison in their white and blue Sabbath uniforms: pure white gowns for the Sisters, blue trousers and vests over sparkling white shirts for the Brothers, special blue cloth dancing slippers on every foot. The light of heaven poured in through large, uncurtained windows, music burst from the throats of a capella singers, and the dance floor gleamed, spotless and holy, as clean as the top of a dining table.

The effect was undeniably powerful and I imagine that even observers disposed to scoff were shaken by the forces at work. Later, of course, writers including James Fenimore Cooper, Nathaniel Hawthorne, and Charles Dickens could gather their wits and their words to write smartly of "dancing dogs" and other behavior they deemed ludicrous, but in the presence of the Shakers, on their own sacred ground, I would bet that they shivered in the grip of something bigger than they wanted to acknowledge.

The most sympathetic published reports about the Shakers appeared in America's crop of nineteenth-century farm journals. Practical farmer-journalists liked what they saw and wrote approving, down-to-earth odes to the beauty and value of Believers' pigs, sheep, apples, and flax. Writers of a more literary bent were not so charmed. While most of them admitted admiration for the Shakers' tidy houses and barns, the practices of communal life and celibacy were targets for criticism and sarcasm. Dickens poked fun at simple Shaker style in a memorable sentence—"We walked into a grim room, where several grim hats were hung from grim pegs, and the time was grimly told by a grim clock"—and sniffed that if all Shaker Sisters looked like the ones he saw, he would give no credence to rumors of any deviation from celibacy.

Hawthorne, who overcame his youthful passion for the communal life after a brief, disenchanting fling at Ripley's Brook Farm, a commune in Roxbury, Massachusetts, visited Hancock and said that everything was so neat that it was a pain and constraint to look at it. Many accounts ridiculed plain Shaker clothing, which deliberately concealed the shape of the body: "a last year's bean pole stuck into a meal sack," declared one fashionable observer of a typical Sister. It wasn't until the 1850s that anything like an honestly favorable review of Shaker life appeared in print, when the journalist Benson Lossing visited New Lebanon, New York, and published a detailed account, illustrated with his woodcuts of his skillful renderings, in *Harper's New Monthly Magazine*.

With the decline of the Shakers, outside interest grew more favorable. No longer a powerful, youthful threat, the Believers were easier to know and like as they faded. In the early twentieth century, most of what little publicity the United Society generated was positive, which was ironic, given that nearly all of it related to the closing of yet another communal Shaker Family or village. At least the Society's obituaries were respectful. Many of the articles published since 1875 focused on the imminent demise of the United Society of Believers.

During the first half of the twentieth century, when my own Shaker friends came of age, flowered, and began the droop into advanced age, a couple of articles stood out as benchmarks. One, which appeared in *Life* in 1949, was more sympathetic than others in both text and images, profusely illustrated in the magazine's trademark style with large black-and-white photos. Still, the article painted a bleak picture that some of the Shakers didn't like. *Life* did a second article in 1967. The Shakers were pleased with the attention because it turned the light on their faith, rather than on their furniture design, which always seemed less important to them, or on their inevitable demise as a society, which seemed as natural to them as any other death, so why focus on it? After all, they pointed out, even Christ died after his season on earth. That had nothing to do with the life of the spirit. The subtitle of the 1967 piece said it all: "It Is Christ Who Dwells in Me."

The main title of that article, though, "Serene Twilight of a Once-Sturdy Sect," put the spotlight on the United Society's passing. Twentieth-century headlines generally echoed the theme: "Shakers Dwindling but Impact Still Felt"; "Maine's Shakers: Does It Have to Be Suicide?"; "The Sect That Condemned Itself to Death"; "A Death Leaves the Shaker Faith near Extinction"; "Canterbury Shaker Village Is Ghost of Earlier Days"; "The Last Shaker Brother"; "Seven Left at Canterbury; Last of Shakers Sure Faith Will Live On"; "Vanishing Breed."

It was ironic that the Shakers' internal problems came to a head just about the time that the World's attention had turned consistently favorable. As reporters got wind of the rift, the tenor of the headlines changed: "Shake-up in Paradise"; "Showdown at Shaker Village"; "Shattering the Shaker Image." The Shakers were back onstage and now their private family matters were being exposed to the eyes of a judgmental, interfering World.

It was little wonder that in the summer of 1972, Bertha politely but firmly chose not to give an interview to a reporter from the *New York Times* or to one with a film crew from CBS. In the village, we thought it was too bad, because Bertha made a sympathetic and attractive spokesperson for her faith, and the museum could have used the free publicity, but her understandable reluctance to be drawn into speaking about the very personal controversy prevailed. Her public silence on the split between the two communities, which she rarely broke, was misunderstood by some who did not know her as a case of psychological denial, a refusal to acknowledge painful reality.

Baloney. Bertha simply made a choice to avoid the intermediary of the media. I learned a great deal from her that summer and afterward about a way of behaving in disputes. Like Gandhi, she chose the path of peaceful resistance to what she considered wrong. We marveled at her strength and her evident freedom from motives of anger or self-righteousness. It was love, pure and simple, that guided her, and in the end, I could see how effective that was.

And in Bertha I could see the other, spiritual aspect to the United Society's general reserve about publicity. Interviews and articles and film clips inevitably put the spotlight on an individual, which didn't accord with the Shakers' all-for-one-and-one-for-all tradition of community. On top of that, Bertha was by nature modest and reserved, a "simple Kitchen Sister" unaccustomed to the more public role of Eldress. She loosened up delightfully in private, but only when she was among close friends. Eldress Gertrude, who loved attention and mingling with people, would have been more suited by temperament to the role of spokesperson, but her deeply personal involvement with the schism made it impossible for her emotionally.

Historically, the United Society had addressed this business of official representation to the World by creating service roles that included the responsibility. The Trustees and Office Sisters were chosen in part for their ability to deal wisely and easily with the World. On the spiritual front, the Elders and Eldresses of the Gathering Order for novitiates were generally the designated liaison between the World and the United Society because they were closest to new and would-be converts. It made sense to put these leaders in the Meetinghouse to lead public worship.

In time, although it took some years, the Shakers changed their mind about TV interviews. As the United Society's internal tensions eased, and as it became clear that media attention was virtually always favorable—and that good publicity would help spread the Shaker message—Bertha and Eldress Gertrude began to say yes instead of no. About ten years later, when a young, neophyte filmmaker from New Hampshire asked them to appear in his documentary on the Shakers, they agreed. Ken Burns was grateful. The Shakers liked him very much, and he considered Bertha one of the spiritual leaders of our time. His beautiful film, *The Shakers*, preserved the Shakers as we knew them, and they were glad to know that he went on to bigger and better things with his acclaimed documentary series for PBS.

As they became more relaxed with publicity, the Sisters got to be so popular for interviews that the phone rang more and more. About the only time Bertha balked was when they were asked to appear in a segment of *Ripley's Believe It or Not*. Bertha had some doubts—it seemed sensational and even a little tacky—but Eldress Gertrude, by this time an old trouper of stage and screen, had her heart set on it. All right, said Bertha, you can if you want, but no thanks for me. Even Eldress Gertrude was a little sheepish when the feature aired (Bertha was right), but she never seemed really sorry. She was having way too much fun.

At any rate, in 1972 Tom Davenport was warmly welcomed. He had already won the confidence of the Believers and had been filming for a year or more. I liked him a lot. He was a bright young fellow who lived on a farm in Virginia, had a brand-new son named Makepeace, and was interested in Zen Buddhism. I didn't get to meet people like this every day, so I hung around when he and the Sisters sat down to visit. He wanted them to identify some historic Shaker photographs if they could, so one evening he set up the slide projector. Bertha's eyesight was already too far gone for her to be much help, and we could tell it made her sad, but Lillian was able to tell him the names and some of the stories of a number of the faces that glowed softly from the screen.

Tom's enthusiasm prompted Bertha to fetch her photo albums from a drawer in the hall, and we fell on them with eager eyes. What do you know? Bertha had been an avid amateur shutterbug in her early years and here was a treasury of candid snapshots, taken by Bertha and by others, of her Family at work and at play, picking apples, eating watermelon at picnics, and—my favorite—Dewey the dog perched on the piano stool "playing." Dewey was a dead ringer for the mutt on *The Little Rascals*, rakish patch over one eye and all, and I'd bet that in his heart he was banging out boogie-woogie, not some saintly Shaker hymn.

Unexpectedly, Bertha also brought out another community treasure, Elder Henry Blinn's two handwritten journals from the 1880s and 1890s. She staggered a little under the weight of the big, heavy volumes, which looked like ledgers. Each was bound in brown leather, scuffed into velvet by time, and inside were pages and pages filled with words in Elder Henry's clear, angular hand. Tom spent most of the next day or two poring over the pages, reading bits aloud. I couldn't hear enough. Elder Henry was articulate, sensitive, and funny. He had combed through the Family's older journals to consolidate accounts of the most interesting events into a history of the Canterbury Shaker society. I could hardly wait to bury my nose in the volumes myself when Tom had finished with them.

Elder Henry devoted considerable coverage to the Shakers' long and fascinating history of spiritualism, which seized Tom's imagination. To the Shakers, spiritualism meant a belief that the living could communicate with the spirits of the dead with the help of a medium, or "instrument" in Shaker parlance. It also meant a conviction that all reality is in essence spiritual. Many Believers had dreams and visions from which they received deep comfort and abiding inspiration. The tradition began with Mother Ann. At ease in the spirit world, Ann experienced visions and conversations with angels and departed spirits. In this, of course, she was out of step with her Enlightenment times contemporaries. It was impossible, for example, to imagine her contemporary Abigail Adams at home in the same world, or rather, otherworld.

The Shakers' devotion to spiritualism continued throughout the nineteenth century, too, especially in the 1840s and 1850s, during a period of internal revivalism the Shakers called "Mother Ann's Work." During this time, it was commonplace for inspired individuals to receive "gifts" from the spirits. Some were messages of comfort or exhortation from Father Joseph Meacham, Mother Lucy Wright, and other bygone Shaker worthies. Some were from even higher up the ladder of heaven, Jesus and Mother Ann, in whom the Christ spirit lived. And then there were visits from the really big guns—the Heavenly Father and Holy Mother Wisdom, the dual aspects of God.

Inspiration came in various forms. Some Believers received gifts of song, and many of the United Society's ten thousand sacred songs dated from this creative, spiritually vigorous time. The best-known example in our time, "Simple Gifts," was among them, received by Elder Joseph Brackett in Maine. Other Shakers were more open to visual imagery, which they recorded in ink and paint. Sister Hannah Cohoon, who drew and painted the now famous *Tree of Life*, was of this type. Bud had a few other spirit drawings, or gift drawings, which he showed me that summer. They were haunting and mysterious. Henry Blinn himself was an inspired instrument, or medium, for spirit messages, in his younger days, and so were dozens of other wise, credible Believers, who earned respect both within and outside their Shaker homes.

During the summer of 1972 I had a healthy suspicion of what I dismissed as hoodoo and tended to laugh at people who took astrology, fortune-telling, and the like seriously. Oh sure, I had fun with it. I read my horoscope in the funny papers every day and my friend Marlene and I had given the planchette more than a spin or two around the old Ouija board, but that was just for amusement. Wasn't it?

Here was something I didn't expect, or know what to do with. My Shaker friends, my own down-to-earth Bertha and Lillian and Eldress Gertrude, who sat and ate cornflakes with me every day at breakfast, were on Mother Ann's spiritual plane, too. Each of them had experienced visions and communications with spirits and they freely shared this information with Tom. I sat on the edge of my chair. Bertha was working in the kitchen one day when she heard Eldress Dorothea Cochran's voice. She turned and saw Eldress Dorothea with her arms outstretched, smiling, and saying, "My golden child!" Bertha ran to embrace her—but she was gone. Lillian had been visited and encouraged by her deceased sister in a tree-shaded lane. In time-honored Shaker tradition, she had received gifts of song. Some of her work was included in the old Shaker hymnal, but not under her name. Like her spiritual forebears, Lillian believed that her music was a gift to her from God, and from her to her beloved companions. Viewing herself as God's "instrument," she did not claim credit.

Lillian had also experienced a miraculous healing. Bertha told how Lillian had developed cancer when she was in her sixties and had been sent home by the doctors to die. But she came home and made up her mind to get well because she knew that her work wasn't done yet. Sure enough, she recovered, and here she still was thirty years later, so I guessed she was right. Her recovery did not particularly surprise the Shakers because they had faith in what the rest of us usually call miracles.

It seemed simple to Believers. The Gospels were as real to them as the morning newspaper or nightly news were to the World. They could accept the testimony of those who knew Christ firsthand, or knew people who knew Christ, because they understood and trusted the experience of their own founder's apostles. If Jesus' friends and followers said faith could heal, then that was that. If the spirit of Christ could heal and save and perform other miracles two thousand years ago, then the Shakers saw no reason why that work should not continue here and now. Their history was full of accounts of miraculous healings and communications with the spirits and other such works rejected by the age of science and reason.

Mother Ann may have been born into the world of the Enlightenment, but she perpetuated a way of understanding reality that was far more ancient. I grew to believe that intuition and a kind of spiritual sixth sense made more sense than logic and rationality, which I could see masqueraded sometimes as a cloak of respectability over fearful and closed minds. Mother Ann and Believers throughout Shaker history made no bones about their conviction that the unseen reality, or alternative reality, was more real than the chairs they sat in or the bread they put in their mouths.

Such a no-nonsense easiness with the spirit realm tended to throw more conventional, mainstream Christianity into a tizzy, which in turn made no sense to the Shakers. If you read the Bible, there it was: healing, angels, spirits, walking on water, and all. If it happened then, why not now? Jesus himself urged his followers to believe in the unbelievable, and showed them over and over that the veil that wavers between what we deem possible and impossible is as insubstantial as a soap bubble.

In terms of my own spiritual development, I was hardly out of the egg, still plucking bits of shell from my down. So learning about this aspect of Shaker life excited me and made me uneasy at the same time. It became clear to me that séances and my silly pranks with Ouija boards had nothing to do with the deep well of spirit from which my Shaker friends drank. I realized that I had it all wrong. My comprehension was a dim flashlight in the dark compared to the strong, powerful light of their experience and understanding. I had a hard time deciding whether I was more comforted or frightened by the experiences of my Shaker friends. I guess it was a draw. In the light of day, rocking comfortably in the sitting room or the piazza, I was intrigued, attracted, even eager for some otherworldly experience of my own.

But at night in my room when I held my breath in the empty Infirmary, straining my ears in the dead silent aftermath of this odd thump or that inexplicable scratch, I wasn't so sure I wanted any part of some world I couldn't see or touch. Traffic with the spirits wasn't all sweetness and light. Bertha herself told of an experience that made my blood run cold. When she was young, she had awakened one night to see a dark shape hovering near her bed. Whatever it was, she knew that it was associated with an aunt who had been particularly nasty and hateful to little orphaned Goldie. It was uncharacteristic in the extreme for Bertha to speak so strongly about another, which seemed to add to the power of her story. Bertha said that the evil shape drifted closer, intent on doing her harm. She was chilled with fear, but she sat straight up in bed and said, "Jesus is with me!" and it was gone.

Good heavens. When I went to bed that night, I had a bad case of the willies. Bertha was not the type to tell ghost stories for dramatic entertainment, and the very matter-of-factness of her nature and her recollection of the event made it all the more terrifying. Life seemed full enough of tangible horrors. How could I deal with unseen menaces that could sneak up on me and pounce?

I remembered what Bertha said about Jesus, however, and fell into sleep, hoping fervently that I might be given the presence of mind to babble the same if the unwelcome opportunity ever arose.

# CHAPTER 5

# Alice and Ethel

If I didn't get to know Alice Howland or Ethel Hudson as well as I came to know the Sisters who lived in the Office, it wasn't because they were unfriendly or remote. My everyday life was simply so much more involved with the Trustees' Office's doings. Bertha, Lillian, and Eldress Gertrude didn't visit the Dwelling very often, but they kept in touch by way of the old-fashioned crank telephone. *Brring! Brring!* All the phones rang when anyone turned the crank, so every house had different rings, say, three long for Alice and Ethel in the Dwelling, two long and a short for Bud, two short for Miriam or Mildred in the Enfield House, and so on. The Office Sisters called the Dwelling Sisters at least once a day. Sometimes Ethel didn't answer right away and sometimes she didn't answer at all. Being a worrywart, I was usually convinced that Ethel was lying crumpled at the foot of the stairs, or that some other equally grim scenario had occurred.

But Bertha just shook her head and sighed. She knew Ethel. In Ethel's defense, it could be said that the Dwellinghouse did have fifty-six rooms, and the only home phones were down in the kitchen and in the sitting room. No, Bertha sighed. Ethel wasn't deaf and Ethel wasn't lame, and anyway, you could ring right back on the home phone whenever you got there. C'mon, Ethel, pick up. We all knew that Ethel hardly ever went out. Nope, no answer. Sigh. In addition to phoning, someone always visited in person every day. When Jennie's duties in the Office Kitchen after the noon dinner were done, she plodded willingly up the granite walk in the afternoon with the newspapers and some treat, a leftover "little fox" from dinner that Bertha knew Alice and Ethel would especially like.

Jennie and Ethel enjoyed their visits at the kitchen table in the Dwelling basement, gossiping about this and that. They were both crazy about their cats—they always said "kitties," which Ethel pronounced "kit-ties," as if it were two words. Jennie's were great big unfriendly creatures who spent the days outdoors and the nights inside. If they didn't come in at dusk, Jennie would spend a miserable night worrying that her darlings had been eaten by fisher cats.

I'd never heard of these predators and at the time half suspected that they were the product of Jennie's imagination. In that, I was wrong. I learned later that fishers, members of the marten family, are larger than weasels and more fearsome to fish, birds, and small mammals. Fishers came to haunt me that summer, too. Every weekend Jennie went home to Wilmot Flat, leaving me to make sure that her kitties were safe at home at night. Jennie was so good to me, and I was so fond of her, that I would have hated to let her beloved cats come to harm.

I like cats, but Jennie's were hard to like. They were snooty and full of fleas that bit our legs all summer long, as if we weren't pestered enough by the blackflies and mosquitoes. Every Saturday night was a battle of wills and wits, which the kitties usually won. The same animals who came galloping to Jennie's calls turned wretchedly coy. Flapping the mosquitoes from your arms and legs, you'd stand in the doorway crooning to Tiger and Tommy as the minutes dragged. The cats would groom themselves, stare at the air, and yawn in delicate boredom, but they wouldn't come in, even when you waved their smelly cat food under their noses. If you tried to go after them, they would retreat, although they wouldn't run away for good, and if you lunged for one or the other, you'd get scratched.

Nope, they just hung around to let you know that they knew perfectly well what the deal was here. After about ten minutes of this you could be forgiven for daydreaming about some fisher cat enjoying a tasty, furry midnight snack.

But who could stand the thought of what Jennie would go through if Tommy or Tiger vanished? Sometimes I just had to give up and abandon them to the jaws of night, but I paid for my sins by worrying all night long. I was always very glad when they showed up in the morning and let me serve them breakfast. Those blasted kitties never came to grief, but fisher cats will always stalk the night woods of my mind.

Ethel was so scared of fishers that she didn't let her cats out of the house at any time. From the cats' point of view, it was certainly a good thing that the Dwelling had fifty-six rooms. If Jennie's kitties were a pain in the neck, Ethel's little darlings made Jennie's look like . . . pussy cats. Goldie and Sunny were large, yellow tigers. Daisy, Ethel's pride and joy, was a huge gray tomcat with a nasty disposition. Daisy . . . what a name. Fang, or Claw of Death, would have been more like it. Ethel was very proud of her cats' front paws, which had about a dozen toes apiece. She fed them lavishly well. The refrigerator in the Dwelling Kitchen was always crammed with quarts of milk and cream. Forget canned cat food; she cooked tidbits of fresh chicken for them daily. Sometimes, she made different meals for each.

In spite of this attention, Daisy always seemed desperate to escape. When he reared up on his hind legs to reach the backdoor latch, maybe dreaming about dismembering a porcupine or a fisher cat for lunch as a nice change, Ethel would purr on and on about his cleverness and beauty. When he turned those saucer-sized paws tipped with half-inch talons to swipe at Ethel, she would coo and tell him what a good, sweet kit-ty he was. I hoped that she wouldn't notice me flinching or rolling my eyes. Since Ethel was very short, and Daisy was very long when he stretched, these little interchanges were somewhat alarming. But Daisy never got out, and Ethel never got severely scratched. Like an old married couple, they had reached a workable standoff in their daily battle of wills.

We wondered whether Ethel didn't let her cats out of the Dwelling because she herself rarely ventured beyond the kitchen door. This was one of Ethel's eccentricities. She loved to have company and was perfectly affable when anyone came to visit, but she just didn't like to go out. With Jennie to deliver her groceries and news of the village and the world beyond, Ethel stayed tucked indoors. All that summer she didn't emerge at all, except maybe to visit Sister Alice in the hospital.

I liked Ethel but I had to admit that it was a chore for me to visit her. For one thing, the kitchen where we sat and chatted never smelled too good. Ethel apparently never quite grasped that even her monster cats couldn't drink more than a couple of pints of milk or cream a week, and every week she sent Jennie down to the Office with a note ordering about three times too much. Bertha just shook her head when she made up the grocery list for Miriam to take into town on shopping day. She felt bad about the waste, but she didn't like to upset Ethel. Meanwhile, the extra milk went sour. Ethel's sense of smell must not have been too keen, because she never seemed to notice or mind. Sometimes it was all you could do to keep from holding your nose.

The Dwellinghouse Kitchen was a big, low-ceilinged room that had been in service since the early 1800s. The ceiling was plenty high for Ethel because she was only four feet something, by far the shortest adult I'd ever met. She wasn't quite small enough to be classified as a true midget, or "little person," but she sure was short. She cackled when anyone remarked on her height. "I'm like most remnants," she'd say in her high old quaver, "just a yard and a half. Hee, hee, hee!" The Sisters had regularly updated the appliances over the years, but they hadn't done much remodeling since the turn of the century. The stove and refrigerator were modern, but the ancient linoleum, the narrow tongue-and-groove paneling, and the pressed-tin ceiling gave the room an old-fashioned air. The old copper-lined sink, with deep double tubs, was too low for most people, but was high for Ethel.

Ethel liked to point out the Kitchen's conveniences. One, a storage bin for stove wood, was to the left of the sink. The Kitchen was in the basement level, so in the old days the Brothers dropped the wood into the bin through a window that was at ground level

*Big Dwelling, little Ethel*

outside. Piece of cake—let gravity do the hard work. She also got a kick out of explaining the "suicide" rocker she kept over by the built-in cupboards. For some reason, some early Canterbury rocking chairs were made with very short runners. If you rocked too hard, whoops, over you went. Hee, hee, hee!

Ethel was always glad to see me and we'd sit at the table near the windows. This summer the tour groups passed right outside on their way from the Meetinghouse to the Schoolhouse. Once or twice I happened to be visiting Ethel as this happened. The guide would talk about the Dwelling and its history, and explain that it wasn't open to the public because two Sisters still lived there. At this point, three or four pale ovals would press against the old panes to peer inside the dimly lit room. I felt like a fish in an aquarium, and wondered how Ethel liked it, but she just cackled. Ethel wasn't easily fazed, as long as she was safely indoors at home.

We'd talk about this and that, I'd admire the kitties from a prudent distance, and Ethel would invariably feed me something and send me off with a little present: a can of talcum powder, a bag of candy, or some old greeting card of cute, fluffy kittens, who didn't even seem to be of the same species as Daisy and Goldie. The tables and windowsills in the dining room just off the kitchen were heaped with mementos of Ethel's social life over many years, so "shopping" for my little present was easy. She would just step out, rummage around, and bring back some trifle. The thought that you might not want some such recycled gift never occurred to her, and in fact, it was kind of sweet.

Her generosity dovetailed neatly with Shaker tradition. If you looked around the museum, probably half of the artifacts had been intended as gifts for someone dear. It was not uncommon for an oval box, for example, to have an inscription on it in old brown ink: "For Eldress Dorothea Cochran." The tradition of presenting others with small, useful objects was as old as the United Society.

In the Shaker heart, giving was truly more blessed than receiving, or owning. Bertha said that when she was a little girl, the children were asked at Christmas to pass on their favorite possession so they would learn the joy of charity. It sounded like practice for later choices, when they came of age. Could they let go of the World and all its promises for the sake of the Shaker life?

Ethel's devotion to her kitties and her reluctance to leave the Dwelling were just two of her quirks. Ethel was a free spirit—as much as an old Shaker lady could be one. Her individualism expressed itself in ways that made Bertha shake her head. Ethel's appearance particularly troubled Bertha, who quietly fretted that she wished Ethel would keep herself up more. It wasn't vanity, the way Bertha explained it, it was the time-honored notion expressed by Father James Whittaker, one of Mother Ann's successors: "Be what you seem, and seem to be what you are." A neat appearance didn't guarantee an orderly soul, but in the Shaker tradition, they went hand in hand. Come to think of it, however, Ethel was in fact following Father James's dictum.

Ethel's version of the traditional Shaker outfit was, shall we say, more loosely interpreted than that of the Office Sisters and Miriam. Her dresses were appropriately made of cotton fabric in some solid color or floral print, and they came below the knee just as they should, but there her resemblance to her more public Sisters faded. Ethel was no clotheshorse. Her figure was not trim like Eldress Gertrude's, nor appealingly rounded like Bertha's, but was sort of bunchy fore and aft. Her dress was often a little dingy, with an AWOL button or two. To complete the ensemble, Ethel scuffed around in mousy old slippers. She clearly valued comfort over style.

Privately, I sort of cheered Ethel, not being much of a fashion plate myself, but I could see Bertha's point. It didn't matter if Ethel paraded down the main street or not; the idea was to maintain things properly whether or not they showed. When Bertha wished that Ethel would clean up her act, I realized, it was prompted by the same spirit that led Bertha to have the cellars and attics cleaned on a regular basis, in spite of the fact that village residents seldom saw them and visitors never did. Dust was dust, in the parlor or the garret. Mother Ann said, "Clean your room well, for good spirits will not live where there is dirt. There is no dirt in heaven."

Bertha didn't see a demon in every dust bunny, but she was obedient to the spirit of Mother Ann's instruction on cleanliness and order. If she'd lived in the Middle Ages, Bertha might have been one of those cathedral stone carvers who chiseled the angel's face to perfection even though no one on the ground would ever appreciate it. There it would perch, high above the human ragtag, with a smiling God its only witness. If Ethel had lived in the Middle Ages . . . Lord knows what she might have been, although jester comes to mind. She didn't seem to worry that God wouldn't love her, ragged slippers and all.

Since she didn't see many people, Ethel frequently went around without her net cap, and her stringy gray hair poked out from the small, bunchy knot at the back of her neck. She wore spectacles, like all the Sisters except Sister Alice. Ethel's nose dripped most of the time into the balled-up hankie she habitually clutched or tucked into her watch band. Her watery eyes peered through the lenses like fading blue forget-me-nots. When she threw back her head and laughed, her "Hee, hee, hee!" ricocheted through the Dwelling's dark halls. She'd tell you her age the minute you met: seventy-five that summer. I knew Ethel for twenty years, and the older she got, the prouder she was.

To be fair, Bertha's concern wasn't just that Ethel's appearance was going to the dogs. Ethel seemed to act as though "Hands to work, hearts to God" was fine and dandy—for the others. All of the other Sisters were industrious and kept busy with ladle, trowel, needle, or ledger. Ethel didn't seem to have any similar occupation; in fact, we guides never really knew what she did with her time.

Come to think of it, we never knew what trades Ethel had practiced in her youth, either. We could tell you what all the rest had done: Bertha had baked and cooked and worked in the poplar-ware industry, Gertrude had been involved with the healing arts and also made poplar ware and dressed china dolls for sale, Lillian had wowed customers up and down the East Coast from Maine to Florida as a sales representative for these products and more, and so on.

And then there was Ethel. She didn't garden; she didn't cook to speak of; she didn't go on shopping trips for the Family; she didn't share the work of greeting visitors; she didn't confer with the lawyers about managing the Central Trust Fund; she didn't make anything to sell in the Shop. She didn't seem to have any serious responsibility. Ethel did watch TV, and she was Canterbury Shaker Village's number one fan of Johnny Carson and *The Tonight Show*. It was fair to say that Ethel was the kind of Believer who took more than she gave, but then the Shakers never said this was heaven on earth, only that they were aiming for it.

Oh, well, there was enough stew in the pot. If Ethel was content to goof off at this point in her life, then so be it. Much later I learned that Ethel had done her share of work in years past, in a number of trades, including the sweater industry, and in canning. Her specialty was sewing, and she made a deep-dish custard pie that Mr. Wyman especially liked. And the old photos showed that she was neat enough in her dress. It wasn't as if she'd always been as she was now, which you could call "relaxed" or "haphazard," depending on how you felt about it. It was clear, however, that at this age Ethel had chosen what none of the other Sisters had (and what had never been part of the Shaker tradition): retirement. In her last years, it seemed that she had made up her mind that she was done with the regulation way.

For members of a small family that had known each other forever, the Sisters were pretty good about minding their own business. They didn't complain about Ethel's not doing her part. After a lifetime of squabbling with my sister Ann about who was going to do the dishes, or the fact that I *always* ran the vacuum and now it was her turn, the Shakers' attitude was refreshing. Bertha and Gertrude made us laugh by complaining privately about how much work the other was doing. My goodness, why didn't the poor dear have enough sense to slow down at her age?

I was flabbergasted that Mom took a shine to Ethel when they finally met. I couldn't believe my eyes and ears; Mom got a real kick out of Ethel's wayward ways. My mom, the same woman who was forever on my case to fix myself up because if I didn't, I was doomed to a life like that shabby old Miss Presser we saw on the street, the very same woman who raised her daughters to be ladies and who got the vapors at the merest hint of anything suggestive—yes, my mom, who probably never disobeyed one single rule in her whole life, took to Ethel like a bee to a blossom.

Maybe Ethel took her by surprise, and once the barn door was open, it was too late. On my mother's first visit, Ethel confided solemnly to her that the Shakers didn't want members of the same sex to get too close because "You know . . ." and then grinned like a naughty girl. Mom had to giggle—this was the last thing she expected to hear, especially having met the Office Sisters, who were good-humored but dignified through and through. Ethel did have a good sense of humor, although her jokes were even lousier than Bud's. They were clean, though. Did you hear about the Irishman who didn't like to fly? He preferred "terra firma"; the "firma" the ground, the less the "terra." Hee, hee, hee!

Ethel had come to the Shakers as a little girl, and she didn't talk much about her biological family. Her parents had divorced, which was fairly scandalous for the times. She was born in 1897, the same year as Bertha, in Salem, Massachusetts, and was brought to the Canterbury Shakers in 1907, where little Goldie had already been living for two years. They didn't live in the same communal family, however, so they didn't know each other well as girls. Ethel was placed at first in the North Family and then in the Second Family up the road. She only moved down here to the Church Family ten years later when the combined Second and North Families closed and the few remaining members moved down to the main part of the settlement. Ethel's waggish role in the community seemed to have been established from the beginning, when the Eldress looked sternly down her nose at the new arrival and introduced Alice as her "Shaker mother." Eight-year-old Ethel looked Alice straight in the eye, smirked, and curtsied, "very politely like," while she asked, "Ma'am, will I do?"

In spite of the Shakers' regard for all people as beloved children of God, there was a definite hierarchy in Shaker life that had persisted into Ethel's youth. The Church Family, as home of the Senior Order, was the spiritual center of each community. If you were a Shaker, the Church Family was the Promised Land. The outlying families were sometimes more like outposts on the spiritual frontier, where good leaders were sent to shepherd members who were younger in the faith.

This was especially true of the Gathering Order for novitiates, a sort of halfway house where would-be Shakers tested the waters to see how the Shaker life worked for them. The Gathering Order was the North Family. In the old days, newcomers were called "Young Believers," a reference that had nothing to do with their physical age but only with their spiritual progress.

That summer, the only other two-legged resident of the Dwelling was Sister Alice Howland. I had met both Ethel and Sister Alice early in my stay, when Eldress Gertrude kindly paid a call to make the introductions. What a contrast: Sister Alice and Sister Ethel were the lady and the scamp. Sister Alice was everything Ethel was not: a quiet, gentle Sister who personified the Shaker ideal, according to her longtime friends. She loved Ethel dearly and they were as close as mother and daughter. It seemed that relationships like Alice and Ethel's, and Lillian and Bertha's, explained everything about the continuation of Shaker life over two hundred years, in spite of strict celibacy. After all, the decision to choose a Shaker life was an individual one, a fact that underscored the irony of Shaker communal life. The community only existed because one member at a time chose to stay. Why did anyone choose to stay? There was convenience, and then there was deep spiritual conviction. It was easy to imagine that maybe more than a few members like Ethel stayed in part because it was just easier to stay than to go.

But the real key to conversion was the bond that formed between each young person and her spiritual mentor, or sponsor. These friendships were the glue that bonded one generation to the other. Bertha loved Lillian like a mother, and Eldress Gertrude reminisced frequently about her beloved mentor, Prudie, Eldress Prudence Stickney. Like them, Ethel and Alice were sisters, friends, and mother and daughter in spirit. There was only thirteen years' difference in their age, but that was sufficient to make all the difference to Ethel at ten, who looked all her life to Alice as an older sister, friend, and adopted mother.

Alice was born in 1884 in Lowell, Massachusetts, famed as a textile mill town. Her gentle and refined mother died when she was seven, an event that left such an impression on little Alice that she remembered how her mother was dressed in the coffin ever after. Her father, a prosperous engineer in the mills, married again. Alice's stepmother, who was French-Canadian, was not nice to her. Alice recalled the rough, scratchy underclothes she was made to wear. When stepmother and underwear alike proved a painful enough contrast to the way things had been, Alice went to live with the Canterbury Shakers. Her family had learned of the Shakers when they summered in a previous year in the nearby village of Loudon. When she was in her late teens, Alice was asked by her family to leave Canterbury Shaker Village and stay with relatives so that she could make a more informed decision about joining. Alice, who already knew that she wanted the Shaker life, was not happy about the move. In time she came back to her Shaker home, where she remained.

Like Lillian, Alice had known Elder Henry when he was an aged Elder, but she, like Ethel, had been placed in the Second Family, so she wouldn't have known any of the Church Family Shakers well at first. Alice and Ethel moved to the Church Family when the Second Family closed.

By the summer of 1972, Alice was a faded rose, drifting beyond the shores of the world the rest of us inhabited. She was a little taller than Ethel, slender, and graceful. In both beauty and temperament, she reminded me of my Grandma June, my father's stepmother and my namesake. Grandma June had been a Hollywood star when she was young—not a big famous one, but she made a living in pictures like *The Little Rascals* and *Rin Tin Tin* while managing to keep her modesty and sweetness. Like Grandma June, Sister Alice had the most beautiful, great dark eyes.

That summer of 1972, Alice hovered between the present and somewhere else. In conversation she repeated herself constantly, but she was gentle and serene. Everyone loved her and no one would have thought to make fun of her decline. Rather, the other Sisters always made a point of acknowledging her accomplishments as a violinist, artist, and beekeeper. She seemed, perhaps, to personify the kind of cultured, genteel Believer encouraged at Canterbury at the turn of the century under the tutelage of Elder Henry Blinn, Eldress Dorothy Durgin, Eldress Dorothea Cochran, and others. A younger, more vigorous Alice gazed from the pages of an old *Life* magazine feature story on the Canterbury Shakers. There was a beautiful black-and-white picture of her standing near her hives with a tray of bees in her hands, her luminous gaze steady and clear through the beekeeper's net that covered her face.

Teresa and Darryl recalled many happy childhood days with this lovely lady, who made wonderful things for the Gift Shop in her magical workroom upstairs. She had gifts for them, too— Sun-Maid raisins in the little boxes, which she carried to them in a basket, and the best raisin cookies in the world. I was sorry that I hadn't known her earlier.

Looking back, I wish I had known Ethel in her prime, as well. Our mutual friends have recounted marvelous recollections of a sprightly, witty, kind eccentric who passionately loved words, cats, and her Shaker Sisters. They recall a Sister devoted to the Shaker life with all her heart, especially to the circle of Sisters she'd known and loved—"earth angels," she'd called them, whose immense kindness to her had always been deeply appreciated. She knew that her Sisters had committed themselves to the tenets of Shakerism, she knew that her Sisters were good, and so she understood that the beliefs they held must also be good. Her friends recall her absolute devotion to Bertha, in whom she recognized a patient and loving protector. If Bertha occasionally fretted about Ethel's disorganized life and appearance, it represented the concern of a loving Sister, not the condemnation of a critic.

Among all those who loved her, Darryl Thompson has perhaps understood Ethel best as the spiritual balance wheel of the community—a zany, fresh, spontaneous spirit who regularly tested, and expanded, her Sisters' capacity for Christian charity. In Ethel, he saw the dynamic tension in Shaker life between "gift" and "order," that is, between the traditions of inspiration and structure. In the tradition of the "holy fool," now lost to Christianity, Ethel provided the yeast in the bread of Christian life. At her best, Ethel sparkled, and kept Canterbury Shaker Village from becoming stuffy, intolerant, or tyrannical. On nonessentials, Ethel went her own way; that could not be denied. But in the basics, everyone agrees, Ethel was the real thing.

I made many visits to the Dwelling that summer, especially after I began to sketch. Ethel was a proud and informative tour guide through this remarkable structure. It was one of the few large Shaker Dwellings that dated from the eighteenth century, although additions and alterations had greatly changed its original appearance. Other large communal Shaker Families did not hesitate to tear down their old Dwelling and put up a splendid new model in the 1830s and 1840s, when the old buildings were full to bursting and the Shakers had the means to build in a plain style on a grand scale. The Church Family at Canterbury was more conservative. They just added and added and added, until one exasperated deacon made a note that it would have been less trouble and expense in the end to rebuild from scratch.

Ethel said the oldest part of the Dwellinghouse was in the center, but that renovations throughout the nineteenth century had obscured any signs of the original house. The Dwelling Kitchen, where our visits took place, was just one part of the food preparation complex on the ground level. If you went farther in on the left, you entered the bowels of the great house, a massive food-storage cellar where the communal Family had once kept all kinds of provisions in rows of cupboards and in big, screened mouse-proof shelves that hung from the ceiling.

If you closed your eyes, you could picture dozens of pies and great joints of meat hanging from the wrought-iron hooks over-head. But the rooms were still now, dusty and dark, so different from Bertha's lively kitchen in the Trustees' Office that they made

me melancholy. A kitchen without food or women seemed un-
natural and gloomy. It was delightfully cool, anyway, naturally
refrigerated from its depth in the ground.

If you went to the right, you entered the long, narrow dining room. This was where the communal Family ate their hearty
meals—in silence, in the old days. As the bare walls, windows, and
floors of the dining room did nothing to absorb sound, the business of eating in silence had a practical as well as spiritual basis. In
the old Shaker tradition, the hour for meals was a time of peace,
given to thankfulness for sustenance in the company of one's beloved Brothers and Sisters. In Bertha's time, the family was enlightened and entertained during the dinner hour by one member
who read aloud appropriate selections from the newspaper and
other suitable periodicals. This sounded like one of those human-
izing reforms that the progressive leaders made to make Shaker life
more attractive a hundred years ago. At the far end of the room
were neat built-in drawers and cupboards, the handsomely stained
pine painted white long ago when the Colonial Revival crept
across New England.

In contrast to the other rooms nearby, the dining room was
bright and cheerful, lit by a long row of windows that looked out
across the lawn and through Alice's lilies to the Meetinghouse. All
the beautiful, original Shaker tables and chairs were long gone,
sold off years and years earlier to an antiques trade that at that time
barely appreciated their quality and style. Only one or two of the
large set of chairs made by Micajah Tucker in 1834 remained in
the village. Elder Henry's journal noted that Micajah, retired from
his duties as Elder and stonecutter, made the chairs for the ease and
convenience of the Family. The old benches were a pain in the
neck, Elder Henry reported, more or less. They were hard on your
rear, they made it hard for fat and thin people to sit at the same
table comfortably, and if one diner had to get up and leave in the
middle, everybody else had to get up and shuffle around, too.

Bertha recalled that all but a few of Micajah's chairs had been sold ages ago to a department store to be sold with painted "peasant" designs on them. Things had sure changed in the collecting world. Now, an original Canterbury dining chair would bring a good price just as it was. Around that time, the Church Family bought factory-made maple tables and chairs, pleased no doubt with their shiny, modern style. Near the door from the dining room to the kitchens, which faced the windows, a drop-leaf table built into the wall swung up or down for the use of the Sisters who served and cleared.

Beyond the dining room lay the great treasure of the Dwelling's Kitchen: the famous wood-fired revolving oven that baked dozens of pies or loaves of bread at a time. It was truly splendid, a brick structure the size of a shed fitted with massive cast-iron doors that opened to the revolving shelves. Ethel said that the oven had been designed by Eldress Emeline Hart, who had moved to Canterbury from Enfield, Connecticut. One of the Sisters in charge of baking would turn each shelf on its axis like a lazy Susan so the contents would bake evenly. Now the oven stood silent and cold, but it had been a focal point of Bertha's young days, when she was the community's pie baker at thirteen and chief bread baker a few years later. She must have baked thousands and thousands of pies in her life. Bertha's crust was so crisp and light that once when we asked for her recipe, Bertha grinned and fetched a stick of Betty Crocker's ready-made piecrust dough out of the refrigerator. What do you know! You still had to roll it out by hand, but Bertha was a convert. It wasn't just the convenience, it was the quality. This was a time-honored Shaker attitude. Faster wasn't better unless it *was* truly better, too.

There were other odds and ends of rooms on the ground floor, but the upper floors beckoned. In the heart of the Dwelling, a pair of side-by-side staircases ascended through the whole house to the attic. The banisters were beautiful and so were the newel

posts, which looked like oversized chess queens. Up we trotted.
Ethel's little old legs were as fast as mine. As we climbed, there was
more of a chance to see how the Dwelling was organized. The
whole building stretched from east to west, at right angles to the
road, with the west end closer to the road. The ground sloped away
from the road, so the floors on the west end were higher above the
ground.

The front door was on the first floor facing the side of the
Meetinghouse across the lawn. For years, a crocheted panel by Sister Cora Helena Sarle hung at the window on the front door. It
was a pretty design of two love birds beak to beak, which brought
to mind Jennie's cockatiel, Toto, goggling in a mirror. No one
ever actually used the front door, mind you; this was New England, and there seemed to be some unwritten law against that.
The Yankees I got to know even joked about it. The front doors
on some houses around the area were more or less permanently
sealed with a sheet of plastic (cheap winter insulation), and others
lacked steps. Why bother with them? Other home owners planted
flower beds right in front of the door.

Like Shaker Dwellings everywhere, the Canterbury Church
Family Dwelling was divided by an invisible but uncrossable line
through the center that separated the Brothers' and the Sisters'
quarters. The women lived on the east side, opposite the men on
the west. The Sisters were free to enter the Brothers' rooms
for daily housekeeping once the men had left for barn chores or
other work, but the Brothers probably didn't venture often into
the women's domain. By 1972, with all the male residents long
gone, Ethel and Alice had no reason to stay on their side of the
Dwelling. Still, Teresa told me that Alice always used the Sisters'
stairs and gently directed Teresa and her brother to use the proper
stairs when they came to visit. I noticed that Ethel and I were using
the west, or Brothers', stairs. Ethel seemed to get a kick out of it.

First stop, first floor. We went past the rooms where Alice

and Ethel spent most of their time. Since we met in the kitchen, I never spent much time up here, and I never did see their bedrooms or the communal bathroom. The sitting room was just off the central hall. From inside, the crocheted beak-to-beak birds were dark in silhouette. The sitting room walls were white plaster, and all the interior trim, including the ubiquitous peg rail, had also been painted white years earlier. Time had dimmed the brightness of all this white, mellowing it to shades of soft, dappled gray. There was an old upright piano in one corner. The rest of the furnishings were Victorian, but simple, "grandma furniture": a platform rocker, an overstuffed sofa, two or three dark-purple, flowered upholstered seats, a couple of pieces in light-colored wicker, a corner bracket for knickknacks.

Our main destination on the first floor was the Chapel. Ethel was always ready to take visitors to the Meeting Room, which was here called the Chapel. This was a large, airy room in the ell that the Shakers added to the north side of the Dwelling, the rear, in 1837. The Meeting Room was for the Family's daily devotions, while the Meetinghouse was for public worship. Even by this time, the average Shaker communal Family was aging, as fewer young adults entered the ranks. The walk to the Meetinghouse on wintry or damp days was getting to be too much for comfort, so the meeting room in the Dwelling was a welcome addition.

The Chapel, as the Shakers called it by this time, was as plain as you would expect, and was well lit by lots of windows on all three sides. Unlike the old 1792 Meetinghouse, the chapel needed columns to support the weight of the floors above. In the Meetinghouse, the gambrel-roof design eliminated the structural need for interior columns, leaving an uninterrupted floor for the Shakers' communal dance worship. The biggest difference, however, was the pipe organ installed in the front corner on the left, a splendid vintage Hook and Hastings that the community purchased secondhand, in 1929.

The organ was yet another victory for the redoubtable Eldress Dorothy Durgin. In the last quarter of the nineteenth century, she and other progressives recognized that the United Society's old-fashioned ways were not going to win many new young converts, so they let go of some of the old prohibitions against worldly "superfluities," which had included musical instruments. Eldress Dorothy and Elder Henry believed that permission to enjoy flower gardens, musical instruments, pets, and potted houseplants would do much more good than harm. Until then, musical instruments had been rejected as unnecessary for the making of sacred music. The human voice was sufficient, all the instrument that God gave or needed. Even harmony was avoided as an unnecessary, worldly embellishment. In the face of long tradition, Eldress Dorothy attempted to convince the Church Family to purchase a small pump organ in 1871, a truly ground-breaking event that ruffled some conservative feathers.

But Elder Henry, universally admired as one of the last of the great Shaker patriarchs, stepped in to help win the day for changes across the board. We shouldn't be fossils, he gently warned his Family; we need to look forward, not back. Besides, the male contribution to the chorus was growing slim, as the Sisters increasingly outnumbered the Brethren. The organ's rich low notes helped eke out the dwindling voices of the basses and tenors.

The Hook and Hastings was a grand addition to the family's musical resources. It had been Lillian's. One of the old photo postcards that the Shakers continued to sell in the shop showed her sitting at the bench, turning slightly toward the camera, with a quiet, Mona Lisa smile. We had to content ourselves with that image, because Lillian no longer played the organ, even before her fall. She really missed playing, but she accepted her limits. Before the fall she sat often at the upright piano in the sitting room of the Office and rippled through the old hymns from memory. Her eyesight was too poor to read music anymore. We loved it when

Bertha sang along, her reedy, old lady's voice high and strong. They looked so happy when Lillian played and Bertha sang.

Up we went, and up some more, to our second and final stop, the attic. Let's see, we'd visited maybe six rooms, which left about fifty. They were to remain a mystery to me that summer, although if Ethel had thought there was anything worth seeing, she would readily have showed it off. We reached the top, and the stairs curved on a landing lit by a skylight into the entrance to the attic. Everything was streaked and dulled—the old skylight had sprung a leak long ago, from the looks of things—but not even this could obscure the beauty of that space. And then we were in the attic, the uppermost floor of the ell. From the doorway where Ethel paused, a wall of built-in drawers and cupboards stretched and stretched to the windows far down the hall. We walked into the hall, dimly lit by a single bulb, and Ethel turned me loose. The wall of built-in drawers was punctuated with doors into big walk-in closets that had strips of peg rail hanging from the ceiling for clothing storage. Each drawer and door was numbered in order with a neatly painted square metal plate. The attic was wonderful. If you've seen illustrated books of Shaker design, you've seen pictures of this famous room, justly celebrated as an icon of the Shakers' passion for simplicity, order, and excellence. But even the best photos are hard-pressed to do justice to its details and the sense of the place.

There were yards and yards of clear, old-growth pine, free of knots, warmed by the original transparent yellow stain. A thread of delicate molding separated the drawers below from the cupboards above. The drawers' small, turned fruitwood pulls fit just so between the thumb and the first two fingers, and every drawer we opened glided easily after nearly a century and a half of use.

Everything was neat as a pin and like brand-new, not a

scratch or a dent in sight. The Shakers had certainly taken good care of their beautiful attic, but then that was typical. Believing that worldly goods were for the blessing and use of all, the Shakers seemed extra respectful about how they handled things. Down in the Office, Eldress Gertrude explained one day why the old wooden thresholds were still crisp. She was taught to step over, not on, the threshold. That one simple act, repeated by hundreds of Shakers over many years, helped preserve what one old Believer had made with his hands to work and his heart to God. Such an attitude in my throwaway world so impressed me that to this day I can't step on a threshold. As stewards of all God's creation, I read somewhere that summer, from thresholds to the rich green fields, that's how the Shakers thought of themselves, not as owners or masters.

As we poked around, it dawned on me that this attic was one of the few places in the village that had not been altered or brought up to date over the years—not refinished, not repainted, not remodeled, except for a simple strip of wire molding that led to the lightbulb; Brother Irving Greenwood, who wired the village for electricity in the 1920s, didn't miss a trick. That made sense. Why bother to modernize an attic? Its changeless quality was what made it so magical. Far above the rest of the Dwelling, the rest of the village, the rest of the world, so far from the highways and the rockets and the TVs that brought us news of Nixon and China and Vietnam and bombs and children running from them naked and screaming, so far that those things did not seem to exist, this room was just as it had been almost a hundred and fifty years ago, the perfect antique: something lovely, made long ago, unchanged except by the light hand of time.

I held my breath. We seemed to be in another world. I breathed again, deeply, of air that was dry and warm, hushed and still, faintly sweet with the unmistakable scent of old pine. Air that shimmered with the echoes of voices and laughter and life. Spring:

the Sisters tucking away winter clothes, throwing open the windows, sweeping and wiping their wonderful attic until it gleamed. Time seemed irrelevant here. If I turned quickly, would Eldress Dorothea gaze at me over the dark head of a little girl with Bertha's smile?

Even Ethel was quiet. Was she out of breath from all those stairs? Or was she, too, dreaming of old times, old faces? Was she missing Sister Alice? Was she lost, like me, in the great mystery of time, the majestic wheel that turned and turned, cycled us in and out of each other's lives, perhaps just this once, but maybe, just maybe, forever and ever, so that no love and no loved one was ever really lost? Was she . . . was she . . . what *was* she doing over there in the corner?

Ethel stood up and poked at a small dark shape with her toe. "Look, dear," she cried gaily, her watery eyes sparkling. "A dead mouse. Poor little creature, nothing to eat up here. If my darling kit-ties had found her, she wouldn't have had to starve to death. Hee, hee, hee!"

# CHAPTER 6

# *July*

The month began on a bright note that cheered us all. Lillian and Sister Alice were well enough to leave the hospital and go to the nursing home in Concord.

It was a step in the right direction, and at times Lillian began to seem like her old self again. When someone asked her, teasing, what good she was doing in a nursing home, she said, deadpan, "Keeping the bed warm." Things looked good until we made a visit and found poor Lillian crying and calling weakly for help. A scatterbrained nurse had put her on the bedpan and then gone off and forgotten her. When we walked in, Lillian had been perched in pain for long minutes, helpless, mortified, and unable to move. It was the first time I ever saw Bertha really angry. She didn't make a scene or tear into the staff, but that was that. Lillian was coming home *now*. Other things upset Bertha, too. Lillian had lived her life a virgin Shaker, the soul of modesty, and it humiliated her when the nurses yanked up her hospital johnny as if she were a child.

It took a few days, but Lillian came home, one month to the day since her fall. Poor Bertha—we knew she'd wear herself out taking care of Lillian, and she was going to put off the cataract operation she needed so she could be up and around to care for Lillian. We'd all help, and there would be round-the-clock nurses as soon as it could be arranged. Everyone felt better with Lillian where she belonged, at home.

It wasn't easy. Lillian's condition was still touch and go, and our spirits rose and sank constantly with her changes. It was her old problem with digestion. At night, especially, her stomach and bowels gave her torment. We took turns sitting up with her when we couldn't get a night nurse. When my turn came, I was scared silly because I didn't know what to do and was in distress because I couldn't ease her pain. Most of the time she dozed or slept in the modern hospital bed that Bertha had installed in the former sewing room, off the back kitchen.

When I heard her moaning, I'd go in and take her hand and try to murmur words of comfort. My healing touch didn't impress either of us, but she made it through the night. Whenever she slept, I went back to the kitchen table and worked on a drawing of a basket to while away the hours. It was strange but not unpleasant there in the lost hours of the night. I didn't mind the solitude, and I watched the pencil in wonder as the basket took form.

Just when Lillian improved some, Eldress Gertrude's health took a nosedive, and she had to go into the hospital way down in Manchester for dangerously low blood pressure. Poor Eldress Gertrude; it was a longer drive to Manchester than to Concord, so she didn't get much company. Margaret drove Miriam and me to visit and it looked as depressing as the old brick mental institution in Concord. Everyone was happy to learn that nothing much was wrong with Eldress Gertrude, but it was a couple of weeks before she came home. By this time Bertha was exhausted physically and emotionally, although she kept her sense of humor. "I guess I'm ready for the glue factory," she'd say, like the old gray mare who wasn't what she used to be.

The heat wave that rolled in didn't make any of us feel more comfortable. It was hard to believe that a New England state could be so hot and sticky. The air lay in flat, heavy slabs on the panting lawns, and even the mosquitoes seemed slower than usual. The cats moped; Bud's little dog Tag flopped full-length on the floor and dreamed whatever beagles dream, twitching and whining after phantom prey. My hair went berserk in the hot, damp days. Sometimes I got crabby. We all did.

I found relief in my new passion, sketching. Every chance I got, I'd head to the Meetinghouse at the top of the hill, to try my hand at one new object after another, exploring the texture of wood, tin, iron, bristles. With its old dark green shades always drawn, the Meetinghouse was always pleasantly dim and cool, even when no breath stirred the maples in the lane. I spent hours there, learning what a pencil could do.

For a change of pace, I asked Ethel if I could make some sketches in the Dwelling, and she happily obliged. I made a beeline for the attic, even in the heat. The corner by the window drew me like the sun a morning glory. I got bolder as I went. I drew the narrow cupboards in the corner with the old mop and pincushion hanging from the peg rail, just as they were. I tried my hand at drawing the roof slates of the North Shop, and just about went cross-eyed, but I loved what I saw: the straight lines dipped and folded by the wavy old panes into ripples, like a geologist's diagram of some hiccup in the earth.

Life went on in the Trustees' Office, and what had been strange and disconcerting in my first few days was now comforting routine. Bertha and the others kept breakfast simple, just toast or dry cereal and coffee. But she would have risen early to make me eggs and bacon every day without a word if I hadn't assured her that simplicity suited me, too. She wanted me to have plenty of strength for the morning's round of tours. It was hard work to convince her that I could manage to walk and talk for an hour and a half without fainting, fueled merely by a bowl of cereal and some orange juice.

After breakfast, Bertha started right in with preparations for the day's dinner. The menu was already planned for the week on lists, written in her graceful Spencerian script on scraps of paper. Bertha's handwriting got bigger and bigger as time passed and she used increasingly thick black felt-tip markers so she could see what she had written. Bertha was so organized that she would already have taken care of some of the preparation for the day's meal the night before, if required—say, if she was making Shaker fish and eggs, she would have put the coarse, white chunk of dried codfish to soak after last evening's supper. I tried many new foods for the first time at Bertha's dining table, and the creamy, delicious blend of salty fish and chopped hard-boiled egg was just one new dish I grew to love.

Soon after breakfast, Jennie would lumber over from the Infirmary and stump down the steps to help Bertha in the down-stairs kitchen. Since the Shakers couldn't abide waste, and since Jennie happily ate up anything put in front of her, breakfast left-overs (if we had oatmeal, for example) were soon gone. Bertha found Jennie a mixed blessing as kitchen help. Jennie had learned an impressive amount during her time with the Shakers. She did a wonderful job with almost everything Bertha relied on her to do. She read recipes accurately, if slowly, and wrote well enough to be of use in compiling and copying recipes and shopping lists. Bertha was always generous with encouragement and praise for what Jen-nie did well.

In private, sometimes Bertha would sigh. Jennie had a heavy hand with herbs and spices, and Bertha preferred subtlety. Jennie's notion of "nicely brown on top" and Bertha's were not the same, unfortunately. When Bertha expected a delicate tan on her soufflé or crust, sometimes Jennie surprised her with a heavy sunburn.

Probably because of her gimpy legs, Jennie was not as diligent with the broom and mop as Bertha would have liked. Precision in all things, a quality traditionally valued by the Shakers, was one of Bertha's hallmarks, from the way she crimped the crust of a pie to her careful diction. I teased her because she was the only person I had ever met who called the popular doughnut chain "Dunk*ing* Donuts," enunciating each syllable with her habitual care.

Theoretically, tours started at nine and went out every hour on the hour. In real life, however, tours started whenever visitors came to the door, especially when things weren't busy. It didn't make sense to keep three or four people waiting for forty-five minutes if they arrived at a quarter past the hour, so we guides would often set out at our company's convenience. The problem usually started about half way up the Meetinghouse lane. Just when you had finished explaining the basics of Shaker life and history, sure enough, here came stragglers, puffing hastily up the slope from the Office. So you'd take a deep breath, apologize to the ones who'd already heard about Mother Ann and the rest, and race through the basics again.

If all went well, you could make it to the Meetinghouse with only one repetition. Once inside, you could generally consider yourself safe from other latecomers, but we soon learned that such congratulations were premature when Miriam was on deck in the Office. Miriam was the worst offender in this regard. Although Bertha reminded her that people who came as late as half past should wait until the next tour, Miriam would gaily send them on their way to join us when we were already halfway through the village. Then we would feel obliged to offer yet another repeat of the first part to the latecomers. Around this time the members of the first group would begin to look a bit glazed. After introducing the Shakers for the third time, you wondered if your original party would chime in, like some Greek chorus. I think the record for repeats that summer was four times, and we guides grumbled among ourselves, but it was good-natured grumbling. As employers went, ours were certainly nicer than most. And they fed and loved us better, too.

We had all kinds of interesting visitors that month—a couple who lived in the Meetinghouse down in the Shaker village in Harvard, Massachusetts, where all the buildings had long since become private residences; a family from a kibbutz in Israel, who really understood the communal aspect of Shaker life; and the owners and operators of Shaker Workshops, Inc., who made reproduction Shaker furniture for sale, ready-made or in kit form. We also had groups from the state school, where Jennie spent her youth. I had no idea what to say to this silent group of men with hollow eyes— the usual spiel was not going to work—but somehow we made the rounds. I shivered when they left, glad that Jennie had found a nicer home.

*Meetinghouse*

An elderly woman who called herself the "peace pilgrim" paid a call and was invited to stay overnight. The Shakers didn't know her by any other name. This woman had decided to spend the rest of her days walking the country to promote peace in the world. So far, she'd racked up some twenty-five thousand miles. She seemed a bit preachy to me, but the Shakers knew her from other trips and always hailed her warmly. She enjoyed their hospitality but was death on the Cool Whip that Bertha served on dessert; it was full of bad chemicals, she said, shaking her head. Maybe she had a point—she was going full steam, and she was no spring chicken.

The tours picked up as summer got into full swing, and every day we were handling bigger and bigger groups. The annual Canterbury Fair always brought extra-large crowds, so we doubled up on guides and sent tours out on the half hour. The Shakers' old friends Barry and Claire Roche came up from Salem, Massachusetts, as they always did to help out. Barry waded into the confusion and set us all in order, visitors and staff alike. He made a top-notch drill sergeant and the Shakers were very grateful; we couldn't have managed nearly as well without him.

The museum was such a small operation in those days, with only about five thousand visitors annually, that we closed the door every day for the noon meal. Surprised visitors were told politely that we would reopen at one and we would be happy to see them again then. They were also informed that if they wanted a sandwich or a light lunch, they would do best to head back to Concord. The nearest eatery, the Inland Lobster Pool, was about ten miles away. There was nothing else they could do but climb back in their cars. There was nothing closer for their convenience at that time.

We guides got into the habit of good-naturedly trying to avoid either the eleven or the one o'clock tour. If we could foist these slots off on each other, fine. The trouble with the predinner tour was that you had to rush if you wanted to get through the whole shebang and make it to dinner on time. Visitors were advised that tours ran an hour to an hour and a half, but we knew you really had to march if you wanted to finish in sixty minutes. Then, if you did manage to make it to the Office by noon, you had the unpopular job of letting your group know that yes, indeed, they were more than welcome to buy souvenirs and use the rest room, but not for an hour, please. That got a bit sticky at times.

Those of us who sat down at the table on time were good about leaving some of everything for latecomers, inspired of course by the Shakers' customary selflessness, so at least you knew you'd enjoy the full meal even if you did run late. Poor Darryl! We'd always laugh (and so would Darryl) when he went out at eleven— we all knew he'd never make it back on time. Darryl knew so much, and gave his tours with such gusto, that his groups were known at times to wander in two hours later, a little dazed maybe, but content. They got their money's worth and more.

The one o'clock tour, on the other hand, was to be avoided because it was really tough to walk and talk after one of Bertha's big country dinners. How we suffered. I found that it helped to let visitors know under what burden I labored as I staggered back out the door at one. All I had to do was to reel off the list of home-cooked Shaker dishes I had just nobly consumed and the visitors started to moan with envy. By the time I got to the pie, we were all moaning. At least I had company.

It was funny. Closing for noon dinner may have disrupted some people's visits, but on the whole, at that time they forgave us. Most visitors adjusted themselves surprisingly well to this news, especially those who had already met the charming Eldress Gertrude in the hall. They could see for themselves that this was more of a home than a big business, and that seemed to hit the right note with many of the vacationers. After all, Grandma was not Howard Johnson; you had to make allowances for these things.

From our point of view, the daily noon hour was the best part of the day. The delicious meal was just part of it. Best of all, we got to spend time visiting with each other for a whole hour of sitdown food and companionship. The table was full and it felt so nice: Bertha, Eldress Gertrude, Bud, sometimes, Darryl, Jan, Margaret, Marjorie, and I, each in his or her place, each at home. Jennie ate in the kitchen just off the dining room so she could keep an eye on things out there.

But, oh, how we missed Lillian . . .


I spent most of July with my head in books and in Elder Henry's wonderful journals. There was so much to learn, and as I grew to know and love the Sisters more, I was curious about the historical forces that had shaped them. I wanted to be better able to answer visitors' questions, but my interest was far from academic. I wanted to know what made Bertha, Lillian, and the rest tick so that I could try for it, too.

There was a brief moment that summer when the notion of staying on played in my head. I remember it well. It was the end of a fine afternoon and my tours had gone extra smoothly. I was meeting interesting people and it felt great to introduce the Shakers to them. Supper would be on the table in an hour, with apple pie for dessert. I was so happy here, I felt so much at home. It was an oasis in the wilderness of young adulthood. Here, I didn't have to trouble myself with the difficulties of growing up and learning how to live as a woman instead of a child. Every day blessed me with a bellyful of good food, work that I liked, people I loved who loved me back, and a safe, comfortable bed. As the days went by, several of the Sisters fondly told me they wished I didn't have to leave. I considered Lillian. So long ago she had come for the summer, like me, with no thought of remaining, and look how her life had turned out.

For seconds the thought floated and shimmered in the air, beautiful and delicate as a soap bubble from a child's pipe. I stared at it, mesmerized by the iridescence of possibility, and then it dissolved and vanished even as I watched. What a sweet, fleeting thought, a dream that I knew was impossible even as I was having it. It was not going to happen in this lifetime. It wasn't just the Shakers' decision to close the doors to new members, which was proving to be more important than anyone would have thought a decade earlier. Nor was it the realization on my part that it would take hard work to make a Shaker out of me.

No, it was as if I had sent forth a silent question and the answer had come back: "No, my child, no." Ordinarily "no" was something I didn't like to hear in reply to something I wanted, but this felt different. In less than the time it takes to write about it, a door swung open and then shut, leaving me thoughtful but not sad.

I thought about how it might have been, a century or so earlier, and saw that my family might well have joined the Shakers in another time and place. A widow with two small girls—we would have found a good home in a place like this. My mom wasn't interested in remarrying and she said that she didn't mind the single life. Actually, what she said was "No one ever died from celibacy." (What else would you tell a pair of ripening teenage daughters?) I could see us there—Sister Dorothy Sprigg, capped and gowned, in some Church Family, rising and retiring to rest with the rest of the Sisterhood. And under another roof, little Ann and June tucked safely into the Girls' Order, where someone else's hands would smooth their damp brows on feverish nights, someone else's tongue would instruct them in the mysteries of growing up, someone else's eyes would rest on them in wonder as they grew.

A mosquito sang madly near my ear and the last of the melody of might-have-been faded and was gone. I shook my head and went inside. This was here and now. There must be another plan for me. Since no angels or spirits seemed to be appearing to me to point the way, I guessed I'd have to follow the nudges of my heart.

Those nudges led me, always, back to Elder Henry's journals and Bertha's photograph albums, where Shaker days past came alive. Their pages held two hundred years of Shaker and American history and the information and insights were mine for the prospecting.

Elder Henry made a grand guide through the first century of Shaker life; in fact, it was hard to imagine a better one. Perceptive, articulate, sensitive, kind, and good-humored, Henry was a born observer, which made him particularly well suited for his various roles as teacher, writer, historian, and spiritual leader. He was thrice blessed, this right man in the right place at the right time.

From the first day of his voluntary entry into the community in 1838 at age fourteen, Henry was taken directly into the Church Family, where he came of age under the wing of some of the best old-time Brothers. With the wisdom born of time and experience, they knew they had a live one, a real, fine Believer in the making. The Elders had the sense to place him as the boys' schoolteacher in his youth. It was an inspired choice. Family hardship had forced Henry to leave school back home in Providence so he could work, and he threw himself into teaching with such pleasure that the Brothers must have smiled. He was teaching the boys, all right, but he was also educating himself.

It was one of life's magnificent coincidences that Henry

entered the United Society at the very onset of the two-decade era known to the Shakers as Mother Ann's Work, when the Believers' tradition of mysticism flowered anew. He had been in the community just four years when Philemon Stewart, one of the most prominent inspired instruments in New Lebanon, "received" the text of *A Holy, Sacred and Divine Roll*, a spirit communication that weighed in at four hundred pages. This was big in more ways than one. The next year, in 1843, at nineteen (my age) Henry was chosen by the Ministry to teach himself printing so he could transform Philemon's manuscript into a book that Shakers and the world leaders to whom it was sent everywhere could read.

Philemon Stewart himself came to Canterbury, and I could imagine the author and the printer poring over the manuscript and galleys side by side. Like others in the Church Family, Henry caught the inspiration fever and served as a channel for spirits, although his contributions to meetings (recorded neatly by a scribe in the Family's official accounts) seemed modest and low-key.

In contrast, alas, Philemon's spiritual fire proved too much for him in the long run, and somewhere along the line he seemed to have popped a cork. In time he fell from favor with the Central Ministry, made himself troublesome, and eventually was banished to a remote Family at Sabbathday Lake Shaker Village in Maine, where they thought that he couldn't do too much damage. Unfortunately, they were wrong. While the troubled author was going around the bend, however, the printer stayed steady.

From the age of twenty-eight, when he was chosen to serve as associate Elder of the Church Family, Henry spent the rest of his Shaker days in service as an Elder of one kind or another. He was almost immediately transferred to associate Elder in the Ministry, an even higher position of authority. At thirty-five he returned to Canterbury to serve as the senior Elder of the Church Family. Eventually, as all who knew him must have seen coming, Henry at fifty-six rose to serve as the senior Elder in the New Hampshire

Ministry, the highest position of authority below the level of the Central Ministry in New Lebanon, New York. He remained in this role for the next twenty-five years, the rest of his life. All in all, Henry spent more than fifty years as a leader of the Canterbury and New Hampshire Believers.

Elder Henry's leadership roles separated him from close daily contact with the boys and the communal Family, whom he missed, but it gave him the opportunity to travel widely, a privilege that this man of boundless curiosity enjoyed. As part of the New Hampshire Ministry, he made regular visits to other Shaker villages. In 1873, to afford him relief from a bout of depression, Henry was given permission to travel to most of the eastern and all of the western Shaker communities in America, including Pleasant Hill and South Union in Kentucky, a thousand miles away. His journal of the trip and his observations of America en route, written for circulation among friends in the United Society, provided an excellent account of Shaker and American life in the years following the Civil War.

As senior Elder of the New Hampshire Ministry, having devoted his life and labors to many improvements in the United Society, Henry had more time to devote to his lifelong antiquarian interest in the history of his Shaker community. For once, this most forward looking of Believers paused and turned his gaze backward, over the long years of his Shaker life and the life of his spiritual forebears. An old photograph that I especially liked showed him at his desk in a toss of books and papers, leaning his white head on one hand.

In his study, Henry pored anew over the records kept by his predecessors, drawing on them to write his two-volume history of the Canterbury Shakers to commemorate the village's centennial in 1892. He also formed a small museum of artifacts relating to the community's early years and assisted outside archivists in assembling library collections of Shaker works at the turn of the twentieth century so that the record of his beloved way of life would not be lost.

His preservation plan had worked, and I for one was very grateful for the long hours that Henry had spent dipping his pen into ink. Curled up in the sofa of the sitting room, with one volume or the other perched on my knees, I turned the pages, lost in a world that was here but not now.

Henry of course could not give an eyewitness account of the United Society of Believers' first fifty or sixty years in America—he was born a week or two before the fiftieth anniversary of Mother Ann's arrival in New York—so he copied passages from earlier Elders' records. I learned about Job Bishop, called Father Job, and Mother Hannah Goodrich, who had made up the first Ministry in New Hampshire. They had been sent from New Lebanon like other founding leaders, two by two, to guide the newly gathered Family into proper Shaker life.

Father Job was a stickler for doing things the New Lebanon way, which was a useful method of ensuring that the far-flung societies would stay close to the tried and true original model, the "pattern on the Mount." Father Job and Mother Hannah and their associates traveled back and forth to New Lebanon as often as they could (given the difficulties of the journey over eighteenth-century backwoods roads) to find spiritual refreshment and keep abreast of the approved manner of working, building, and worshiping, and other details of daily life.

I felt a rush of amused sympathy for Job, who in 1794 went so far as to check with the Central Ministry about the use of suspenders among the Brethren. Were they all right or contrary to order? Father Job was a good Shaker. He checked with the Central Ministry, who checked with God, who evidently approved. Easy in his mind, Job came back sporting a pair himself. When leading a flock into heaven on earth, one couldn't be too careful. Father Job and Mother Hannah also brought back examples of articles made in New Lebanon—boxes, shoes, sieves, pails—to show his people how to work, how to make things simple, without ornament, and how to make them substantial and well.

Elder Henry chronicled the highlights of each year and decade of the Canterbury society, as well as the United Society as a whole. He must have been mindful of his own life, I thought, as he jotted down notes about the years in their order, and I wondered how much he knew of events that took place far beyond Canterbury's fields and woods. The year 1824: The venerable General Lafayette makes his grand tour of America, in remembrance and farewell; John Quincy Adams wins an embarrassing victory as president when none of the candidates gets a majority; laborers work themselves to death completing "Clinton's Ditch," the Erie Canal, America's newest and fastest superhighway. Lord Byron perishes romantically in Greece, Beethoven completes the Ninth Symphony in Vienna, British workers win the right to unionize. A male infant christened Henry Clay Blinn is born in Providence on July 16.

And 1848: The very first rumors of gold tumble east from far California. Marx and Engels publish the *Communist Manifesto* while revolutions explode throughout Europe. Franklin Pierce defends the Shakers in the New Hampshire legislature from petitioners who want converts to relinquish their rights to property. The four members of the New Hampshire Ministry make their first journey by railroad. Young Henry Blinn is given paper, paint, and time to record his Shaker village in loving detail: here, the chain of seven man-made ponds and their mills; there, Pleasant Grove, the holy outdoor worship ground, and its centerpiece, the Lord's Stone, which Henry himself has been chosen to letter; and here, in the heart of the Church Family, a familiar old apple tree he labels "Best of Red Cheeks."

It was interesting to learn what building was built when, and how many pounds of cheese were made in a year, but the best parts were the thumbnail sketches that Henry provided of many of the Canterbury Believers. For each decade, Henry recorded a list of all the persons who had died in Canterbury Shaker Village. Thanks to Henry's delightful reminiscences, what could have been a gloomy dirge became instead a song of life. He may not have shared these Believers' youthful experience, but he had known many of them personally in their old age, so his cameo portraits glowed with authentic affection and admiration.

Some of the most interesting Believers had been there from the start, even before the Canterbury society was formally organized in 1792. For around ten years before that, the faithful had gathered to live as Shakers with the converts Benjamin and Mary Whitcher in their farmhouse at the top of the hill in Canterbury. There was Zilpha, the Whitchers' daughter, who accompanied her pioneering parents to the hilltop as a one-year-old baby in the arms of her uncle.

There was Joseph Sanborn, born in 1780, so gifted in music as a very young child that his parents would pick him up and put him on a table to sing for the dancers in the march. And there was Josiah Edgerly, born in 1750, who learned a lesson from Father Job. One Saturday afternoon Josiah bought grain from a farmer some four miles from the village, found himself short a few cents, and promised to come back first thing on Monday morning with the balance. The farmer had no complaint, but when Josiah got home and reported to Father Job, he was sent right back to keep the United Society free of debt over the Sabbath.

Some of the old Believers had personally known even more revered founding members. David Sanborn, born in 1767, made his choice to sign the Covenant at seventeen upon getting to know and love Elder Henry Clough, the missionary from New Lebanon who visited his father's house in 1784. As an old man, Brother David took a deep interest in a religious periodical called *The Day Star*. Enoch Jacobs, an Adventist who originally published the journal as *The Midnight Cry*, changed the title to *The Day Star* as he became convinced of the truth of Shakerism (and joined the Shakers at Union Village, in Ohio). A number of disillusioned Adventists joined the Shakers after the world failed to end as promised in 1843 (and again, in.1844). Those who had disposed of their worldly goods in anticipation found themselves embarrassed financially, not to mention spiritually, and found the Shakers a welcome home. David would urge young Mary Ann Gillespie to get a move on with her chores so that she could read *The Day Star* to him first thing in the morning.

A handful of Believers, the most blessed of all, had met Mother Ann herself. Sarah Wright, Jr., born in 1766, was barely a teenager when she had the honor of being the first New Hampshire Believer to give Mother Ann a gift, a "very plain neck kerchief."

Jonathan Lougee, born in 1761, could claim the dubious distinction of having been reproved by Mother Ann, who scolded him for not coming to visit Believers more often. She told him to give up his wealth and covetousness and take up the cross and serve God. Like Jesus, Ann saw that worldly possessions—or, more precisely, the scrambling and yearning for them—were an impediment to true spiritual growth. Unlike the young man in the Bible whose reluctance caused Jesus to mutter about rich men, Heaven, the eye of a needle, and camels, Jonathan saw the light and gave up all to embrace the faith.

I couldn't get enough of Elder Henry's words. There was a story on every page. Calvin Goodell, born in 1774, was legendary for his thrift and his abstemious diet. From 1837 to his death he was a strict vegetarian. He couldn't abide waste of any of God's gifts, including time, so he could be seen making calculations for his work while he walked from the Dwelling to his shop. In the spring and fall he built fires out of mere chips to save firewood. Young Henry made his first visit to the Family's maple-sugar camp with good Brother Calvin, who preferred to walk the two miles in deep snow rather than ride a horse. Henry recalled that it took an "active boy" to keep up with Calvin.

Molly Cotton, born in 1768, was the Family memory bank, "her brain a storehouse of knowledge" of every kind. Sarah Ward, born in 1770, was a good mother "and so neat that she looked as though she had been taken from the bureau drawer." Phebe Bailey, a "kind teacher" who was fond of little ones, fled early in life to the Shakers from a family of twenty-one children ruled by her father, the Major, a "wicked man and cruel parent." Francis Winkley, who went on to become one of the village's great Deacons, couldn't wait to join the Shakers when the Canterbury society was formally gathered, and signed on immediately in February 1792. It wasn't that easy for his wife, Sarah, who came along with him and their two young sons. She spent the whole spring and summer making up her mind if she would follow him into the faith.

She did.

Henry wrote with greatest affection of old Peter Ayers, born in 1760, who had a "full acquaintance with Mother Ann and all the Elders." Peter, who loved boxing, dancing, and all-night parties, astonished his friends by joining the Shakers and doing missionary work himself. In 1792 he came with Father Job to the new Canterbury community, where he established the hatter's trade. Henry enjoyed the time he spent with the aged Peter, a great reader full of interesting information, until the venerable Brother's death at age ninety-seven.

I did some quick arithmetic. Peter was sixty-four years older than Henry, which was about the same age difference as that between the Sisters and me in 1972. I could see that Henry felt about him and other old-time Believers the way I was feeling about Lillian and Bertha and the rest, and all of a sudden history made sense to me. It wasn't about dates and facts—it was about people. And because of that, it was also about love.

The middle years of the nineteenth century witnessed the prime of the United Society and of Henry himself. It also witnessed the beginning of the end of the old, rural way of life in America. As more and more Americans headed west for gold or homesteads, or found employment in the factories and offices of the cities, quiet Shaker villages no longer attracted as many men and women of talent. While the United Society's overall membership peaked around the 1840s, the depth of conviction may have been weaker as the villages became more like havens for the lost than vineyards for the labors of the spiritually fit. Whether they knew it or not, the Shakers had already begun the long, slow slide to the present by the 1850s.

It seemed ironic that the United Society was quietly crumbling from within as the United States shattered around them. The Civil War that ripped into the country was devastating to the peaceable Shakers, too, as it tore into the fabric of their economic life. The Kentucky Shakers suffered particular hardship. Committed to peace while supporting abolition, they fed and tended to the needs of troops from both sides as the lines of battle shifted. The armies' relentless demands for food, horses, and other goods nearly ruined some of the families.

Worst of all, the Shaker Brothers were called to fight, a moral impossibility for these dedicated pacifists. It was easy to laugh along with Elder Henry in his old age as he recollected his experience with the draft in 1863, but it was not funny to him at the time. Henry endured the physical exam in Concord and submitted to the regulation pryings and proddings. Henry Clay Blinn: thirty-nine, five foot ten, light chestnut hair and hazel eyes, healthy. But when the order came to disrobe, that was simply too much for the modest Shaker Brother. It seemed that Henry had a winning way with people, even tough army doctors, because his appeal prevailed and he was not forced to part with his clothes.

Henry was appalled when he passed the physical and became a conscript. Principles or not, he was just another able body sentenced to the "slaughterpen of the nation." Henry left the ordeal clinging to the paper that allowed him furlough for a month.

It was fortunate that leaders of the United Society had made friends in high places, notably Washington. Canterbury's own Brother David Parker, the community's widely known and well-respected Trustee, had even visited the White House to see the United Society's old friend, President Franklin Pierce, before Pierce's enforced retirement from politics in 1857. The president had close, amicable connections with the New Hampshire Shakers from the days when they had hired him to defend them in the New Hampshire Legislature against the charges of angry apostates and disgruntled families of converts. Pierce may have fallen from grace as president in a severely troubled time, but his friendships in Washington persisted into Lincoln's term.

The social and financial cost of pacifism was nothing new to the United Society, which for decades had routinely paid fines in lieu of participating in local militia musters. In the Civil War, the United Society's appeal for exemption from military service on religious grounds was finally successful. It was nice to think that the high moral ground carried some weight with the bureaucracy, but I didn't think the Shakers' other principal argument hurt any, either: representatives of the United Society simply pointed out to the secretary of war that many of their early Brethren, who were collectively entitled to decades of pension from their service in the Revolution, had declined the money in order to more fully separate from the World. If the Shakers were to pursue those legitimate claims now . . . in the end, President Lincoln agreed to grant the Shakers an indefinite exemption, which was very good news for Henry and the rest.

As he grew older, it must have alarmed Elder Henry to see his beloved way of life declining. Encouraged by a reform movement spearheaded at Mount Lebanon, Henry and other like-minded progressives threw themselves into a broad new range of outreach that included missionary work, public Shaker meetings in big cities like Boston and Worcester, participation in local church services with Baptists, Methodists, and Unitarians, and publication of *The Shaker*, a monthly periodical distributed free to libraries and colleges to help spread the word.

In an all-out effort to catch up with the times and show the World that Shakers were an existing concern, not a relic of times past, the Canterbury Shakers of the 1860s and 1870s marched into the modern world, bravely led by Elder Henry and Eldress Dorothy Durgin. In many a break with tradition, Believers at Canterbury attended camp meetings and seances; bought a parlor organ and a piano; set out decorative shade trees, ornamental shrubs, and flower gardens; modernized their dress; got rid of the old outdoor worship ground at Pleasant Grove and removed the marble "Lord's Stone"; hired a lady gymnastics teacher for two weeks; put up a Christmas tree for the little boys; bought comfortable settees with backs for the Meetinghouse; invited a lecturer to speak about her visit to Yosemite; sent a washing machine to the Philadelphia Centennial Exhibition; and repainted the woodwork in the Meetinghouse for the first time since 1815 (a lighter, presumably more modern blue). A Chinese man came to give a lecture and presented them with his chopsticks after dinner. Another lecturer spoke on "Hindoo gods . . . very interesting." The celebrity midget Tom Thumb paid a call and obliged the Family by climbing onto a table to show off his thirty-three-pound self.

Henry and the others worked as hard as they could, but the United Society kept shrinking. I wondered whether that circumstance had something to do with his depression and his restorative trip to Kentucky in 1873, the year he turned forty-nine. Was that Henry's midlife crisis? Toward the end of his life, it must have been clear to Elder Henry that the United Society was failing in strength and in numbers. In the end, it was all for nought.

Or was it?

I thought about that, there on the sofa in the bright pink sitting room, and listened to the life around me, the clink of Bertha's pots and pans down in the kitchen, Eldress Gertrude chirping to her birds out back.

No, I thought, Elder Henry had made a difference. With a few others of his generation, Elder Henry formed the bridge that led Shakerism into the modern world. His reform efforts made Shaker life newly attractive to converts, especially young people, in the early twentieth century. His efforts to nurture and teach the young never ceased, and he was regarded as a loving, encouraging, and gentle Shaker father by both boys and girls in the late nineteenth century. His love and enthusiasm made it possible for a whole generation of young people raised at Canterbury to choose Shaker life when their contemporaries in other, more rigidly old-fashioned Shaker communities were leaving. His friendships with non-Shakers around New England and beyond narrowed the old gap between the Shaker world and the World. As much as anyone else, Elder Henry Blinn made Shaker life sympathetic and accessible to Americans in the twentieth century.

Elder Henry settled down to write his historical journals amid other tasks during the 1880s and 1890s, when he was in his sixties. He was nearing seventy in 1892, the Canterbury Society's centennial year. The years flew by under his pen—in Volume 1 he covered twenty-seven years, from 1848, when he was twenty-four, to 1875—and I wondered whether his own life seemed to him to have passed as quickly. As I read his journals, it seemed to me that Elder Henry made peace in the end with things as they were, and I felt a wave of respect. He tried his best and took what came. It was all-important to fight, I saw, but not essential to win. I was not sure he'd lost, anyway. Lillian was here because of him. So in a sense was Bertha. For that matter, if you took the long view, even I was here because of him.

Loved by the old when he was young and loved by the young when he was old, Henry was a living link in the great chain of life. I wanted to be like him, too. I picked up the journal and continued to read.


My spiritual quest continued, too. I spent as much time as possible with Lillian without tiring her. It was only a few minutes a day, but it meant a great deal. Bud and Nancy shared new insights on prayer. It didn't have to be a big formal affair, they said. Why not just talk to God? That sounded interesting. I could give that a shot. Bertha, Lillian, and Eldress Gertrude were all big on prayer, which sounded as natural as breathing, the way they talked about it. Bertha and Bud kidded that Lillian had the "hot line" to God, her connection was so strong.

Lillian's will to live was powerful; we just wished that she felt better more of the time. Lillian's good days cheered everyone up. One evening found Bud and Nancy singing to entertain her, and it looked great to see her toe tapping strongly to a rousing chorus of "There Is a Tavern in the Town." One morning Bertha put a jaunty bow in Lillian's hair and when we admired it, she kidded that it enhanced the beauty that she *didn't* have. When we protested, she smiled and shook her head, serious now, saying that she'd had a certain kind of beauty when she was twenty or twenty-two. As the years pass, beauty grows as character develops, she said, until at last only true beauty exists, that of the spirit.

On July 22, we all joined to celebrate Lillian's "Shaker birthday," the eightieth year of her life with the Shakers. We dabbed our eyes when Bud wheeled her to the piano so she could play from memory—"Edelweiss" and "Love's Old Sweet Song"—while Bud and Bertha sang.

The heat wave broke and a touch of autumn chilled our evenings. There were nights when I took out the screens, closed the windows, and pulled Grandma's flowery quilt up under my chin. Summer was sweet in New Hampshire, I was learning, sweet and fleeting as a child's handful of clover.

# CHAPTER 7

# Miriam and Mildred

High summer rolled into late summer, bringing changes in the land. Everything ripened from green into gold. The varieties of wild flowers, old troupers, appeared on cue in the ancient performance. By now the blackflies and mosquitoes had taken their bows and left the stage. Overhead, the heavens joined in the dance. Slow and stately, the constellations wheeled and turned. Once they were host to a special appearance—the northern lights, which flared and shimmied across the night.

When I lay in bed late at night sometimes, waiting for sleep to return, I liked to think about Canterbury Shaker Village dreaming under the stars. In my mind I floated up and out through the window to hover overhead, gazing tenderly down at the houses as Elder Henry drew them, in bird's-eye view, on his map. Drowsing now, I took a dreamy census of all who slumbered below. I flew up to the top of the hill, where Bud and Nancy and the boys nestled in their new life together. All was well there in the old Girls' House, where little Goldie Ina Ruby Lindsay had spent her first Shaker days so long ago. Drifting gently downhill, I sailed over the Dwelling, where Ethel and her cats were snug in one of the fifty-six rooms, waiting for Sister Alice to come back where she belonged.

I took a lazy backstroke and soared higher now, up where the northern lights tickled and tingled, then fell, light as a wisp of milkweed silk, closer and closer to home and to sleep. Here was the Office, staunch protector of Bertha and Lillian and Eldress Gertrude and Margaret, and now the Infirmary, where Jennie and I lay snoring and still. As I sank into dark warmth I passed the last house of all, the Enfield House, where Miriam and Mildred lay in their beds. It was the house of mysteries, I thought. And then I was asleep.

Miriam and Mildred lived next door in a house that I passed every day of that summer, but I never once went inside. Every door in the village was open, thanks to Bertha's trust and kindness, even those to the buildings that were locked and closed to the tour, and I went everywhere with my sketchbook and pencils in search of bits and pieces to draw. The Enfield House was different. Once I had an errand to Miriam, who beamed her welcome from the door, but she didn't invite me in. The room I could see looked normal enough, a kitchen, but Miriam trilled, "Thank you, dear," and pulled the door shut. I didn't feel bad, that was for sure. Miriam was sweet, but Mildred gave me the jimjams.

Sister Miriam Wall and Mildred Wells were the village's odd couple. Their relationship was a puzzle. Mildred was silent, dour, and distant. Miriam was giddy, a giggling flibbertigibbet. She never seemed to stop laughing. She'd throw her head back and close her eyes: "Tee, hee, hee!" She loved bright colors and the Boston Red Sox. The style of dress that drooped and sagged on Ethel always looked crisp and smart on Miriam. She bustled up and down the walk in sprightly canvas shoes, her bright lime dress a rival to the rich summer greens of lawn, garden, and maples. When you met up with her on the path, you could see that the dress was sprinkled with tiny white polka dots, like a zillion bubbles of 7-Up. That was Miriam.

In spite of her friendly demeanor and kindness to me, I didn't

find it easy to get to know Miriam. My days were so full of the growing friendships with "my" Shakers in the Office that I didn't take time to spend prying at doors that did not swing wide by themselves. I didn't take any of this personally, because no one else in the village ever seemed to enter the Enfield House, either. There was none of the easy come and go that typified the rest of the village. It seemed that Miriam and Mildred lived in another country, whose borders were closed, terra incognita.

Miriam's history in the village was no secret. Gladys Miriam Wall was born in Boston in 1896, and had been brought to the Shakers in 1908 in her twelfth year. She and Bertha had grown up here side by side. Together, they made the commitment to join the Shakers and stay when they came of age. They had sung duets and shared the responsibility of managing the kitchens. While Bertha had overseen the Office meals for company and hired men, Miriam had been the Dwellinghouse cook for the Family.

*Up the walk past Mildred's garden*

Miriam, Mildred, and Bertha worked together for years baking cookies as Christmas gifts. The same trio joined forces in 1942
on the immense, three-acre Victory Garden at the top of the hill to
the east, where they raised some two dozen vegetable varieties in
forty-five rows, each three hundred feet long—an astonishing two
and a half *miles* of vegetables, from broccoli to turnips. (Bertha said
that she tried planting peanuts once just to see what would happen,
but it was too far north.) The same year Bertha and Mildred
planted peach stones in front of the Enfield House, and the peach
trees were still there.

But in spite of these long associations, Bertha and Miriam
were not close at this time. I didn't know Miriam well enough to
know why, and Bertha, who took forgiving and forgetting seriously, didn't dig up old dirt. I knew that some of their troubles
were recent, a difference of feeling about dear friends, a marriage,
and a divorce. It seemed ironic at first that matters of the heart—
such worldly business!—could riffle the calm surface of Shaker
life, but in time it made more sense. The Shakers had always
sought harmony and unity through celibacy and communal living, but these practices by their very nature brought tensions all
their own. Like a placid mill pond fed by roiling underground
springs, Shaker life here and elsewhere had more to it than met
the eye. Now, with just a handful of members at Canterbury, all
women in advanced age, there were still undercurrents of con-
tention.

It seemed odd to imagine Canterbury in its heyday, when
men and women in youth and ripe middle age shared a home and
the common passion of their faith. In this celibate society, sex was
the empty chair at the table, the vast, conspicuous absence that
defined and shaped Shaker life. It was the void left by the thousand
things nature does with our eyes, bodies, and voices when sex is a
possibility.

No wonder the old-time Shakers made the distinction between the "spiritual" life, theirs, and the "natural" life, ours. In the old days, Shakers regarded themselves as higher beings, above the animal plane and below the angelic, striving ever upward. Officially, they did not condemn marriage and the "natural" man or woman, but on the issue of celibacy they tended to agree with St. Paul. For those in pursuit of salvation, the celibate life was by far the best course, but for those who couldn't forswear their carnal nature, it was at least better to marry than to engage in unbridled sex. I could see that college life in the seventies left a lot to be desired from the viewpoint of Bertha or St. Paul. By 1972, the Shakers were no more opposed to the institution of marriage than my grandma was. In later years, the Canterbury Shakers even allowed Steven Lamb, Nancy's son, to be married in the Meetinghouse Lane. The Sisters sent their love and best wishes, but didn't attend the wedding.

By 1972, of course, whatever thoughts the remaining Sisters might have entertained about marriage and motherhood were long gone, cool gray ashes of dreams and possibilities that had long since blown away. Bertha talked about it sometimes. When she was young she had yearned at times for the married life and a home of her own to keep. But her love for her Shaker Family always won out, and in the end, she chose to stay. She said she had no regrets, and I knew she was telling the truth.

Being nineteen and alert to every beat, however subtle, of the great dance of life, I bet privately that the Shakers, too, were keenly aware of the nuances of attraction from childhood on up, a hunch that Bertha confirmed one day when we were talking about school. In the old days, boys went to school in the winter so they could help the Brothers on the farm in the summer, when girls had their turn at school. By Bertha's time, however, boys and girls went together because there weren't enough students to make separate school terms practical. Bertha smiled in remembrance. When the girls teased each other about "looking to the west," everybody knew what that meant. That's where the boys sat in the Schoolhouse.

Then Bertha paused, and her smile broadened and lit up her face. Looking as pleased as I ever saw her, she remarked quietly and deliberately that *she* couldn't say, "Sweet sixteen and never been kissed." I gawked and she laughed her lovely light laugh. I was dying to hear more, but that's all she ever said, and I was too shy to pry.

You could sense that there were as many responses to celibacy as there were Shakers. Celibacy was regarded as a cross to bear—*the* cross—by many. It was not to be made light of, as it was the focus and center of Shaker daily life, the life in community of self-denial and humility. The Shakers felt called to bear the cross of Christ. Still, others probably found it a relief, for reasons of their own. It wasn't too hard to imagine a few scenarios from the pages of Elder Henry's detailed journals of his community. Let's see. Here was Lucy, who at the age of forty-two joined the Shakers with her husband and eight surviving children. Do you think maybe she'd had enough? I thought about Lucy and I thought about Mom. Mom just had the two of us, and we lived in the age of "modern inconveniences," as Gus called them, but I could see that even so the demands of motherhood could wear a body out. I bet that someone like Lucy sank into Shaker life as into a soft and delicious feather bed.

For other Shakers, though, the sacrifice was too much, an attitude that most of our visitors seemed to understand, even applaud. They were always curious about celibacy and some made a big fuss about it. Abstinence and celibacy were not buzzwords in the seventies. It was the age of the Pill, and AIDS was not yet on the scene. We guides often had to explain what "celibate" meant. Whoa . . . no sex! Grins, raised eyebrows. "Hey—wasn't there ever any hanky-panky?" Yuck-yuck. "Are *you* a Shaker?" Wink, wink. "Boy, I'd make a lousy Shaker." Yuck, yuck, yuck. This was usually some fat old guy with three strands of hair combed to his forehead from the nape of his neck. I'd look at the Mrs. with all the pity youth could muster. Yuck, indeed.

Some perceptive visitors saw that there was more to the sacrifice represented by celibacy than sex. It wasn't only about the call of the wild, powerful as that might be; it was also about family. No marriage, no kids; no kids, no grandkids. The grandmoms and grandpops who plastered their Airstreams with bumper stickers that announced "Ask me about my grandchildren" would glance at each other and shake their heads.

Once in a while someone objected to the Shakers' universal celibacy on biblical grounds, which was ironic, because they based their celibacy on biblical grounds. But some visitors insisted that it said right there in Genesis, go forth and multiply. It was hard to argue with anyone who quoted chapter and verse at me, partly because I was sure they knew the Bible better than I did, but also because I had some ongoing arguments with the Bible myself. Depending on where you looked, it also said that God made the world in seven days, that it was okay to have slaves, and that women should sit down and shut up in church. Or at least that's how some people wanted it interpreted. None of that made sense to me—come to think of it, those things hadn't made sense to the Shakers, either—and I was a long way from understanding.

Faced with the challenge, all I could do was repeat the Shakers' own answer, which I personally thought was both intelligent and beautiful. They loved children, they said, and felt very blessed to have been able to provide a home and care for children who were in need. Eldress Gertrude had added, "There are already so many little ones in the world who need caring for, we didn't think it necessary to add more of our own."

If the inquisition persisted, I did the prudent thing and weaseled out sideways. Eldress Gertrude is back in the Office, I'd say politely, and she would be happy to discuss this with you. That was usually the end of that.

Ah, well. That summer the coolness between Bertha and Miriam was healing. As a Trustee, Miriam was a regular visitor to the Trustees' Office, where she worked sometimes in the Gift Shop. It was a good place for her. She presided behind the old bronze cash register and dispensed striped sticks of penny candy, postcards, stuffed animals, and other mementos along with her cheerful chatter.

Miriam made things for the Shop, too. She filled fine net sachets with dried lavender from Mildred's garden. The "lavenders," tied with a ribbon and trimmed with a small artificial flower, were inexpensive and smelled nice. They sold as well as the other small, useful Shaker-made items: old-fashioned cakes of beeswax to smooth and strengthen sewing thread, "strawberries" made of satin stuffed with emery to sharpen and clean a seamstress's needle, and glass jars of potpourri made with dried petals and leaves that were also from Mildred's garden.

Mildred's garden was the centerpiece of the broad lawn between the road and Bud's little house, way up at the top. It filled the whole yard in front of the Enfield House, and Mildred's dark figure could be seen morning and evening amid the blaze of color. She vanished inside when the tours went by, and we didn't pass directly by her garden, but visitors admired it even from the Lane. It was really lovely.

I arrived just before Memorial Day and was to leave by Labor Day, so for me, it was always summer at Canterbury Shaker Village. The fields were forever green, the trees full bellied, heavy with leaf. The roadside bloomed with cornflowers, black-eyed Susans, devil's paintbrush, butter-and-eggs, clover, daisies, graceful

Queen Anne's lace with their tiny purple hearts. In early morning, the lawns glittered with dew; a familiar toad crouched on the walk, a small, warted Buddha casting its yard of shadow down the granite. The sun rose through the black web of apple trees at the crest of the hill. A light breeze busied the maples in the Meetinghouse Lane. Later, the maples brandished full leafy crowns against the midday sun. At twilight, we admired the fireflies' ancient minuet to the night music of mosquitoes and peepers. The toad clung to the sun-warmed stone and we had to watch where we put our feet. Dark against dark, bats skittered overhead like leaves loosed from their moorings, crazy with freedom.

The summer days weren't always fair. We had what the Sisters called "weather," crashing thunderstorms that aimed for our hilltop. High white banks of cloud gathered in the morning, then darkened and dropped walls of afternoon rain. Lightning struck often and near, with thunder so close on its heels that we knew we were lucky not to be hit. There was hail, pellets of white ice on the sodden grass.

Some of the Shakers were terrified of thunderstorms, but I liked hard rain and loud noise. I didn't like the other kind of wet New Hampshire day, heavy, gray, and still. Some days were chilly and dank; old bones and bunions ached. We waited for visitors in the sitting room with lamps lit against the dreary dark. My least favorite days were the gray days sticky with heat. The Shakers pressed embroidered hankies to their damp brows; I just sweated.

And then, when it seemed we couldn't bear the gray weight another minute, a night wind would blow it all away, and we'd awake to clear sky and air as refreshing as ginger ale. The earth seemed to shiver with energy. As late afternoon turned toward dusk, cloud after huge pearly cloud sailed serenely to the east, with no purpose but to give the measure of the endless sky. White and gray, then pink and gray, finally gray and gray against dark blue, the clouds' silent passage made my throat ache for reasons I could not put into words. Soft stars lit the summer night. I could not imagine the land white and brown, with branches like bones.

I loved this hilltop on which the village grew with all my small-town heart. Where I was from, back in Martin's Creek, Pennsylvania, our houses filled the valley of a creek that wandered through swelling limestone hills, the domain of slow, black and white cows. The tops of some wooded hills were tonsured with fields. From the time I was eleven or twelve, I had turned to the hills after school, seeking solace and grace. Even then I was baffled by the world, was more comfortable in the company of trees and sky. I went out to find safety, and I never felt safer than when I walked or rested alone in creation.

Canterbury Shaker Village offered the same in abundance. The village itself could not hold me, and I wasted no time exploring the land around. The old pictures in Bertha's photo albums showed farmers' land, skinned of trees, ordered into right angles by the rural geometry of fieldstone wall. By now, however, the woods had returned, lazily reclaiming the acres pried loose with farmers' blood and sweat. The Family's prize Guernseys were long gone, and the stanchions in the great Cow Barn stood empty.

The Shakers kept some land cleared by leasing fields to neighboring farmers. The clatter of the haying machine in the Meetinghouse Field, across the road and just down from the Office, accompanied our summer days. Never one for the woods, I always preferred open land. You can't see where you are in the woods; there is no view; you get cobwebs in your face; things can creep up or drop out of trees on you. None of this happens in a grassy field, where fisher cats and other horrors do not lurk. The mosquitoes weren't as bad, either, where the wind blew them away. They were fierce in the woods.

So I explored the unwooded parts. The little road that ran

north and south through the village was the beginning of my travels. I loved to walk up and down the road in the early morning, when I had it mostly to myself. There wasn't much traffic except for an occasional salt-rusted sedan or pickup that barreled over the bumps and frost heaves. Hard-top covered the old granite walkway that connected the Office to the rest of the village on the other side of the road, but the protruding stones formed a little jump. When we rested on the piazza in the late afternoons, our conversations were regularly interrupted. *Whomp!* Another vehicle landed with a crash. Bertha would wince. She always worried about accidents, especially after Honey was hit on Shaker Road.

To the north, the road ran straight through maybe a mile of open field to the edge of the woods. The stone walls along either side of the road were exceptionally handsome. The one by the Schoolhouse, on the east side of the road Bertha said, had been built by a Shaker Brother who had only one arm. It was tall and wide, made of stones that a one-armed man could heave into place, big rounded loaves at the bottom tapering to small, fist-sized cobbles at the top. The wall, more than a yard wide at the base and tapering gracefully at the top, stood higher than my waist.

From the Schoolhouse up to the cemetery, old sugar maples arched overhead. They were one hundred and seventeen years old. I didn't have to cut them down and count their rings to know that; it was right in Elder Henry's history. The wall on the east side of the road continued past the Schoolhouse and the arboretum that Elder Henry and his students had planted. The workmanship changed here, and I could see that old Brother Elijah had finished this stretch. The stones were bigger here, and the whole wall was topped with a course of squared stones as flat as a sidewalk. I was never good at heights and my balance was lousy, but I climbed up anyway. No problem—it was so wide and sturdy that I strolled along in comfort. I didn't think it was intended to serve as a raised walk, but I'm sure I wasn't the first young person to walk on it, either.

On the west side of the road, where the wall stretched from the Horse Barn to the Cemetery, the construction was slightly different. Here, the top was not crowned with flat stones, but was fashioned of small rocks that formed a slight trough in the center. When I squinted down the wall's length, the sides and edges were amazingly straight, as if laid to a ruler. That so many oddly shaped parts could join to form one such large, harmonious whole seemed strange and wonderful, enduring testimony to the maker's patience and care. In a way, Shaker community life wasn't so different from that stone wall. Ethel and Bertha were different, all right, but they both had a place.

Past the Cemetery on the west side was the Wymans' low, homemade house, and beyond that, Dave Curtis's small, neat white Cape Cod cottage, which I coveted. It had everything I had learned to love in New England: a scatter of day lilies, a stretch of stone wall, a clutch of old apple trees, a few tall sugar maples, and a little barn in the back. The house wasn't Shaker, but the barn was and so was all the rest. Beyond Dave's, the land rolled on flat and open to the north. There were no buildings on the east side of the road until the end of the long, flat stretch, where the North Family's brick Trustees' Office still stood. Like all the other property, it had long since been sold. Now the Meehs, another Quaker family, lived there in what was left of the North Family's holdings. The North Family Trustees' Office was much smaller than the Church Family Trustees' Office, more of an ordinary house size. It was the only building left from the North Family's holdings.

And that was it. The present, visible world of the Canterbury Shakers ended here. When I reached the North Family site I usually turned around and walked back toward the village. I'd go past the Church Family Office on my right and head on down the hill.

When I got to the bottom, I'd turn left on the little dirt Asby Road just to the edge of these woods, then turn back up the hill and walk through the long green field toward the Meetinghouse. The route took me right past the apple orchard.

The orchard was special to us in the village, hallowed by Bertha's recollection of her first memorable Sunday in the village, when she was barely eight. Surrounded by blossom and scent, kind Sisters, and other girls, little Goldie awoke to comfort and peace. When she told the story, it always sounded as though her commitment to Shaker life took root in that moment, which she remembered for the rest of her life. I loved Bertha's memory and the old apple trees, now ragged with neglect, but I would have been drawn there anyway. There was privacy there beyond the edge of the rise, where I could walk away from the eyes of passersby, and find the solitude I craved. This was Eden.

But I was not alone there. A narrow path snaked through the tall grass between the trees, evidence of someone else's frequent passing. If this were an old map, these parts would have borne the warning: "Here be Mildred." And she frightened me. She and her dog.

Mildred was an enigma, a shadow on the sunlit plain of Shaker life. Even now, remembering, I feel the chill. Meeting Mildred in the village was like swimming in the Wymans' pond: you'd float blissfully along in the warm surface waters and then drift all of a sudden into a cold current stirred up from the depths.

Ethel's kitties were daunting, and the dreaded fisher cats prowled the landscape of my imagination, but Mildred's German Shepherd was not imaginary. Its hoarse roar sent all of us running for safety. Chris was the largest German Shepherd I'd ever seen, huge in the chest, dark, menacing, vicious. Not long before I arrived it had slipped its chain and chased and bitten Jennie in the buttocks. It broke loose every chance it could and chased anyone unlucky enough to be out. I could move quicker than Jennie and had less to offer in the way of backside (Ethel remarked that the dog had an "ample target") but I was taking no chances. That dog scared me to death. I steered clear of Mildred, too, always when she had the dog, but even when she didn't. Stringy and powerfully built, wide shouldered and with hands like a man, she frightened me, with or without the dog lunging at the end of her leash.

In some fundamental way, Mildred was not civilized—she did not belong in the world of towns and cities. I don't mean that she was uncouth, although her manner was brusque and her voice high and tight. Rather, she was wild as a badger is wild, a creature of bone and hide, not silk bonnets or flowered dresses. She was the color of outdoors. Tall and big-boned, she stalked the village and surrounding fields in the only clothes I ever saw her wear, a drab house dress worn with socks and boots. I never saw her without the kerchief that she tied over her brown hair, and I seldom saw her without some large, heavy implement gripped in her fist, a spade or the stout cudgel she carried on her walks. Mildred worked immensely hard. Remarkably strong for a woman in her seventies, she could lug, dig, hoist, and shovel for hours. I would have bet that Mildred did more in any given week than Ethel did in a year. Maybe two or three.

In this way and more, Mildred and Ethel lived in different worlds, and it didn't seem surprising that they didn't like each other much. Ethel never went out; Mildred was always out. She seemed ill at ease indoors, as out of place in the sitting room as a rotting log. Although she came to the Office daily, she never sat and visited, only quickly arranged a fresh armload of flowers in the vase inside the door and slipped away again as soon as she was done. It was odd to think of her sleeping on sheets in a bed or standing at a kitchen sink. It would not have surprised me to learn that she didn't stay indoors at all, but curled up each night in a lair in the orchard. Of course she didn't; but it seemed possible.

We rarely spoke, since my encounters with her were confined to running into her along the stone walk, or once in a while out in the fields. What shreds I knew about her did not come from Mildred herself and did not lessen her mystery. Her name was not really Mildred, but I wasn't ever sure what it was. It was Ella or Gabrielle, and she was part Hungarian. I understood that she and her sister had lived first with the Shakers in Alfred, Maine, where she was Sister Mildred Barker's girl. Sister Mildred was a prominent spiritual leader at Alfred and, later, at Sabbathday Lake.

I gathered that Ella-Gabrielle-Mildred had not been an easy person wherever she had lived. Her mother took the girls away, but Mildred had eventually come to roost at Canterbury in 1921, when she was seventeen. There was already an Ella at Canterbury so Ella-Gabrielle was given the opportunity to choose a new name, a practice adopted to minimize confusion. She chose the name Mildred in honor of the one who was like a mother to her. She had never signed the Covenant, however, and was not a Shaker in the same sense as the others. As I understood it, the Covenant was to Shaker life as a marriage license is to the World, a formal, legal declaration of full commitment. She did not wear the cap and bonnet like the other Sisters at Canterbury and she was not called Sister.

Everything about Mildred troubled me. She wasn't a Shaker; well, neither were the rest of us who stayed in the village. But she was guilty of worse: she wasn't *like* the Shakers. There was no joy in her that I could see, no opening at all. Mildred was shut tight. I resented her. I felt safe at Canterbury, but not around Mildred. Why was she there, spoiling paradise? I did not want this dark bruise on the perfect apple that I cradled in my palm.

In time, I learned more. When I had been there a few weeks,

someone, not one of the Shakers, explained Mildred's story to me in brief. I was appalled—it was the worst thing I'd ever heard, maybe even the worst thing I could possibly imagine. She had survived an unimaginable childhood: her father had killed her mother, perhaps while the child watched. I was sure that this was true, but it was understood that we did not speak of this, not to each other, certainly not to Mildred. I felt free to ask Bertha about almost anything but this. As a consequence, Mildred and her life before Canterbury vanished into the limbo of unspoken family secrets, where what is impossible to acknowledge stirs in fitful, monstrous sleep.

The enormity of Mildred's tragedy stunned me; it was the biggest thing I'd ever heard about anyone. Yes, there was something "big" about my young life; one of my parents had died when I was a child, too. But the sadness of my childhood seemed a mere ditch to the abyss of Mildred's loss. The silence about her frightened me more than anything. How was it possible to live with something so big and not speak of it? I realized that some of the community's reticence might have been generational. I knew that people of my parents' and grandparents' age tended to keep the family's dirty laundry off the outside line. "It's a poor bird that dirties its own nest," said Mom firmly, although I never could see how anybody, including Mildred, could be held responsible for anyone's actions but her own.

With everyone's silence, her story in time seemed fantastic, unreal. It was years later before the things I learned about Mildred were confirmed—as it happened, in the preface to a Shaker cookbook by someone who had spent time working with the Shakers in recent years. Those who had known Mildred and the Shakers were distressed. In such a context, the information appeared irrelevant and sensational. It was nobody's business but her own, even after death.

．　．　．

That summer I wished that I had known Sister Alice Howland while she was in her prime. But I wish that Mildred could
know me now. She fooled me then, you know. Her camouflage
worked because I was young and had not yet learned to decipher
the language of pain. I read all the signals wrong. I thought that she
walked the fields and woods alone. The demons in attendance
were invisible to me. The dog I thought was there to harm us was
there to protect her from a world that she could not begin to trust.
Did Mildred heal from the wounds of her childhood? How can I
say she didn't? At Canterbury, they let her be.

I saw Mildred more often in her garden than anywhere else.
She never had the dog with her when she was there. Like Ethel in
her kitchen, Mildred seemed to feel safe in her garden. I see now
that she made a place for herself between the worlds of wildness
and humankind, one foot in each. She had converted a large
stretch of lawn in front of the Enfield House to a magnificent mass
of flowers. A gardener myself now, I understand that it must have
taken her years.

Mildred seemed different in her garden, more at ease and
more approachable, kinder, softer. Whenever I passed her I said
hello and learned a little about what she was growing. When I first
came she gave me four plants to keep in my room. The beds nearest the house were luxuriant with lavender, which Miriam used
to make the sachets. Flamboyant spears of gladioli dominated the
center of the circular garden. What I liked best were the Icelandic
poppies, very different from the tall, stiff, orange Oriental poppies
that Grandma grew back home. These smaller, delicate, blowsy
blossoms ran the gamut of sunset colors from palest yellow through
peach and tangerine to deep scarlet.

I can see her now in late afternoon, poppies dancing at her

knees. I was wrong about so much. That year I saw only summer. I went home when it ended, but Mildred stayed. She watched the leaves fall, the land grow hard, the birds flee, her flowers wither and die. She watched the snow come, the first flake and then the others, thick and fast under the wicked lash of the wind. Mildred knew what gardeners know, that winter always comes and kills.

But she knew the rest of it, too, which I had yet to learn. Summer did not, does not, will not fail to restore what is ruined by the dark and cold. Beyond the reach of humankind, Mildred was yet not beyond the reach of new green shoots ever rising toward the light.

# CHAPTER 8

# *August*

Mildred's garden reached a new crescendo of glory as the days began to grow shorter, rivaled by the wild beauty of the roadside. Constellations of small purple asters appeared in both places. Goldenrod drifted over the fields. The sky itself changed now, no more the soft, hazy blue of June; it grew sharper and deeper, more keenly blue. Every day twilight came maybe sixty or seventy heartbeats sooner.

In the Office too, there was change, mostly good change. Lillian was still in bed most of the time, but now there was a steady crew of nurses and Bertha could get a good night's sleep. There were only a couple of times when the schedule fell apart so that we did some more night duty, but we could depend on a night nurse more often than not. Lillian was no better, but she was no worse, so we counted that as a blessing. The days rolled on swiftly now. How could time be so elastic? By the mindless calculation of the clock and the calendar, June and August were about the same: thirty and thirty-one days. So why did August weigh light in the balance by the reckoning of the human heart? The end of the summer was always in sight, and it seemed to prod and hurry the days that led to it.

Like the flowers that tumbled over each other to bloom

and seed before the first frost, summer events crammed themselves into August while there was still time. All of a sudden, we were on the road. Bud and Nancy took the boys and me to Harvard Shaker Village, not too far from Concord and Lexington in Massachusetts, and to the Fruitlands Museums in Harvard, high on a hill. Fruitlands was the estate of Miss Clara Endicott Sears, who spent her time and fortune collecting beautiful things around the time that big guns were pounding lads to pulp in the trenches of the Great War.

Miss Sears seemed like a ghostly godmother of Bud because they liked the same things: the Shakers, the Indians, utopian societies (Bronson Alcott's Fruitlands had been on this very site), and nineteenth-century American landscapes and still lifes. The museum, which was lovely, included one of the earliest collections of Shaker artifacts, housed in a little clapboard Shaker Trustees' Office that Miss Sears had moved to the site a long time ago.

When we were done wandering through the houses and exhibits of Fruitlands, we piled back into the big brown car and Bud drove across town onto another Shaker Road. This one, too, was full of bumps and curves as it wound through thin woods and past great hefty lumps of granite dropped by a careless glacier's retreat. We stopped at the Harvard Shaker burying ground, where each grave had kept its individual cast-iron marker, and went on to a kind of Shaker shrine, a pile of stones that marked the spot where Mother Ann's right-hand man, Father James Whittaker, was beaten by a local mob, who feared this strange new sect.

So much for my notion of proper, reserved Yankees. Here was a different face of New England. There were things about the Shakers that frightened and threatened some people so much in the late 1700s and 1800s that they used fists and sticks and stones to drive it away. But they didn't kill Father James and they couldn't conquer the spirit of the converted, because the Harvard Shaker community formally gathered not long after the incident, in 1791.

Even after, the site of Father James's courageous stand was honored by the Shakers, and the custom arose of pilgrims adding a stone to the heap that marked the site. There was quite a pile of rocks, each slightly different, all very much the same, standing in quiet resistance to violence and oppression. There was something about that gesture I liked very much.

When we neared the village itself, the road lay down and behaved, running flat and straight into the heart of the settlement. It was truly beautiful, slightly different from Canterbury, and also very much the same. We weren't on a hill here, but on a stretch of plain. All the buildings fronted the road, like beads on a string or links in a chain. The Harvard Shaker society had folded long ago, around 1918, in what was becoming a familiar story. The few remaining members were relocated in another Shaker village and the property was sold. For many years, the houses had served as private homes.

You could tell that hard times had not particularly troubled this lovely place, which seemed to float in the rising mists like some simple Brigadoon. Everything on the street was beautifully kept. Bud drove slowly past each building—really slowly, even for Bud, although it didn't matter because we didn't pass another car either way. Here was the Trustees' Office, a huge clapboard structure, gable end to the road. Here was the Meetinghouse, although much changed from its original gambrel-roofed state.

As we climbed a slight rise, here was the Square House, where a self-proclaimed messiah promised his flock in the 1780s that he was immortal and would rise three days after death. In due course he died. Somewhere around day number six they gave up and buried him for reasons that were becoming all too obvious. It was disillusioning, to say the least. But the seekers were still hungry for spiritual sustenance, so when Mother Ann came through town on her missionary tour, they found better, truer bread in her. Ann Lee stayed in that house, Bud told us, and we felt some awe. She walked on this ground, looked out through those windows, breathed these dusk mists. In the gathering dark, two hundred years seemed wavery and vague. The Square House was very dear and important to Mother Ann, who paid most of the cost of its purchase and wanted that so recorded.

Bud and Nancy took the boys and me on other outings, too. One rainy morning after I had sat up with Lillian all night we went up to the Mountains, to the Kancamagus Highway, to the Flume and the Old Man of the Mountain and Dismal Pond at Crawford Notch. Good old Bud. His life was changing, too. These were the jaunts he used to take with Bertha and Lillian, to the White Mountains (Bertha's choice) or the ocean (Lillian's pick). Now, instead of two cheery but sedate old Shaker ladies, his car packed a rollicking crew of four young teenage boys.

It was becoming clear that the Shakers' touring days were drawing to a close. Just a few years earlier, they had taken to the road often, enjoying the innocent sights and amusements that Believers had been denied a hundred and fifty years earlier. Elder Henry and Eldress Dorothy helped to change all that, believing that good Shakers would be good Shakers whether at home or out and about. Strawbery Banke in Portsmouth, the Boston Museum of Fine Arts, St. Johnsbury in Vermont—all these destinations and more had welcomed the familiar Shaker bonnets not so long ago. Lillian's last outing had been in the first week of June, when Bud took the Office Sisters and me to the Arnold Arboretum near Boston to enjoy the trees and flowers and the "bug-eatin'" pitcher plants, Eldress Gertrude's favorites. On the way home, Lillian got so sick that I privately feared she might die right there in Howard Johnson's. Now the traveling was over. Bud took Lillian for a half-hour spin in August and she came home exhausted and sick. With Lillian ailing at home in bed, Bertha saw little pleasure in pleasure trips.

Others came to carry me away, too. The Wymans took me

to New Hampshire's half inch of coast (that's how it looked on the map), where we gasped in the waves that a coldhearted Atlantic peeled from icebergs—and this was August, when the water had sucked up the heat of the sun all summer and was at its warmest and best, they said. Small parties of Sisters and Brothers had made just such pleasure-and-health excursions to the seashore as early as the 1840s. I wondered what they wore for bathing suits. I made my third trip up to Maine (or "down" to Maine, they told me to say, "down east") to see Gus and Alice. Claire and Barry Roche, our wonderful Canterbury Fair day commando team, took me home to Salem for a delightful weekend of sightseeing in the town where women had been executed by the colony as witches and Nathaniel Hawthorne made his home.

Mother Ann was probably lucky she didn't show up in New England until the late 1700s. She was accused of witchcraft, too, but by 1774, even the most backward Yankees had to make do with beating and verbally abusing women whose power they could not understand or accept.

Nathaniel Hawthorne was of particular interest, too. He had dabbled in communal living experiments in his youth, including a stint at Brook Farm in Massachusetts. In 1831, when the Trustees' Office was brand-new, a youthful Hawthorne took a trip of his own to the Canterbury Shakers. He liked the cider and admired what he saw, both in the buildings and in the people, and joked about perhaps joining them himself one day.

Twenty years later, Hawthorne visited the Shakers in Hancock, Massachusetts, where he found that the communal life didn't look half so good to him anymore. They have no privacy at all, he complained, and although he admitted grudging admiration for the neatness and workmanship of the Dwelling, he concluded that its inhabitants were "the most singular and bedeviled set of people that ever existed in a civilized land." Hawthorne was older for sure . . . and wiser? More cynical? More realistic? More knowl-

edgeable about himself? He was married and a father by this time—
in fact, his little boy, Julian, came with him on this trip—and you
could bet that home life at the Hawthornes' wasn't nearly as neat
and tidy and quiet as this.

I enjoyed all this gadding about, grateful for the kindness of
all who welcomed me, but I had mixed feelings about spending
long days away from the Shakers because time was running short.
Before long I'd be back in college and this summer would seem
like a dream. There was still so much to learn. Every chance there
was, I sat with Lillian and, more and more, with Bertha. Who
knew how long they'd be around? Bertha seemed likely to go on
for a long time, but you never knew. We regarded each new day
with Lillian as a gift.

Bertha lived more fully in the present than most people I
knew. But she liked to remember the past when we asked her, and
I couldn't learn enough. It made her feel good to talk about the
older Sisters she'd known and loved. Like Lillian, she said she had
always sought the company of old women, because they had so
much to teach. I could understand that. Just as Elder Henry ab-
sorbed the lore of earlier Believers, I sat with Bertha and plied her
with endless questions about the people she'd known. What started
as mere names to me assumed substance and warm life as Bertha
shared her memories.

Bertha had missed Elder Henry by a matter of weeks—he
died on April 1, 1905, and she came at the end of May—but she
grew to know many of the Shakers who had shared his world. This
near miss and overlap put me in mind of Henry's own experience.
He missed aged Elder Benjamin Whitcher by a matter of months—
Benjamin died in 1837 and Henry came in 1838—but he was surrounded by others who could tell him the stories. I appreciated the
juxtaposition of Henry and Bertha in time. Where Elder Henry's
journals left off, Bertha's memories and photographs picked up.
Although they had never met in this life, she was his true spiritual

daughter and heir, doing for Shaker history in the twentieth century what he had done for the eighteenth and nineteenth.

Bertha's personal memories of Shaker life began in 1905, when she came to Canterbury Shaker Village just before she turned eight. What a wonderful age that was, I thought. I wasn't much past that age myself, and I looked back on that time of my life with mingled happiness and regret. I was confident then, full of myself, queen of the playground and classroom. I loved learning and my teachers, especially that year. Mrs. Shuttleworth's outsides were homely as mud but her heart made her beautiful to us. She threw wide the door of reading for me—I met Ferdinand the Bull and Madeline and Pooh that year—and let me water the windowsill plants. I loved her with all my seven-year-old heart.

When I learned that the United Society had customarily preferred to take in children that age and no younger, I understood why. They made exceptions all the time to provide care for younger children, but the Society traditionally counseled that seven or eight was the proper age for a child to enter the Church Family Girls' or Boys' Order.

Bertha told us stories of her childhood. The girls slept in the little house at the top of the yard and walked two by two to the Schoolhouse, like Madeline of the classic storybooks by Bemelman. In fact Madeline was more like little Goldie and the other girls than not, living as she did with a kind Sister and other girls in beds in a row. Never mind that Madeline's sister was a nun, not a Shaker Caretaker, or that she lived in Paris, not Canterbury. The principle was much the same. The Shaker girls made their beds every day, but not right away in the morning, Bertha said. They pulled back the covers over a chair at the foot of the bed to let the mattress and sheets air during the morning, then made the bed around midday, so it was nicer and fresher at night.

In addition to lessons in the Schoolhouse, the girls had chores. Bertha remembered stitching seams and hems on sheets. The work was to be as perfect as possible. On one occasion the Sister in charge asked Goldie to pull out and rework a yard of seam because of a few crooked stitches. The next time, she did it right. The quest for perfection, a hallmark of Shaker life and work, dated back to Mother Ann, who told her followers, "Do all your work as though you had a thousand years to live, and as you would if you knew you must die tomorrow." The Shakers quickly earned a reputation for the excellence and honesty of their many products. Artemus Ward, a nineteenth-century humorist, made fun of their ways but praised their "apple sass," adding that you wouldn't find a few layers of the dried fruit over a pile of shavings, either, an unscrupulous practice in the World.

At first this Shaker drive for perfection seemed kind of dangerous to me, because I was far from perfect myself, but I soon learned that I needn't have worried. It became clear that Shakers like Lillian and Bertha were interested in improving their own behavior, not in putting me or anyone else under a glass to look for flaws, not that mine needed magnification. I watched Bertha carefully. She aimed for perfection in her work and in her conduct, and was pleased when she hit the mark, but she had patience with herself when she missed, too. This was worth knowing, I thought. It's one thing to demand perfection or else, and quite another to hope for it and try for it.

The focus that Lillian and Bertha kept on their own behavior caught my attention, too. It was not only kind, it was practical, I realized. There was nothing that Lillian could do about anything or anybody but herself, and I saw her conducting herself through frustration and pain with dignity and humility.

It was as if we were all given garden plots to tend, side by side. Instead of peering over the fence to frown at my weeds, Lillian and Bertha seemed to keep their eyes on their own flower beds. They looked up now and then to smile and wave, but on the whole, tending their own gardens seemed to be a full-time job. I know that I must have unwittingly said or done things occasionally that distressed or annoyed them, but the Sisters were consistently mild and kind. Lillian had some concerns about my miniskirts, I learned later, but she never criticized me. She knew I was a good girl and just wished that my "petticoats" were longer.

Eldress Gertrude, God bless her, seemed to spend considerably more time gazing over the garden fence. It was comical to watch TV with the Sisters in the sitting room at night because Eldress Gertrude appointed herself drama critic and kept busy pointing thumbs up or thumbs down. I noticed that it was down more often than not, and once in a while Eldress Gertrude's criticism even got to stolid Margaret, the housekeeper of few words. "Hoo, boy," she said one night when the Eldress stepped out of the room, and rolled her eyes, grinning. For Margaret, that was a real speech.

Eldress Gertrude had a good heart but a tongue like a tart green apple. I spent lots of time listening to her that summer, and not all of what she said about others was flattering. Her outspokenness made me a little cautious around her. "A dog that will fetch a bone will carry a bone," Mom always said. If Eldress Gertrude had been critical of me, my feelings would have been hurt, although I probably wouldn't have taken it too personally. "Consider the source," my mom also said. If Bertha or Lillian had spoken harshly of me, on the other hand, I would have wanted to die.

Bertha told stories about her own misdeeds, which made us laugh. It was hard to imagine this saintly Sister as a naughty girl, but she assured us that it was true. She liked to tell one story that lived in my mind ever after as "Goldie and the Candy Kitty." One of the older Sisters had a confection made of marshmallow or some such sweet in the shape of a cat—a "dear little kitty," said Bertha, with a wry smile, which made it sound that much more appealing. The candy kitty became the apple in her Eden. Little Goldie knew where the forbidden fruit was kept in the cupboard, and so one day she stole a peek at it. There it was, pink and sparkling, her very heart's desire in the palm of her hand. As young as she was, Goldie knew perfectly well that it was wrong to covet the kitty so badly, and even more wrong to consider taking just one little nibble. It was wrong, wrong, wrong, out of the question, impossible.

She bit off one ear. It was even better than she'd dreamed.

Goldie shoved the kitty back in the cupboard and scampered out of the room. Was she remorseful? Oh, very. Did she repent of her guilty secret? Yes, of course. Did she go back and bite off the other ear the next day? You bet. And every chance she could, after that, she went back for a nibble until the kitty was mostly gone.

Bertha laughed when she told how her crime caught up with her in the end. Well, of course it would, she said, because before too long there was nothing left of the kitty but a sorry, sticky little lump. When the Sister in question discovered the remains, she didn't scold, Bertha recalled. The Sister simply took her aside and asked if she knew what had become of the candy cat. Goldie admitted what she had done, ashamed of herself. "Next time when you want something, you might ask" was all the Sister said, and that was that.

She told us that corporal punishment was not allowed, that the children were not hit or spanked in any way. Instead, she said, the usual consequence of a misdeed was being sent to assist one of the aged Sisters for a while. How wise that was, she said, because the young girls soon forgot to be mad or ashamed in the gentle company of many of the Sisters.

From one of them Bertha learned another story of crime and punishment, Shaker style. One of the older Sisters told Bertha how she was sent as a young girl to the Printing Shop, where she accidentally knocked over a whole page of metal type just set by Elder Henry. To her horror the lead alphabet flew through the air and scattered across the floor. She froze. Henry, who would need hours to reset the page, couldn't have been gentler. He knew that accidents happen. It seemed more important to him to be kind than to be angry. His patient reaction meant a great deal to the child, but it also dawned on me that Henry somehow made that choice for himself.

It had never occurred to me that serenity was a choice, not a consequence, that I might try choosing mildness instead of criticism, no matter what anybody did. Wait . . . there was more to this. If someone hurt me, even intentionally, I could hurt them back . . . or I could forgive them. Never mind them. Which was better for me? Wasn't that selfish? Yes, and it was also wise and good. There was some kind of paradox in this kind of behavior, I began to understand. This was a revelation. I looked around at my own inner garden. What a tangle. There was potential here, I'd give it that. But I'd better get a move on if I ever hoped my garden to be lovely and serene.

As Bertha talked, more and more of the faces and names in the photo albums came to life. There was Sister Rebecca Hathaway, born one hundred years ago in 1872, a large, smiling woman who taught little Goldie how to cook potatoes. That was the first step for girls in learning the kitchen arts, Bertha explained. When they were about ten or eleven, they were given the responsibility for the Church Family's potato dishes of all kinds. When they were a little older, the girls were promoted to pie baking. When she was thirteen, Goldie made twenty-six pies every Saturday, which lasted the Family through the next Sunday. Her lemon meringue pie won the contest that Sister Jessie Evans, the schoolteacher, organized for the boys and girls to practice their various skills.

Sister Rebecca also grew sage for the village's use and for sale, dried and ground, in the shop. Sage was the favorite seasoning for the stuffing in turkeys and chickens. It was Rebecca, too, who led Bertha into the art and mystery of canning, pickling, and preserving when she was about fifteen. They worked side by side in the old Syrup Shop at the top of the hill, back of the Dwelling. At eighteen, Bertha moved on to responsibility for baking the Family's bread. Rebecca supervised the confection business, which somehow didn't surprise me, given her comfortable figure, about halfway between Jennie and my own grandma in girth. Rebecca taught Bertha how to prepare the old-fashioned treats: maple-sugar cakes, sugared butternuts, sugared flag root, and candied grapefruit and orange peel.

While I was there, Bertha made a batch of candied violets to use as decoration on a dessert. She laughed when she recalled how years ago she had once trimmed a birthday cake for Lillian with fresh roses. Elder Arthur Bruce, passing by the kitchen, chided her for extravagance. But the way she said it, I don't think she minded much. She never said much about the last Elders, but she did not speak of them with particular affection. She said that Elder Arthur expected a lot from the Kitchen Sisters in the Office. He prided himself on being able to invite guests home at any time in the assurance that they would be served a fine, full-course company meal. Under Bertha's leadership the Sisters rose to the challenge, although I imagine that Bertha had to remind herself that she was laboring for God and the United Society, not bossy Elder Arthur.

One of the faces was darker than the rest. Edith Green, whose father was from the West Indies, was the community's only black Sister. She helped make the famous "Shaker knit" sweaters, worked as a Dairy Deaconess in charge of the Creamery, made hat brushes, and crocheted articles for the fancy-goods line.

And that handsome face belonged to Eldress Josephine Wilson, born in 1866, a respected and skilled Trustee and businesswoman. She supervised the manufacture of cloaks, assisted Elder Henry with the printing of *The Manifesto*, and chose Bertha at nineteen to come and cook at the Office. She was the one who taught Bertha to make the meals attractive, not just delicious. Bertha always said, "Put something red on the plate to make it look nice," and I keep that in mind to this day. Eldress Josephine liked to keep up with the times, so the Office Kitchen enjoyed many renovations and added conveniences under her management. In 1940, Josephine surprised Bertha by saying that there was a "new baby" downstairs. It was a new electric stove, quite the modern convenience for the time.

The story that Bertha told about Sister Annie Baker was short but it packed a punch. When Bertha was still very young, Sister Annie took a long look at her and said, "You will be the last Canterbury Shaker." Her prediction made a big impression on little Goldie. Bertha was not eager to lose her Sisters, but you could tell that she hoped Annie was right. The thought of having that honor pleased her.

There was one Sister whom Bertha remembered with particular affection. Cora Helena Sarle, born in 1867, came to Canterbury in 1882 when she was fifteen years old. Helena was the Sister who comforted Goldie, crying in the road as her natural sister drove away. The girls adored "Grammy" Helena because she was fun and kind. With Rebecca Hathaway, she organized popcorn ball parties, sledding parties, and other treats for them. Lillian would whip up some kind of entertainment, like getting the girls organized in an impromptu tissue-paper–and-comb chorus.

Before long, Helena was more to me than the black-and-white image of her in a photo from late in her life, standing at her easel, paintbrush in hand. I had to say that her later oil paintings, which existed in abundance, did not do much for me. They looked like examples of conventional late Victorian American impressionism, if you wanted to give it a name, postcard pictures of a world awash in birch trees and violent pink sunsets. Bud wished that she had painted scenes of her youth, à la Grandma Moses, but to no avail. Helena liked her birches and sunsets.

Then one day Bud showed me Helena's earliest work. When he brought it out, my breath caught in my throat. When she was sixteen, still in her first year with the Canterbury Shakers, Elder

Henry asked Helena to illustrate native wild plants for a botanical compendium on which he was at work. What do you know . . . Henry was Helena's Gus. Their collaboration of age and youth, male and female, and words and pictures created two beautiful manuscript volumes. On each page, Helena's delicate watercolor rendering of a plant joined a brief identifying caption in Elder Henry's familiar script. I turned the pages in awe and wonder.

Here was an aster, the very same aster that I saw myself on my walks: "Order Compositae. *Diplopappus umbellanus.* Aster. Low grounds, river banks, fields, New England to La. Stem 3 to 4 ft high. Aug & Sept." And a few pages on, *Chenopodium album.* You could dress up its name, but it was plain old pigweed, the "most common of weeds in field and gardens. July–Sept."

And that yellow flower, I recognized that! It was celandine, *Chelidonium majus,* provider of "abundant bright yellow juice. . . . Used to destroy warts." And stuck here at the very bottom of one page, with not even a whole page to itself, was poor, shabby little *Physconsitrium pyriforme,* so unimportant that no one bothered to give it another name: "On the ground; extremely common" was all Elder Henry wrote. Somehow it reminded me of Ethel. God loved them both just the same.

And on and on I looked, through Latin names and the common names that read like farmers' poetry:

> *Heartweed, smartweed, Mayweed, squawmint,*
> *walking fern, crowfoot, corn cockle, cale . . .*
> *Self heal, hard hack, silver weed, milkwort,*
> *mouse ear, chick weed, arrow head, flax.*

> *Hare's foot, horsemint, scratch grass, apple moss,*
> *speedwell, liverwort, button bush, gold thread . . .*
> *Dog's bane, coltsfoot, pitcher plant, pickerel weed,*
> *drop flower, hobble bush, Jersey tea, snakehead.*

The words for these plants were ancient beyond telling, I realized, far older than the Shakers or America, older than medieval Europe, older than farming itself. When we, still wild, hunted and gathered for our life through the first eons of human existence, these plants were already old friends.

My head grew light as time once more shivered and dissolved. Helena's asters, my asters . . . Helena, me . . . the ninety years that separated those plants and these, that girl and this, were a fraction of a breath in that vast span of time. Thinking about it made me dizzy. Were my asters, which grew in the very same place from the same earth, the same as hers, or different? If a fire still burns, uninterrupted, is yesterday's flame the same as today's, or not? Was the Merrimack River that we crossed today in Concord the same river that Elder Henry crossed a century ago?

I had studied enough about ancient Greece to recognize these as philosophers' riddles. For a moment they writhed before me, stubborn, unpickable knots, but all of a sudden my heart grew as light as my head. Who cared about answers, anyway? What a divine conundrum, what a splendid mystery! I knew nothing but the questions, and perhaps that was progress enough for this day. Elder Henry danced through my mind. He had noticed Helena's young possibilities and encouraged her. What had really made me pick up the pencil that summer and throw myself into drawing? I never did see Henry hovering near my bed when I awoke late at night, for which I was glad, but that didn't mean he wasn't near.

It gave me the goose bumps, but they felt good.

It must have been something in the air, or maybe the veil here was thinner between the world (which seemed solid and real) and that mysterious other reality (which seemed equally real, though no more solid than a sigh). Whatever the reasons, time played peculiar tricks the whole summer long. The photograph albums that Bertha let us pore through had something to do with it, I know. She had stacks of old leather- or cloth-bound volumes with four or five black-and-white snapshots to each thick, black, slightly furry page, each photo slipped into an old-fashioned gummed paper mount at each corner, each face and scene neatly labeled with her beautiful script in white ink.

The small, preternaturally clear images haunted the other guides and me. Here was this place, these trees, these rooms, preserved forever as moments that took substance as two-by-three-inch rectangles of stiff, shiny paper. And there were faces—wonderful faces—of Sisters and Brothers whom Bertha and Lillian knew as the dearest of friends, or perhaps not. There was one charming informal portrait of three or four little girls in plaid dresses and bows, grinning into the camera for all the world like Anne of Green Gables or Rebecca of Sunnybrook Farm. You could practically smell the paint on Norman Rockwell's brush.

They looked so innocent and so dear, but when we asked Bertha who they were, she held the print close to her eyes so she could see it, and then shook her head. Alas . . . these beautiful children grew up wild, and there was some trouble with the hired men, or some such thing. They were long, long gone.

Our favorite pictures were those of the Shakers we knew or were pictures taken by Bertha, who had grown up as quite a shutterbug. There was a grand picture of a dozen Canterbury Sisters loaded into the back of an old pickup, buried in apples and apple baskets, laughing their heads off. The print was so clear that you could see the silk strands in each milkweed pod, which meant it was taken around this time of the year.

The inscription said 1918. There was Edith Green and Lillian's sister Florence. Here was Bertha, just turned twenty, and Ethel, the same age. After fifty-four Augusts, their faces were slightly different and also exactly the same. No wonder time seemed to bend and meander. Here was Bertha, a.k.a. Goldie Ina

Ruby Lindsay, in 1909 at age twelve, standing for a portrait taken at the Kimball Studios in Concord—the same face, again, and yet not the same. And here was a beautiful portrait of much younger Lillian, smiling at a child soaring on a swing.

When I looked at the Sisters across the breakfast table, sometimes I glimpsed the young woman inside. When I stared at the old photos, I could see the Sisters as they were now. Eldress Gertrude showed us a picture of herself as a girl, maybe my age, probably a little younger, sitting at a table with other girls, smiling self-consciously for the camera as they bent over their poplar-ware work. That was Gertrude all right, and so was *this* Gertrude, just celebrating her seventy-eighth birthday on August 19.

Yes, the photograph albums definitely had something to do with the games time played here. So did the insight of the Shakers then and now, who spoke of "time" and "eternity" to distinguish the two realities that they felt. In the material world, you could tell time by the changes in matter. Time left its tracks all around us, in trees that grew, cheeks that withered, pickets that crackled in long seasons of rain. In the spirit world of eternity, time was irrelevant.

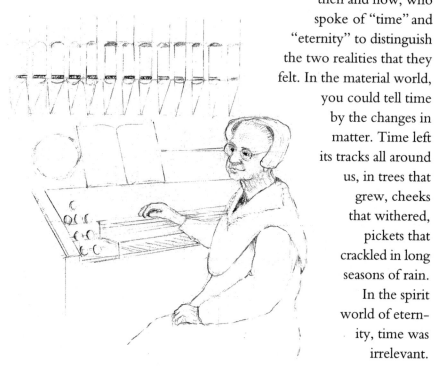

*Lillian at the Hook and Hastings*

There was no beginning and no end, no youth or age, nothing but an endless circle, in which all was one.

I wanted more than anything to be like Lillian and Bertha and Eldress Gertrude, to meet adversity and pain with grace, and I tried, I really did. So it was tough to go crashing over the trip wire of my old nature when that happened. When I heard Bertha talk about how she prayed for more patience, I smiled to myself. By most people's standards, Bertha had the patience of a saint. What would she think if she ever saw me lose my temper? Holy Moses, that had better never happen. That was scary, because my fits blew up out of nowhere, like tornadoes in a Nebraska August. There was never much lead time to head for the storm cellar. If Bertha ever knew how rotten my temper could be . . .

It started innocently enough with two good things: music and a visit to the Dwellinghouse. Bertha let me play the piano in the Office sitting room and I was allowed to spend time with the little old pump organ, too, up in the Sisters' Shop, since restoration there was still in progress and the building wasn't yet open for the tour. It was fun and I liked the way the bellows wheezed in time with the tunes I played, mostly anthems from the Shaker hymnal.

During a visit to Ethel and the Dwelling, I was sketching away when the notion crept into my mind, if the pump organ sounded good, think of how much more grand the big organ would be. The more I thought about it, the more I set my heart on it, until nothing in the world could satisfy me except to sit at the Hook and Hastings. I could practically feel the ivory under my fingers and the deep, dark vibrations of the lowest bass pedals rumbling in my gut. Never mind that I had never played a pedal organ of any kind, or had any notion whether the splendid old Hook and Hastings was fit for handling after all this time. I could hardly wait!

I packed up my paper and pencils and skipped down to find

Ethel to ask if I could play. It was a rhetorical question, of course, just a matter of courtesy, because none of the Shakers here ever said no.

Ethel said no.

Ethel said no in a nice enough way but it must have sounded brusque and my spirits sank like a rock in a pond. She said that the Hook and Hastings was especially Lillian's, and no one else played it. I mumbled an okay and made my exit, but the cork was out of the bottle and the genie had escaped. I don't really know why it bothered me so much, but I was a sensitive soul and Ethel's unexpected "no" stung like a rebuke. It seemed like a reasonable request, and I had to admit that Ethel had made a reasonable response, but by this point reason and logic were losing their clout. I wanted something good that meant a lot to me and I couldn't have it. I felt like a little kid again. Wasn't it just great to be a teenager: all the expectations that we'd behave ourselves like grown-ups, plus all the feelings of our tender years—what a hell of a big dumb joke.

I rushed down the granite walk of the Infirmary and threw myself on my bed and sobbed. The more I cried, the madder I got. The madder I got, the more I began to talk to myself. The more I talked, the louder I got, until I was almost hollering, and a couple of curses came bursting out. "Damn" and "hell" were about the extent of my active repertoire at that time, but even these expletives sounded shocking in Canterbury Shaker Village.

More shocking than any words was the anger itself. I had sensed plenty of emotion in the village's residents during the summer, but I had not witnessed any outburst such as mine. Even Jennie, who burst into groans and sobs on a regular basis when something scared or angered her, did not behave this way. As quickly as it came, the storm subsided, and I fell back on the quilt, spent and baffled. I wasn't even angry with Ethel, because I could see that she had spoken and acted reasonably. Somehow that made it all worse. I was mad as hell at something, and I didn't even know what.

I blew my nose and looked out the window. My heart froze—Bertha was limping across the road from the Office as fast as her bad knee allowed. Where could I go? Where could I hide? Damn—someone must have overheard me yelling through the windows. Damn, damn, damn! It was all over now. She'd yell at me and probably never want me here again. There was nowhere to run and I guessed I might as well face the music, so I slumped wretchedly on the bed while she rapped and came in. Bertha strode right over to me and demanded to know . . . what *Ethel* had done to hurt me so. Bertha was angry, all right, but not at me. She had rushed over here to take care of me, not chew me out.

I burst into tears again. I felt so low I could have crawled under the linoleum. Through my sobs, the story came out. Mildred had overheard me on her way to the Office and had immediately told Bertha. At the time, I could have killed Mildred for telling on my bad behavior, but I can see it differently now. Mildred did exactly the right thing. She did not come up to comfort me herself. I could guess that she was terrified of shouts and anger, and she probably knew herself well enough to know that comfort wasn't her strong suit—but it was Bertha's. She must have known that Bertha could take care of me better than anyone else.

I choked out my protests in defense of Ethel, who truly had done nothing wrong. I might have had a loose grip on my temper at times, but fair was fair and I couldn't stand unjust reprimands, for Ethel or me or anyone. As the story came out, Bertha calmed down, but the glint stayed in her eye, and I thought, God help anyone who really does hurt someone she loves. It was awful and all right at the same time. I didn't know then what Bertha made of it all, what she heard in my blubbering explanations that

sometimes I just lost it the way that poor old Jennie did, that sometimes I didn't feel very grown up. But looking back, I'm sure that I
wasn't the first hysterical teenage girl she'd ever dealt with.

The main point was, everything was all right. The thing I
dreaded most had happened, and it was still all right. Bertha had
seen the worst side of me, and she loved me just the same.

I was exhausted but peaceful. God was in Heaven, all was
right with the world.

# Simple Gifts

My first Shaker summer lasted one hundred days.

The last day and night came and went, and the next morning brought Mom and Grandma in the old blue Chevy. We packed up my stuff, Pink Lady bike, Gus and Alice's miniature room, forgotten Greek text, and all. The hair dryer, which I had considered so essential, had bit the dust within weeks of my arrival when I lunged to swat at a mosquito and knocked the works fatally to the floor. I had not bothered to replace it, but I had not yet surrendered to frizz, either. I continued the good fight and slept valiantly on my giant rollers, big as bean cans. Somewhere between the fading of the daisies and the onset of asters it dawned on me that I might eventually find a better outlet for all that stubbornness and determination, but it was not yet time.

When the car was loaded we gathered with the Office Sisters to say good-bye, then piled into the station wagon and drove off down Shaker Road.

I didn't leave with much more than I'd brought with me, if you consider only the material. I had my earnings, about sixty-two dollars a week, minus the considerable portion I had spent on Gus and Alice's work in the gift shop. Now I had a wonderful collection. I had invested my income from most of the month of July in a nearly complete set of their items, which fit neatly into a shoe box or two. How many thousands of words I had uttered in exchange for these treasures, how many stories I had told. It was a good, fair trade.

There were a few things more. Bertha gave me a white cardigan sweater as a going-away present, a sweet gift that was completely unsuited to a college coed of the seventies. It was dear to me; I never wore it and I never gave it away. Eldress Gertrude, who knew I spent hours writing in my journal, presented me with a small red fake-leather five-year diary with a tiny brass lock and key. There was not nearly enough room for all I had to say in each daily inch of allotted space. I tried it for about three days, then switched back to a big blank notebook. But it too was dear to me, and I have it to this day.

The third gift, from Bertha and Lillian, was a Shaker hymnal, a copy of the Canterbury Shakers' 1961 facsimile edition of their 1908 original. The hymnal, cheerful in its bright blue shiny paper jacket, was by now an old friend to me. The Office Sisters welcomed anybody to use the piano in the sitting room, so all summer I had sat and picked out the notes of one sacred song and anthem after another, feeling sorry that I was so clumsy and wishing that Lillian were sitting on the bench instead. But Bertha had sung along once in a while and she liked hearing the familiar chords. If she minded that they stumbled, she was far too kind to say so.

The front page was inscribed in Bertha's lovely, curving script: "To Dear June from Lillian Phelps and Bertha Lindsay." On the last page but one was "Tarry Not," given in inspiration to Lillian many years ago, before her thirtieth year:

> *O tarry not 'mid worldly strife, But seek the gifts above;*
> *Pow'r divine to guide the life, True wisdom, light and love.*
> *These higher truths attract my heart, Where wealth of*
> *soul is giv'n,*

*Bid me choose with Christ a part, My cross, my crown, my heav'n.*

I was truly pleased to receive the hymnal, the music of that summer, which seemed to me the greatest treasure that Bertha and Lillian could bestow, although it also brought a pang. The bitter-sweet memory of my temper in the infamous Hook and Hastings incident would forever accompany these notes and words. Well, maybe that was part of the gift.

And that was all for the tangible gifts, which scarcely filled a corner of my suitcase. The truer gifts, however, the intangible ones, filled my young being to overflowing. There were new parts to me, whole new cells stirring into life, brand-new synapses growing between them. I felt the gift of words flex in me, brand-new born and old as humankind, as all summer I watched faces turn to me, drinking the stories I could tell of the Shakers and their ways.

I felt, too, the ancient magic of drawing, of absorbing creation through my eyes and telling it back in line and shadow. I felt the force of inspiration, which I looked up and learned means "in-breathing," felt the warm breath of a power greater than myself moving in me and through me to do its work. I awoke to my role of instrument. In ways that I could not fully comprehend for a long, long time, my feet were set on their adult path.

And that summer, in final blessing, gave me three things that proved in time to be everything I have needed to keep me on my way: simple awareness of the path itself, a conviction that life has meaning worth the good fight, coupled with the truth of its wonderful, terrible cost; a North Star in the example of my Shaker friends, so that I can stay the course and regain my bearings when I wander off and get lost; and, of ever greater comfort as the years go by, recognition of fellow travelers on the journey, before me and behind me, through the numberless days and years and seasons of our kind's time on earth. Those who go seeking are never alone.

The Shakers I knew best are all gone now. As I write, I think of the twenty-five years that have passed since my first Shaker summer, and how everything of worth I've learned since has been a stone added to the foundation laid that summer. Neither give nor take offense, the Shakers said. Keep your words few and seasoned with grace. Not a day goes by but that I think of Bertha and Lillian and how they conducted themselves with the same steady peace whether the day brought favor or pain.

It's a good time for me to remember. I was right to go looking for more grandmothers. In time my own three grandmothers died, and they were sorely missed.

When I began to lose the Shakers, one by one, I felt nothing at first but sorrow for the loss. It seemed that the world was bereft of one more great old woman who could not be replaced.

When I began to understand that the way to honor them all was to grow into a great old woman myself, and that the only way to get there was to mind where I was heading now, my real education began.

# BIBLIOGRAPHY

## Periodicals Devoted to Shaker Life

For more than a century and a quarter, a series of periodicals chronicling Shaker life, published both by and about the United Society of Believers, has been available to the general public.

*The Shaker* was published monthly by the United Society from 1871 through 1877 with Brother George Lomas of Watervliet, New York, as editor. Of particular interest to the Shakers themselves were the "Home Notes" submitted by correspondents from the communities, which detailed events and personal news of interest.

The "Home Notes" tradition continued as the United Society's official publication changed titles and editors. From 1873 to 1877 it appeared as *Shaker and Shakeress* under the joint editorship of Elder Frederick Evans and Eldress Marie Antoinette Doolittle, progressive leaders from the North Family at Mount Lebanon. In 1877 Brother George Lomas resumed publication of the periodical under its original title, *The Shaker*. In 1878 it was renamed *The Shaker Manifesto*, still under the management of Brother George Lomas of Watervliet, New York. Finally, *The Manifesto* was published from 1882 to 1899. Elder Henry Blinn of Canterbury, New Hampshire, served as editor from 1882 and assumed full control of both printing and editing in 1890. Sister Josephine Wilson and her assistants took charge of the Print Shop in 1892.

The tradition of a periodical published by the United Society was revived at Sabbathday Lake, Maine, in 1961 by Theodore Johnson and Sister Mildred Barker. *The Shaker Quarterly* has appeared in print ever since. "Home Notes" from Canterbury, contributed by Eldress Bertha Lindsay, were included from 1961 until 1971.

After the rift between Canterbury and Sabbathday Lake made the inclusion of Canterbury's notes in *The Shaker Quarterly* uncomfortable, Bertha found a home for her "Home Notes" in a series of new publications, published not by but about the Shakers.

In 1971, *The World of Shaker* became available, a sign of growing popular interest. It was published quarterly by the Guild of Shaker Crafts, Inc., in Spring Lake, Michigan, from the fall of 1971 through November 1977. The periodical included "Home Notes" from each of the two active Shaker communities and also from the growing number of museums and restorations devoted to preserving the Shaker heritage. In 1978 the publication was revived under Diana and Paul van Kolken and was first published as *The Shaker Messenger* in 1979. In 1996, K. C. and Alana Parkinson took over the publication under the name *Shakers World*, in which the "Village News" feature perpetuates the "Home Notes" tradition begun over a century ago.

In addition to these publications, articles by Eldress Bertha Lindsay were also published in the newsletter published by Canterbury Shaker Village, Inc., as *The Canterbury Shaker* and *The News*.

ALLEN, ELDRESS M. CATHARINE. "The American Shakers: A Celibate, Religious Community." Sabbathday Lake, Me: The United Society, © 1972.

ANDERSON, EARL O. "N.H. Shakers Turn Village into a National Shrine." *New Hampshire Sunday News* (Manchester, N.H.) August 2, 1970.

———. "Shakers Dwindling but Impact Still Felt." *New Hampshire Sunday News* (Manchester, N.H.), September 24, 1961.

ANDREWS, EDWARD DEMING, AND FAITH ANDREWS. *Fruits of the Shaker Tree of Life: Memoirs of Fifty Years of Collecting and Researching.* Stockbridge, Mass.: Berkshire Traveller Press, 1975.

BARKER, SISTER R. MILDRED. *Holy Land: A History of the Alfred Shakers.* Sabbathday Lake, Me.: Shaker Press, 1983.

———. *The Sabbathday Lake Shakers: An Introduction to the Shaker Heritage.* Sabbathday Lake, Me.: Shaker Press, 1978.

BEALE, GALEN. "Canterbury Revives Poplar Industry." *The Shaker Messenger*, vol. 8 no. 4 (Summer 1986), pp. 10–12.

BECKER, STANTON (director). *The Shakers.* c. 1940.

BIBBER, WILLIAM R. "The Amazing Shakers." *Boston Sunday Herald Magazine*, September 20, 1964.

BIGELOW, THOMAS, AND JOHN KNIES. "Letterpress Printing at Canterbury." *The Canterbury Shakers*, vol. 6 no. 1, February 1986, pp. 5–8.

BLINN, ELDER HENRY C. "Church Records, 1784–1879." Collection of Shaker Village, Inc., Canterbury, N.H., ms. 764.

———. *Gentle Manners: A Guide to Good Morals*. East Canterbury, N.H., 1899.

———. "Historical Notes Having Reference to the Enfield Shakers, Vols. 1 & 2, 1893." Collection of Shaker Village, Inc., Canterbury, N.H., ms.

———. "A Historical Record of the Society of Believers in Canterbury, N.H. from the Time of Its Organization in 1792 Till the Year One Thousand Eight Hundred and Forty-Eight." 1892. Collection of Shaker Village, Inc., Canterbury, N.H., ms. 763.

———. "A Journey to Kentucky in the Year 1873." *The Shaker Quarterly*, Spring 1965–Summer 1966.

———. *The Life and Experiences of Mother Ann Lee*. Canterbury, N.H.: Canterbury Shakers, n.d.

[BLINN, HENRY C., ET AL.]."Church Records II, 1872–1889." Collection of Shaker Village, Inc., Canterbury, N.H., ms. 22.

BREWER, PRISCILLA J. *Shaker Communities, Shaker Lives*. Hanover, N.H.: University Press of New England, 1986.

"Bud: Inspired by Shaker Ideals." *The News* (published by Shaker Village Inc., Canterbury, N.H.), vol. 3, October 1989.

BURNS, AMY STECHLER, AND KEN BURNS. *The Shakers, Hands to Work, Hearts to God*. Hong Kong: Aperture, 1987.

BURNS, KEN (director). *The Shakers*. Walpole, N.H., Florentine Films, 1984.

BUTLER, LINDA, AND JUNE SPRIGG. *Inner Light: The Shaker Legacy*. New York: Alfred A. Knopf, 1985.

CALLEY, CHARLIE. "Showdown at Shaker Village." *New Hampshire Times*, September 26, 1973, pp. 2–5.

CAMPION, NARDI REEDER. *Ann the Word*. Foreword by June Sprigg. Hanover, N.H.: University Press of New England, 1990.

"Canterbury, New Hampshire, Shaker Village." *Outlook*, vol. 106, January 3, 1914, pp. 40–42.

CANTERBURY SHAKERS. *Canterbury Shakers.* Canterbury, N.H.: Canterbury Shakers, [c. 1974].

———. *Gourmet's Delight: Favorite Shaker Recipes.* Canterbury, N.H.: Canterbury Shakers, [1968].

———. *Shaker Hymnal.* East Canterbury, N.H.: Canterbury Shakers, 1908. Reprinted. Cleveland, Ohio: Shaker Savings Association, 1961.

———. *Shaker Tested Recipes.* Canterbury, N.H.: Canterbury Shakers, [1965].

"The Canterbury Shakers." *Granite Monthly,* vol. 8, September–October 1885, pp. 310–311.

*Canterbury Shaker Village: Guide to the Collection.* Canterbury, N.H.: Shaker Village, Inc., 1983.

CARR, SISTER FRANCES A. *Growing Up Shaker.* Sabbathday Lake, Me.: United Society of Shakers, 1994.

———. "Open the Doors." *Portland Press Herald,* January 8, 1979.

———. *Shaker Your Plate: Of Shaker Cooks and Cooking.* Sabbathday Lake, Me.: United Society of Shakers, 1986.

CHANDLER, LLOYD HORWITZ. "New Hampshire Shakers, 1792–1947." *Historical New Hampshire,* vol. 8, March 1952, pp. 1–17.

CLARK, TIM. "Shattering the Shaker Image." *Yankee,* May 1980, pp. 81–85, 130–141.

COOK, JOAN. "Shaker Serenity at Sabbathday Lake." *New York Times,* August 27, 1966, p. 20.

CORRY, JOHN. "A Film on the Shakers Offered by Channel 13." *New York Times,* August 7, 1985, p. C20.

COURT, ANDY. "The Lives of the Last Shakers." *Concord Monitor,* December 27, 1984, pp. 1, 3.

———. "Shakers' Covenant Pulled from Auction." *Concord Monitor,* November 16, 1984, pp. 1, 18.

CREAGER, ALLEN. "Cookbook Shows the Shaker Way." *Express,* February 24, 1988, pp. C1–2.

DAVENPORT, TOM (director). *The Shakers.* Delaplane, Va: Davenport Films, 1974.

DELANEY, BARBARA SNOW. "The Shakers Today." *Antiques,* October 1970, pp. 618–622.

DRIVER, CHRISTOPHER. "Bertha Lindsay, a Baker for the Shakers." *The Guardian* (Manchester, U.K.), October 11, 1990.

ELAM, SISTER AIDA. *History of the Shakers.* Canterbury, N.H.: Canterbury Shakers, 1962.

ELAM, SISTER AIDA, AND SISTER MIRIAM WALL. *History of the Shakers: Education and Recreation.* Canterbury, N.H.: Canterbury Shakers, 1961.

"Eldress Bertha Lindsay." *Daily Telegraph* (London), October 11, 1990, p. 27.

EMERSON, MARTHA MAE. "The Shakers' Largest Wooden Barn." *New Hampshire Profiles,* April 1974, pp. 50–55.

EVANS, JESSIE. "Diaries, Canterbury, N.H., 1905–1931." Collection of Shaker Village, Inc., Canterbury, N.H., ms. 1984.14–.15 and 1985.6–.43.

FROST, SISTER MARGUERITE. *About the Shakers.* Canterbury, N.H.: Canterbury Shakers, [1958].

———. *The Shaker Story.* Canterbury, N.H.: Canterbury Shakers, [1963].

GAINES, JUDITH. "Simple Gifts." *Boston Globe,* March 12, 1989, pp. 18–19, 30–31, 34.

GALWAY, LINDA. "Spiritual Leader of Maine's Shakers Dies." *Lewiston Sun-Journal,* January 26, 1990.

GARD, MAX. "Sabbath Day [sic] Lake." *Farm and Dairy,* vol. 42, August 28, 1957, p. 5.

"Gertrude Soule, 93: An N.H. Shaker Leader." *Boston Globe,* June 13, 1988, p. 25.

"Gertrude Soule, 93, One of the Last of the Shaker Sect in the Nation." *New York Times,* June 14, 1988, p. D12.

GHISELIN, ALEX. "Gentle N.H. Lady Relives the Days of Shaker Sect." *Boston Sunday Globe,* February 22, 1970, p. 33.

*The Gospel Monitor: A Little Book of Mother Ann's Word to Those Who Are Placed as Instructors & Care-takers of Children.* Canterbury, N.H., 1843.

GREENWOOD, IRVING. "Diaries, Canterbury, N.H., 1915–1917." Collection of Shaker Village, Inc., Canterbury, N.H., ms. 270.

HALLER, JAMES. "Great New England Cooks: Eldress Bertha Lindsay." *Yankee,* August 1988, p. 88.

HALLER, JAMES, WITH JEFFREY PAIGE. *Cooking in the Shaker Spirit.* Camden, Me.: Yankee Books, 1990.

HARRIS, AMANDA B. "Among the Shakers." *Granite Monthly,* vol. 1, April 1877, pp. 21–24.

HARTMAN, LEDA. "Shaker Birthday: Youngest Eldress Turns 90 Quietly." *Concord Monitor,* July 29, 1987, p. B1.

HAWTHORNE, NATHANIEL. *The American Notebooks.* New Haven, Conn.: Yale University Press, 1932.

——. "The Canterbury Pilgrims." In *The Token and Atlantic Souvenir.* 1833, pp. 153–166. Reprinted in Hawthorne, *The Snow Image and Other Twice-Told Tales.* Boston: Ticknor, Reed and Fields, 1852.

——. "The Shaker Bridal." In *The Token and Atlantic Souvenir,* 1838, pp. 216–233. Reprinted in Hawthorne, *Twice-Told Tales.* Boston: American Stationers Co., John B. Russell, 1837.

HESS, WENDELL. *The Enfield (N.H.) Shakers: A Brief History.* Enfield, N.H.: Wendell Hess, 1988.

HILL, ISAAC. "Canterbury in 1840: A Distinguished Contemporary's View." Edited and with an introduction by Theodore J. Johnson. *The Shaker Quarterly* 4, nos. 2 and 3 (Summer and Fall 1964), pp. 43–60, 83–96.

HILLIER, LEWIS. "Sister Mildred Reflects on Her Life as a Shaker." *Lewiston Daily Sun,* August 6, 1974.

HILLINGER, CHARLES. "Shaker Sect Down to 7 Elderly Women." *The Express,* November 12, 1988, pp. B10–11.

"Historical New Hampshire." Special issue: *Canterbury Shaker Village.* Concord, N.H.: New Hampshire Historical Society, 1993.

"Historical Record of the Church Family, East Canterbury, N.H. Compiled by the Brethren for Special Reference. 1890–1930." Collection of Shaker Village, Inc., Canterbury, N.H., ms. 33.

HORGAN, EDWARD R. *The Shaker Holy Land: A Community Portrait.* Harvard, Mass.: Harvard Common Press, 1982.

HUGHES, ROBERT. *American Visions: The Epic History of Art in America.* New York: Alfred A. Knopf, 1997.

*I Don't Want to Be Remembered as a Chair.* London: British Broadcasting Corporation, 1991.

"In Memoriam: Delmer Charles Wilson, 1873–1961." *The Shaker Quarterly* 1, no. 4 (Winter 1961), pp. 135–137.

"In Memoriam: Eldress Bertha Lindsay (1897–1990)." *The News* (published by Shaker Village, Inc.; Canterbury, N.H.), vol. 5, no. 1, 1991.

"In Memoriam: Eldress Bertha Lindsay, 1897–1990." *The Shaker Quarterly* 18, 1990, pp. 117–119.

*In Memoriam: Eldress D. A. Durgin, 1824–1898; Eldress J. J. Kaime, 1826–1898.* Concord, N.H.: Rumford Press, 1899.

"In Memory of Sister Ethel Hudson (1896–1992)." *The News* (published by Shaker Village, Inc., Canterbury, N.H.), vol. 6, no. 3, October 1992.

"Interview with a Shaker." *Cobblestone: The History Magazine for Young People,* April 1983, pp. 8–11.

JOHNSON, THEODORE. *Hands to Work and Hearts to God.* Brunswick, Me.: Bowdoin College, 1969.

KATZEFF, PAUL. "Shake-up in Paradise." *Boston Herald Sunday Magazine,* May 18, 1986, pp. 17–18.

KIERNAN, LAURA A. "Friends Remember Shaker Eldress' Life of Service to God." *Boston Globe,* June 15, 1988, p. 25.

———. "Shaker Sect Calmly Prepares to Die." *Washington Post,* November 5, 1986, p. A3.

KING, ELDRESS EMMA B. *A Shaker's Viewpoint.* Old Chatham, N.Y.: Shaker Museum Foundation, 1957.

KOVACH, BILL. "Shakerism: A Colonial Vision of Communal Living Is Fading." *New York Times,* June 15, 1972, pp. 43, 51.

KURTENBACH, HATTO (director). *The Shakers.* Grünwald, Germany: Interteam München, 1989.

LABBIE, E. "Shaker Sabbathday Colony Tour Rewarding." *Lewiston Journal* (magazine section), July 17, 1965, p. 3-A.

LAMB, DAVID. "Shaker Casework." *Fine Woodworking,* May–June 1986, pp. 30–36.

"Last of the Shakers." *Newsweek,* February 13, 1939, p. 33.

"Last Shaker Eldress Dies at 93 in New Hampshire." *Danville Advocate* (Danville, Ky.), October 4, 1990.

LILJEHOLM, L. "Ladies of Maine's Shaker Settlement Still an Industrious Lot." *Portland Evening Express,* July 21, 1965, p. 19.

LINDSAY, ELDRESS BERTHA. "Eldress Bertha Recalls the 1920s." *The Canterbury Shakers Newsletter* 3, no. 1, January 1983, pp. 1–5, 12–16.

———. "In Memoriam: Lily Marguerite Frost, 1892–1971." *The Shaker Quarterly* 11, no. 1 (Spring 1971), pp. 3–4.

———. *Seasoned with Grace: My Generation of Shaker Cooking.* Edited by Mary Rose Boswell. Woodstock, Vt.: Countryman Press, 1987.

———. As told to Cable Neuhaus. "The Shakers Face Their Last Amen." *People,* March 2, 1987, pp. 78–81.

LINDSAY, SISTER BERTHA. "The Canterbury Shakers: 1792–1967." *The Shaker Quarterly* 7, no. 3 (Fall 1967), pp. 87–95.

———. "In Memoriam: Ida F. Crook, 1886–1965." *The Shaker Quarterly* 5, no. 2 (Summer 1965), pp. 35–36.

———. "Home Notes from Canterbury, New Hampshire." *The Shaker Quarterly,* 1961–1971.

LINDSAY, SISTER BERTHA, AND SISTER LILLIAN PHELPS. *Industries and Inventions of the Shakers; Shaker Music: A Brief History.* Canterbury, N.H.: Canterbury Shakers, 1961.

LOSSING, BENSON. *An Early View of the Shakers.* Edited by Don Gifford. Foreword by June Sprigg. Hanover, N.H.: University Press of New England, 1989.

LUBERECKI, GREGORY L. "Shaker Taught." *Lafayette Magazine,* Fall 1995, pp. 24–29.

LYFORD, JAMES OTIS. *The Canterbury Shakers: An Excerpt from "History of Canterbury."* Reprint. Canterbury, N.H.: Shaker Village, Inc., 1974.

"Maine's Shakers: Does It Have to Be Suicide?" *Portland Sunday Telegram,* August 5, 1973, p. 18A.

M[ARCOTTE], N[ANCY]. "Shakers: Part I—In the Valley of Love" and "Shakers: Part II—At Sabbathday Lake." *Bittersweet: Western Maine Perspectives,* May 1981, pp. 3–4, 30–31, and June 1981, pp. 3–5, 31.

MARTIN, DAVID. "Serene Twilight of a Once-Sturdy Sect, the Shakers: It Is Christ Who Dwells in Me." *Life,* March 17, 1967, pp. 58–70.

MARTIN, M. "The Sect That Condemned Itself to Death." *New Hampshire Sunday News* (Manchester), October 9, 1966, pp. 98–99.

MCCLINTOCK, JOHN NORRIS. "The Shakers." *Granite Monthly,* vol. 3, January 1880, pp. 145–147.

MILLER, L.O. "Visit to the Canterbury Shakers." *Otterbein Home Journal,* 1916, pp. 5–16.

MITMAN, WENDY. "A Death Leaves the Shaker Faith Near Extinction." *USA Today,* June 15, 1988.

———. "Handful of Surviving Shakers Are Hoping for a Revival in the Faith." *The Morning Call,* February 21, 1988, pp. E1–2.

———. "Shakers Slowly Fade Away." *Middlesex News,* June 14, 1988.

"Modern World Invades Shaker Yule." *Sunday Call-Chronicle* (Allentown, Pa.) December 24, 1978, p. A3.

MORRISON, N. "Shakers Open Museum of Old Craftsmanship in Canterbury." *Concord Daily Monitor,* June 7, 1960.

MORSE, FLO. "Brother Theodore E. Johnson Dies." *The Shaker Messenger,* vol. 8 no. 2 (Spring 1986), p. 12.

NAVAREZ, ALFONSO A. "Bertha Lindsay, 93; Was the Last Eldress in the Shaker Society." *New York Times,* October 5, 1990, p. D19.

NEWMAN, CATHY. "The Shakers' Brief Eternity." *National Geographic,* September 1989, pp. 302–325.

*The 1959 Agreement Establishing the Shaker Central Trust Fund.* With notes and commentary by David D. Newell. Ashfield, Mass.: Huntstown Press, 1995.

"The 1929 Christmas Eve Program." Collection of Shaker Village, Inc., Canterbury, N.H., ms. 996.

"Notebook, Canterbury, N.H." Collection of Shaker Village, Inc., Canterbury, N.H., ms 969.

"Onetime 400-Member Shaker Community in N.H. Dwindles to 11." *Boston Herald,* October 18, 1959.

ORENSTEIN, SUSAN. "Witness: Eldress Bertha's Memories Sustain Shaker Way of Life." *Concord Monitor,* March 2, 1989, p. D1.

O' SHEA, JANE. "Canterbury Shaker Village Is Ghost of Earlier Days." *Manchester Union Leader,* August 7, 1959.

PAIGE, JEFFREY S. *The Shaker Kitchen.* New York: Clarkson Potter, 1994.

PÉLADEAU, MARIUS B. "The Last Shaker Brother." *The Maine History News,* April 1973, pp. 4–5.

PERKINS, ELDER ABRAHAM. *Autobiography of Elder Abraham Perkins.* Concord, N.H.: Concord, N.H. Press, 1901.

PERRONI KATHLEEN. "Henry Blinn: One of the Most Famous Shakers." *New Hampshire Sunday News* (Manchester), May 18, 1975, p. 16.

PHELPS, [SISTER] LILLIAN. "Reminiscences of Shaker Recreational Life." *The Shaker Quarterly* 1, no. 2 (Summer 1961), pp. 55–57.

PHELPS, [SISTER] B. LILLIAN. *Who Are the Shakers?* Canterbury, N.H.: Canterbury Shakers, June 1959.

POTTER, L. "In Maine a Shaker Auction Brings Astounding Results." *National Antiques Review,* August 1972, pp. 20, 23, 33.

PROSSER, JEANETTE. "The Shakers of Canterbury." *New Hampshire Profiles,* August 1960, pp. 26–31.

*Receiving the Faith: The Shakers of Canterbury, New Hampshire.* Champion, N.Y.: Whitney Museum of American Art at Champion, 1993.

RICHMOND, MARY L. *Shaker Literature: A Bibliography.* Pittsfield, Mass.: Shaker Community, Inc., 1977.

ROBINSON, CHARLES EDSON. *The Shakers and Their Homes.* East Canterbury, N.H., 1893.

ROCHELEAU, PAUL, AND JUNE SPRIGG. *Shaker Built.* New York: Monacelli Press, 1994.

SAFFORD, MARION F. "Shaker Buildings at Canterbury, New Hampshire." *Antiques,* October 1970, p. [4].

"Shaker Eldress Soule Dies at 94; Was Trustee of Hancock Village." *Berkshire Eagle,* June 13, 1988.

"Shaker Sisters Victory Garden Has 45 Long Rows of Vegetables." *Boston Globe,* June 18, 1944.

*Shakerism for Today.* New Gloucester, Me.: United Society of Shakers, 1996.

"Shaker Revival." *Newsweek,* April 17, 1961, p. 99.

*A Shaker Sister's Drawings: Wild Plants Illustrated by Cora Helena Sarle.* Introduction by June Sprigg Tooley. Afterword by Scott T. Swank. New York: Monacelli Press, 1997.

"Shaker's Death Leaves 2 Women in Community." *Morning Call* (Allentown, Penn.), June 15, 1988.

"The Shakers." *Time,* July 28, 1961, p. 53.

"The Shakers: A Strict and Utopian Way of Life Has Almost Vanished." *Life,* March 21, 1949, pp. 142–148.

SHEBLE, REBECCA. "Shaker Revival at Sabbathday Lake." *Salt: Journal of New England Culture,* Winter 1984, pp. 18–37.

"Sister R. Mildred Barker, Shaker Leader, 92." *New York Times,* January 27, 1990.

SKEES, SUZANNE. "The Last of the Shakers?" *Ms.,* March–April 1995, pp. 40–45.

SPENCER, CHRISTOPHER (director). *American Visions.* London: BBC TV, 1997.

SPRIGG, JUNE. *By Shaker Hands.* New York: Alfred A. Knopf, 1975.

———. "Diary, August 1972–December 1972." Manuscript, collection of June Sprigg Tooley.

———. "Diary, December 1971–August 1972." Manuscript, collection of June Sprigg Tooley.

———. "In Memoriam [Sister Ethel Hudson]." *The News* (published by Shaker Village, Inc., Canterbury, N.H.), vol. 6, no. 3, October 1992.

———. "Kindred Spirits: The Eloquence of Function in American Shaker and Japanese Arts of Daily Life." Essay, in William Thrasher's catalogue of an exhibition of Japanese and Shaker folk design. La Jolla, Calif.: Mingei International Museum of World Folk Art, 1995.

———. "Rachel: One Day in the Life of a Shaker." *Berkshire Magazine,* Autumn 1982, pp. 33–37.

———. *Shaker Design.* New York: Whitney Museum of American Art. W. W. Norton, 1986.

———. "The Shaker Way." *The New York Times Magazine,* November 2, 1975, pp. 68–69, 71.

SPRIGG, JUNE, AND ARTHUR FUJIKADO. *Shaker Design: Hancock Shaker Village Collection.* Tokyo: Sezon Museum of Art, 1992.

SPRIGG, JUNE, AND DAVID LARKIN. *Shaker Life, Work, and Art.* New York: Stewart, Tabori & Chang, 1987.

STACK, JAMES. "A Serene Faith Sustains 17 Women—The Last Shakers." *Boston Sunday Globe,* March 12, 1967.

STARBUCK, DAVID R. ed. *Canterbury Shaker Village: An Historical Survey.* Vol. 2. Durham, N.H.: University of New Hampshire Press, 1981.

STARBUCK, DAVID R., AND MARGARET SUPPLEE SMITH. *Historical Survey of Canterbury Shaker Village.* Boston: Boston University Press, 1979.

STEIN, STEPHEN J. "Inspiration, Revelation, and Scripture: The Story of a Shaker Bible." *Proceedings of the American Antiquarian Society,* vol. 105, no. 2, 1996, pp. 347–376.

———. *The Shaker Experience in America.* New Haven: Yale University Press, 1992.

STEIN, THEO. "Shaker Village Being Sued for Sexual Discrimination." *The Berkshire Eagle* (Pittsfield, Mass.), July 31, 1997.

STRICKLER, DAVID. "Seven Left at Canterbury; Last of Shakers Sure Faith Will Live On." *New Hampshire Sunday News* (Manchester, N.H.), April 17, 1966.

THOMPSON, DARRYL. "Eldress Gertrude Soule: A Personal Remembrance." *Shaker Messenger,* Summer 1988, pp. 9, 22.

THOMPSON, NANCY M. *Learning About Shakers: For Young People.* Pleasant Grove [Canterbury, N.H.], 1988.

TORTORA, VINCENT R. *The Shakers in America.* Port Washington, N.Y. Vedo Films, 1975.

"Vanishing Breed," *People.* September 28, 1992, p. 60.

WATSON, PENELOPE. "Church Family Dwelling House at Canterbury: A Building History." *The Canterbury Shakers,* Canterbury, N.H., vol. 3, no. 1, January 1983, pp. 6–7.

WERTKIN, GERARD C. *The Four Seasons of Shaker Life: An Intimate Portrait of the Community at Sabbathday Lake, Maine.* New York: Fireside Simon & Schuster, 1986.

WHITCHER, JOHN, ET AL. "A Brief History or Record of the Commencement & Progress of the United Society of Believers at Canterbury, County of Merrimack and State of New Hampshire." Collection of Shaker Village, Inc., Canterbury, N.H., ms. 21.

WHITCHER, MARY. *Mary Whitcher's Shaker House-Keeper.* 1882. Reprint. Hastings-on-Hudson, N.Y.: Morgan & Morgan, Inc., 1972. Original in the library at Hancock Shaker Village, Hancock, Mass.

WHITE, ELDRESS ANNA, AND ELDRESS LEILA S. TAYLOR. *Shakerism: Its Meaning and Message.* Columbus, Ohio, 1904. Reprint. New York: AMS Press, 1971.

WILLIAMS, RICHARD L. "The Shakers, Now Only 12, Observe Their 200th Year." *Smithsonian,* September 1974, pp. 40–49.

WILLIAMS, STEVEN GUION. *Chosen Land, The Sabbathday Lake Shakers.* Boston: David R. Godine, 1975.

WILSON, DELMER. "The Diary of a Maine Shaker Boy: Delmer Wilson—1887." With notes and an introduction by Theodore E. Johnson. *The Shaker Quarterly* 8, no. 1 (Spring 1968), pp. 3–22.

WILSON, JOSEPHINE E. "Diaries, Canterbury, N.H., 1916–1940." Collection of Shaker Village, Inc., Canterbury, N.H., ms. 1985.25, 1985.41–74.

[WINKLEY, FRANCIS, ET AL.] "Journal, Canterbury, N.H., 1784–1845." Collection of Shaker Village, Inc., Canterbury, N.H., ms. 25.

*The Youth's Guide in Zion, and Holy Mother's Promises.* Canterbury, N.H., 1842. Reprint. Mother's Work Series No. 1. Sabbathday Lake, Me.: United Society of Believers, 1963.

ZIEGET, IRENE. "Our Shaker Adventure." Unpublished typescript, 1967.

———. "Our Shaker Collection." *Yankee,* April 1970, pp. 102–104, 126–127.

June Sprigg was born in Corpus Christi, Texas, in 1953. As a college student in the 1970s she spent three summers living and working with the Shakers in Canterbury, New Hampshire. She received her B.A. in 1974 from Lafayette College and M.A. in 1977 from the Winterthur Program in Early American Culture, University of Delaware. From 1977 to 1982 and 1986 to 1994 she was Curator of Collections at Hancock Shaker Village in Pittsfield, Massachusetts. She has guest-curated major exhibitions of Shaker design at the Whitney Museum of American Art, the Corcoran Gallery of Art, and the Sezon Museum of Art in Tokyo. Her many publications include *By Shaker Hands* (1975), *Domestick Beings* (1984), *Inner Light: The Shaker Legacy* (1985), and *Shaker Built* (1994). As June Sprigg Tooley, she is a freelance writer and adjunct instructor in history at Berkshire Community College. She lives in Pittsfield, Massachusetts, with her husband and his three children.

*A NOTE ON THE TYPE*

This book was set in a version of the well-known Monotype face Bembo. This letter was cut for the celebrated Venetian printer Aldus Manutius by Francesco Griffo, and was first used in Pietro Cardinal Bembo's *De Aetna* of 1495.

The companion italic is an adaptation of the chancery script type designed by the calligrapher and printer Lodovico degli Arrighi.

*Composed by Creative Graphics, Allentown, Pennsylvania*
*Printed and bound by Quebecor Printing, Martinsburg, West Virginia*
*Designed by Virginia Tan*